ASTRONOM...

An in-depth treatment of astronomical factors which bear most heavily on astrological interpretation.

Also in this series

ASTROLOGICAL COUNSELLING
Christina Rose

CHART SYNTHESIS
Roy Alexander

FORECASTING BY ASTROLOGY
Martin Freeman

HORARY ASTROLOGY
Derek Appleby

HOW TO INTERPRET A BIRTH CHART
Martin Freeman

MUNDANE ASTROLOGY
Michael Baigent, Nicholas Campion and Charles Harvey

NATAL CHARTING
John Filbey

SYNASTRY
Penny Thornton

THE TWELVE HOUSES
Howard Sasportas

ASTRONOMY FOR ASTROLOGERS

by

John Filbey, D.F.Astrol.S.

and

Peter Filbey, B.Sc.

THE AQUARIAN PRESS
Wellingborough, Northamptonshire

First published 1984

© JOHN and PETER FILBEY 1984

This book is sold subject to the condition that it shall not, by way of trade or otherwise, be lent, re-sold, hired out, or otherwise circulated without the publisher's prior consent in any form of binding or cover other than that in which it is published and without a similar condition including this condition being imposed on the subsequent purchaser.

British Library Cataloguing in Publication Data

Filbey, Peter
   Astronomy for astrologers.
   1. Astronomy
   I. Title   II. Filbey, John
   520'.2413   QB43.2

   ISBN 0-85030-393-1

---

*The Aqurian Press is part of the
Thorsons Publishing Group*

Printed and Bound in Great Britain by
Whitstable Litho Ltd., Whitstable, Kent

CONTENTS

		Page
Introduction		9
Chapter		
1.	An Outline of the History of Astronomy	11
2.	The Development of Modern Astronomy	25
3.	Earth and Sky: Lines, Circles and Projections	39
4.	The Calendar	61
5.	Time	79
6.	The Astrological Ephemeris	99
7.	The Solar System: The Planets	105
8.	The Mechanics of the Solar System	131
9.	Comets	151
10.	The Universe: Stars and Galaxies	165
11.	Cosmic Cycles and Mundane Events	181
	Glossary	193
	Appendix 1: Correction for Geographic Latitude	203
	Appendix 2: The Times of Rising, Culmination and Setting of a Planet	205

Appendix 3: Calculation Tables 209
Appendix 4: Interesting Data 227
Appendix 5: Star Charts 235
Bibliography 246
Index 251

ACKNOWLEDGEMENTS

We wish to acknowledge, with thanks, the permission given by the following to reproduce copyright material:

Kahn & Averill, Star Charts from *Night Skies of the Year*, Roy Worvill, 1968.

The New York Times, for the front page story of the discovery of Pluto in 1930.

The Royal Greenwich Observatory, for the Time Map by Henry Ellis, 1852.

'Sky & Telescope' for the September 1752 extract from the *Ladies Diary* concerning the calendar change.

We also acknowledge our debt to the various publications and journals which it was essential to consult and, without which a work such as this could not have been written.

INTRODUCTION

'As on this whirligig of Time
we circle with the seasons'
Tennyson

The purpose of this book is an endeavour to present an introduction to astronomy, from which the astrological student may gain, not only factual knowledge, but also an appreciation of a science which is the fundamental basis of astrology.

Throughout the ages, man has looked at the starry heavens and marvelled. The infinite immensity of space, with its terrifying beauty has caught the imagination, instilling a sense of spiritual awareness and wonderment. The questing spirit of man has enabled him to confront the unknown frontiers of space and to discover that, not only is the Universe magnificent, it is far more magnificent than he had ever imagined.

Astronomy has its own incomparable splendour. As well as demonstrating a mathematical and physical beauty, it also allows scope for limitless philosophical speculations. An understanding of astronomy and its principles enriches, and as we study the heavens and marvel at its mysteries, its precision, its aesthetic beauty, we realize that our transient existence is ordered and controlled by powerful and subtle universal forces.

The last few decades have seen an unparalleled revival in the study of both astronomy and astrology. The Space Age, with its exciting discoveries, has stimulated the imagination and, although some astrological concepts and teachings need re-appraisal, we may eventually see astronomy and astrology reconciled, with both contributing toward an appreciation of true values and real purposes concerning life and all its manifestations.

1.
AN OUTLINE OF THE HISTORY OF ASTRONOMY

The heavens have always had the fascination of the mysterious and the supernatural. To the earliest observers, the Earth could not have seemed anything other than flat. The sky would appear as a solid dome with the Sun, Moon and other celestial objects moving below it. The stars embedded in the vault of heaven would be sky patterns, whose formation and outlines could be identified with the tribal history and folk-lore of the community. Gradually, that which had been regarded with fear and apprehension assumed new dimensions. During the course of a solar year, early man would see the ever-changing appearance of the different constellations, and these patterns, which could be observed in conjunction with the cyclic motions of the Sun, Moon and planets, enabled the early observers to formulate laws concerning the heavens and the natural world.

In his endless struggle for existence, early man became intimately aware of the relationship existing between heaven and earth. The period of growth and harvesting could be related to the appearance of certain constellations and would correspond with the Equinoxes (Spring and Autumn), while high summer and mid-winter coincided with the Solstices (June and December). At the time of the December Solstice, the Sun would rise late and set early, moving low across the sky. As the days lengthened, it became apparent that the Sun was not 'dying' but would continue to pour out its life-giving force. This fact, along with other celestial phenomena, doubtlessly instilled in early man a sense of divine wonderment with which he sought to combine the spiritual with the mundane.

Initially, the fear of the unknown and superstitious beliefs resulted in a mythology of the heavens being developed, but in the course of time, that which had been regarded as inexplicable was gradually accepted and adapted for more practical purposes. The myths and rituals of many diverse cultures often have a common base, frequently associated with celestial phenomena.

The Ancient Astronomies

Traditional archaeology has been slow in accepting the fact that many of the stone monuments of various kinds which occur world-wide, may owe their origins to early man's strivings to relate celestial phenomena, not only to his physical existence, but also to his concepts concerning death and an after-life.

Due to the expansion in scientific research during the last few decades, archaeology has benefitted from the discoveries of other branches of science such as astronomy, physics, biology and climatology. This interchange of knowledge has greatly facilitated a more realistic approach toward a new understanding of ancient sites and their astronomical connection. When considering the astronomy of the ancients, we have to use the term 'astronomy' advisedly, for in no sense was it the technical and exact study that we understand it to be today. Nevertheless, the researches carried out at many sites suggest that ancient man possessed the ability and the resources to erect vast structures with admirable precision. Many of the stone circles investigated appear to have some form of celestial alignment and seem to indicate that early man was aware of the equinoctial and solsticial points. The locating of these points would not be difficult to achieve, but the tracking of the fluctuating Moon with its variations in declination would pose a far more formidable problem. However, over a considerable period of time, this problem was solved and the Moon and its motions formed the basis for predictive techniques.

The term 'Megalith' from the Greek megas (great) and lithos (stone) was applied to certain ancient monuments during the middle of the last century. In the early part of the present century, the term was commonly adopted to denote the various kinds of stone circles of which vast numbers abound in North West Europe. The most spectacular, and in many ways unique, is Stonehenge situated on Salisbury Plain in southern England.

Probably no other site has been studied in such great detail, nor has any other site attracted so much speculation concerning its origins and purpose. Stonehenge had interested many investigators during the eighteenth and nineteenth centuries and, although an astronomical alignment had been noted by a Revd Edward Duke during the last century, no serious scientific work was undertaken until Sir Norman Lockyer, who was an astronomer, carried out researches with a view of trying to date the structure. Lockyer arrived at an approximately correct date (1900-1500 B.C.) but his methodology was criticized.

The astronomical thesis received a new impetus in the early 1960s, when Gerald Hawkins published his computer laboratory findings concerning Stonehenge. In an article in *Nature* titled 'Stonehenge Decoded', Hawkins endeavoured to prove that the monument was a sophisticated observatory built by Neolithic man, around 2000 B.C. Its purpose was to keep track of the shifting Sun and to plot the position of Moonrise and Moonset. The megalithic astronomy question excited considerable debate, particularly when Hawkins' second article in *Nature* titled 'Stonehenge: A Neolithic Computer' was published. This article described how the various stone alignments at Stonehenge could be used as an eclipse predictor. These revolutionary theories met with dissent from the archaeologists who, in the main, could not accept the astronomical inferences, particularly when other researchers entered the lists, stating that other sites indicated the 'astronomical connection'. Notable among the other researchers were C. A. Newham and Professor A. Thom, who without the aid of a computer, had been working on the astronomical theses. Thom, although he had not surveyed Stonehenge at this time (he did so later) had been investigating considerable numbers of megalithic sites and monuments. In these surveys, Thom discovered a geometric unit that he termed the 'megalithic yard' (32.64 inches), and which he considered was the standard unit used by the Neolithic builders to construct their stone monuments. Thom's results of his innumerable surveys of megalithic sites appear to confirm that the ancient builders possessed a knowledge of complex geometry and were familiar with the simplest Pythagorean triangle. The research into astro-archaeology is rapidly confirming that early man was far more enlightened and organized than has hitherto been thought.

A study of many sites indicates that the siting, layout and orientation have a connection with not only solar and lunar observances, but also a relationship with the rites of the dead. At

New Grange in Ireland, the megalithic tomb built about 3300 B.C. and thereby pre-dating Stonehenge, has a small roof box through which the mid-winter Sun's rays shone, illuminating the rear wall of the burial chamber. The orientation of funerary chambers indicates the importance of the Sun as a 'marker', and while not all barrows, tombs and suchlike are directed exactly east-west, most of them are sited toward the rising Sun, either slightly north or south of east, corresponding with points about midway between the dates of the Equinoxes and Solstices.

In North West Europe, the Near East and the Americas the ancient astronomy flourished because it satisfied important criteria. Firstly, it permitted a solar calendar, probably in conjunction with a lunar one, to be devised. This solar/lunar cycle enabled the society to regulate and co-ordinate their agricultural activities according to the solar or lunar cycle. Secondly, periods connected with astro-religious observances could be known in advance and the appropriate preparations made. The Celtic New Year commenced on about 1 November (Samhaintide), and this period, which was closely connected with death and the coming of winter, was in all probability, a legacy from the distant past. Likewise, the Feast of Beltane — on or about 1 May — celebrated the beginning of summer. These dates, approximately midway between the Equinoxes and Solstices, do appear to have an astronomical significance. In the study of the ancient astronomies, it must be remembered that the climate of North West Europe was undoubtedly different from that prevailing today. If we assume that the climate was more stable during Neolithic times with a clear atmosphere down to the horizon, then we can begin to understand how the different branches of observational astronomy developed. In the Near East, the heliacal rising of Sirius marked the commencement of the Egyptian New Year, and the climatic conditions in these regions did not, generally speaking, require astronomical observations to be made with the aid of accurate markers or alignments. In the more northern latitudes of Europe, particularly the coastal areas, the atmosphere would at times become obscure, and therefore, it would have been imperative to have accurate sight markers. This is particularly true of the megalithic sites in Scotland and the northern isles. Another important factor would be the variations above the horizon of the Sun and Moon at different times of the year. In northern latitudes, the movements of the Sun and Moon would be conspicuous particularly when close to the horizon. The importance of climate and geographical location has to be borne in mind when we study the astronomical traditions; that which sufficed for the Near East would not, and could not, be applicable for northern Europe.

The preoccupation of early man with the Moon and its motions, was derived, not only from any mythological significance, but chiefly from the practical implications associated with its movements. The relationship of the tides with certain phases of the Moon would have been noted, and the plotting of the Moon's position would give a good working knowledge of the 'when' and 'how' of tidal activity. At a very early date, man commenced travelling extensively, and although his sea-going craft were primitive he, nevertheless, managed to navigate treacherous coastal waters, as the relics and remains found in the northern isles amply testify.

The correlation between Moon and tides, Moon and growth and Moon and human physiology would all have an extremely important significance. Initially, the reasons for the association would not have been known, but over a period of time, the knowledge and experience gained from close observations would have been put to practical uses. No doubt, the myths connected with growth and fertility owe their origins to lunar influence. The Moon's phases could be symbolically interpreted as the sowing of the seed and birth (New Moon), a gradual increase in light until Full, then slow decrease and death. This cycle, which could be related to human existence, had practical as well as symbolic connotations; an essential interchange existed between lunar motions and human expressions and activities.

There is much in favour of support for the traditional tales concerning lunar influence, not least the Moon's role in relation to sexuality and procreation. Early man would have been aware of this, hence the importance attached to the Moon and its movements.

Much concerning megalithic astronomy is obscure, and we are unable to obtain a coherent pattern of the society that built these structures. Until recently, it had been assumed that the origins of civilization were centred in the Middle East, but radio-carbon dating techniques show that prehistoric man is now known to be far older than earlier estimates have suggested. The ability of the early builders to construct and align massive stone structures with such critical precision, demonstrates that they possessed an intellectual awareness far in excess of that previously ascribed to them. They combined a sense of the mystical with an appreciation of the practical and functional. In applying 'naked eye' astronomy, early man consolidated his concepts concerning life and death. His astronomy was unique to him and his times, in the same way that future ages would have an astronomy peculiar to them. Megalithic astronomy was, however, the beginning of the great adventure which would eventually lead to the exploration of space.

The Early Civilizations
The earliest records show that the civilizations of the Tigris and Euphrates valley, the Indus valley and China were actively studying and observing the heavens. Astronomy and Astrology were compatible and remained so, with certain modifications, until the Renaissance (fifteenth century). The Babylonian astronomy/astrology was a highly developed study, and the advances made by the Babylonians became the basis for the Greek astronomy. The combination of Babylonian observations and Greek astronomy enabled Hipparchus (c. 130 B.C.) to devise the concept of celestial bodies moving in epicycles and deferents. Earlier, Eudoxus (408-355 B.C.) a pupil of Plato, suggested a planetary system of heavenly bodies attached to transparent spheres turning on separate axes. The Greek philosophers and astronomers contributed immensely towards an understanding of the Universe. Hipparchus supposed that the planets revolved in circles, not about the earth, but about points which revolved circularly about the earth. The observations of Hipparchus were summarized by Ptolemy (A.D. 100-178) in his great astronomical work of antiquity, the *Almagest*. Ptolemy's system was a geocentric view of the Universe; the Earth lay at the centre of the Universe and around it moved the Sun, Moon and planets. Each planet was assumed to move round a circle or epicycle, the centre of which moved round a larger circle (the deferent) which was itself centred on the Earth. At the time of Ptolemy, it was considered that the circle was the perfect geometrical form and that only perfect motion was possible in the heavens. This was the accepted view until the sixteenth century, although the Ptolemaic system did not remain rigid, but was constantly modified in the light of new facts. From the time of Hipparchus until the sixteenth century, almost 1800 years later, little progress was made regarding the understanding of the Universe. The Greeks had devised a model of the planetary system which was of limited use, particularly as the Earth was considered to be the centre of the Universe.

AN OUTLINE OF THE HISTORY OF ASTRONOMY

The idea that the Earth is a sphere probably first occurred to the ancient Greeks around 500 B.C. The four basic elements, fire, air, water, earth were assumed to occupy particular places in the Universe or 'cosmos'. Aristotle, in developing this theory, reasoned that earth must be at the centre of the Universe because rocks fall downward, while the upper atmosphere was composed of fire because flames tend to leap upward. In between were two fluids, air and water (corresponding to the Earth's atmosphere and oceans) and above the upper atmosphere was the 'sphere of the Moon'. In all these regions below the Moon, the normal course of events was for matter (composed in differing proportions of the four elements) to change and decay, but above the Moon were the unchanging heavens, where the Sun, planets and stars moved in perfect circles. In this celestial region there was only one element, ether. Aristotle's theories formed the basis of astronomy and physics until the seventeenth century and were not seriously questioned until then.

The ancient Greeks, imagining the Earth to be a sphere, had at least some supporting evidence for this idea.
1. Ships sailing away from land disappeared hull first, with the sails being the last part to vanish below the horizon. The Earth's surface must therefore at least be curved.
2. During an eclipse of the Moon, the Earth's shadow is not straight but curved, similar to the shadow cast by a ball.
3. Mariners sailing southward reported that the Pole Star (Polaris) appeared progressively lower down in the northern sky, again suggesting a curved surface for the Earth.
4. An additional piece of evidence was supplied by the philosopher, Eratosthenes of Cyrene in the third century B.C. He showed that on the same day of the year, a stick placed in the ground at Syene in Egypt cast no shadow at noon, the Sun then being directly overhead, but a stick in the ground at Alexandria, 500 miles to the north, cast a short shadow at the same time of day, indicating that the Sun was 7 ½ ° from the overhead point (zenith). By measuring the distance between Syene and Alexandria, Eratosthenes was able to calculate the circumference of the Earth and arrived at a surprisingly accurate result (within a few percent of modern estimates).

Some astronomers thought that the Earth was cylindrical, with the axis running east-west, but the evidence of (1) and (2) clearly contradicted this. Of course, the Greeks' and Babylonians' knowledge of the extent of the world was very limited, and did not extend beyond India in the east and the Gibraltar Straits in the west.

Astronomers had also observed that the five bright planets then known, Mercury, Venus, Mars, Jupiter, Saturn, did not move in straight paths around the sky but appeared to move westward at times, instead of their normal eastward movement. Eudoxus of Knidos (third century B.C.) tried to explain this by the theory of 'epicycles', where the planets were not only revolving around the Earth, but were also revolving on epicyclic orbits around a deferent.

During the fifth century B.C., the philosopher Philolaos postulated that instead of everything in the sky moving around the Earth, it was the Earth itself that was turning on its axis and causing apparent motion of the sky. The Earth, he supposed, was also in motion, not around the Sun, but around some mythical 'central fire', around which also revolved the Sun, Moon, planets and the sphere of fixed stars. Another view of the Universe, placing the Earth at the centre, was developed by Apollonius, Hipparchus and Ptolemy between the third century B.C. and the second century A.D. According to this theory, the planets revolve around the Earth on complex orbits which are a combination of straightforward orbital motion around the Earth and epicyclic orbital motion around a deferent. The resultant path of the planet includes a series of loops which matches the actual observed paths. This hypothesis is similar to that of Eudoxus, except that 'wheels' were supposed to be the prime mover, while for Eudoxus it was 'spheres'. To fit the observations, however, in the case of some planets more than one epicycle was required, and in the end as many as forty 'wheels' were required to move the different parts of the Universe, Sun, Moon, planets and sphere of fixed stars.

The first person to suggest that the Earth and the other planets move around the Sun was Aristarchus of Samos in the third century B.C. Aristarchus also measured the distances of the Sun and Moon, using geometrical methods, obtaining a quite accurate value for the Moon's distance but a grossly erroneous one for the Sun's. But his theories of a Sun-centred Universe were forgotten until the time of Copernicus in the sixteenth century, and an Earth-centred Universe was assumed.

Ptolemy was the last great astronomer of the ancient period, and for many centuries afterwards, the development of astronomy and science came almost to a standstill in Europe. The Mediterranean civilization was eventually dominated by Rome (second century B.C.)

AN OUTLINE OF THE HISTORY OF ASTRONOMY

and when, in turn, the Roman Empire declined during the first few centuries of the Christian Era, much of the ancient astronomical tradition and knowledge was lost and only re-discovered many centuries later when Islamic science reached its peak. After the middle of the seventh century, the Moslem world expanded rapidly, and the ancient sciences were translated into Arabic and further fundamental advances in mathematics and astronomy were made. The Islamic contribution is important in that it preserved the ancient traditions of Greek astronomy which later European scholars found so valuable. Ptolemy's great work, the *Almagest*, was translated into Arabic, and eventually into Latin (A.D. 1175). During this time, however, the ideas of Aristotle concerning the physical workings of the Universe still went unchallenged, and the Earth was still considererd to be at the centre.

The Renaissance

The sixteenth century saw the circumnavigation of the Earth by Magellan (1519-22) and the sphericity of the Earth was established. This was the age of geographical exploration; the discovery of the Americas, and a sea route to India via the Cape of Good Hope. All this demanded efficient navigational instruments and tables. No satisfactory determination of longitude was possible, (this came later with the invention of the marine chronometer by Harrison), but latitude could be found from tables of solar declination or from Pole Star altitude corrections. These extensive voyages in southern latitudes contributed to further advances in astronomy, in that the southern constellations were examined and studied for a substitute for the Pole Star. A new age was dawning, and many of the old concepts concerning the Earth and the Universe were being challenged. The sixteenth century was remarkable for the profound social and economical effects which followed the great explorations. The theory of a spherical Earth assisted in the rapid advances in scientific thought and discoveries.

For the preceding 1800 years, the Earth was considered to be the centre of the Universe. The beginnings of a new model for the heavens were established by Nicholas Copernicus (1473-1543) a Polish astronomer. Copernicus suggested that it was the Sun and not the Earth which was at the centre of the Universe. His heliocentric hypothesis, as detailed in his book (1543) *De Revolutionibus Orbium Coelestium* (On the Revolutions of the Heavenly Spheres), suggested that the planetary system was a Solar system. This radical idea had in fact, been propounded by the Greek, Aristarchus, almost nineteen centuries previously, but the theory had been rejected.

It was clear to Copernicus that the theory of the planets' motions, derived by Ptolemy and the other Greek astronomers, was so divided from the observational reality, that a new theory was urgently called for. In fact, there were several Ptolemaic systems, but all were variations on the same Earth-centred theme, and as such all were grossly in error. In his *Revolutionibus*, Copernicus argues that the Earth is spherical, that the Universe is spherical, that the motions of the heavenly bodies are uniform, circular and perpetual, and that the Earth is not the centre of all revolutions, because of the planets' irregular motions. The Earth, he said, has three distinct types of motion: axial rotation once per day, orbital revolution (around the Sun), and conical-axial rotation once per year. The new Sun-centred theory was able to explain the motions of the planets, both direct and retrograde. The theories of Copernicus, as set down in his book, are set out in the form of discursive arguments and run as follows:

> The Universe is spherical, because, either a sphere is the most perfect form, or because it possesses the greatest area for a given volume, or because the celestial objects, Sun, Moon and stars are spherical. The Earth is also spherical, because travelling either north or south on its surface, brings a change in the altitude of the Pole Star and a corresponding change in the number of stars that are circumpolar. The Earth occupies a greater volume than do the oceans, otherwise the latter would dissolve the former. The motion of the celestial objects is uniform, circular, and perpetual, or composed of circular motions. The multitude number of spheres causes many motions, that is, the rotation of the Earth from west to east, and the various motions of the Sun, Moon and planets. The irregular speeds of Sun and Moon in their orbits is ascribed to unevenness in the moving force or to the fact that these orbits are eccentric.

The geocentric view gradually gave way to the heliocentric system and, although the new system yielded better results and reduced the cumbersome mathematics associated with the geocentric system, it still lacked a certain amount of accuracy. The Copernican Revolution introduced reforms in the fundamental concepts of astronomy with a broadening of man's understanding of nature, which eventually led to the scientific revolution of the seventeenth century and the Newtonian conception of the Universe. Not only in astronomy was the Revolution so significant, but its impact influenced the social, economic, philosophical and intellectual attitudes which, hitherto, had in some cases, remained fairly dormant. Copernicus's theories did not gain immediate acceptance, following the publishing of *De Revolutionibus* in 1543. For instance, the astronomer Thomas Blundeville wrote 'Copernicus . . . affirms that the earth turns about and that the sun stands still in the midst of the heavens, by help of which false supposition, he made truer demonstrations of the motions and revolutions of the celestial spheres, than ever were made before.' This was written in 1594. Most astronomers were hostile to the new ideas although a few, (Rheticus, Digges and Maestlin, among others) accepted and taught them.

As the sixteenth century drew to a close, the 'Sun-centred' Universe gradually gained favour among astronomers. The most notable astronomers at this period were Tycho Brahe and Johannes Kepler. Tycho was primarily an observational astronomer, and used his various instruments to compile accurate star-charts and to carry out prolonged observations of the planets' positions over a period of many years. These observations were performed from his observatory on the Danish island of Hven. The planets' positions were calculated to an accuracy of about four minutes of arc, and those of the stars to one second of arc, a distinct improvement on the observations of the astronomers of ancient times.

The Sun-centred theory was rejected by Tycho, because he had not been able to detect any parallax in the stars' positions, that was a necessary result of the Earth moving around the Sun. He could not accept, or did not know, the vast distance between the Earth and the stars compared with the distances of the planets. Rejecting the Ptolemaic and Copernican systems, he devised a theory of his own. According to this theory, the Earth is stationary and non-rotating at the centre of the Universe, while a sphere carrying all the stars rotates once every twenty-four hours. In between, the Sun moves round the Earth once every year, and the five planets known then, all move in orbits around the Sun. In 1572, Tycho observed what is now known as a nova (an exploding star) in the constellation of Cassiopeia, and for eighteen months it continued to be visible, outshining Venus when at its brightest. This object could not be a comet, because it had no tail and did not move relative to the neighbouring stars. The significance of this event lay in the fact that, up to that time, the heavens had been regarded as unchangeable, meaning that the new object must be some phenomenon occurring in the upper atmosphere. This idea, however, was quickly falsified when the nova's parallax was measured which showed that it must be as far away as the stars. Similarly, comets observed by Tycho between 1577 and 1596 also showed no measurable parallax, so that these objects also were very distant. Although Tycho's contributions to astronomy were important and significant, it was Kepler, an associate of Tycho, who eventually discovered the fundamental laws governing planetary motions.

After Tycho's death in 1601, Kepler continued the observational work using tables compiled by Tycho. Kepler concentrated mainly on the orbit of Mars, which has a particularly eccentric orbit. From his observations and researches, he concluded that the planets do not move in circular paths but in ellipses. To explain the planetary motions in greater detail, he formulated his three laws:

1. The planets move in ellipses with the Sun at one focus of the ellipse.
2. The radius vector (imaginary line connecting the Sun with the planet) sweeps out equal areas in equal times.
3. The squares of the planets' revolution periods are directly proportional to the cubes of their distances from the Sun.

Unlike Tycho, Kepler was an adherent of the Sun-centred Universe theory, as was apparent from the three laws of planetary motion. The force, which kept the planets in their orbits around the Sun, was at that time unknown — this was before the time of Newton — but Kepler imagined that the Sun produces a force, acting outward and parallel to the Ecliptic, which impinges on each planet and pushes it along. The more distant planets receive a correspondingly weaker force, and therefore move more slowly along their orbits. Also, Kepler's second law says that the same planet will alter its speed during its orbit, travelling faster the nearer it is to the Sun. This force, which Kepler called the 'anima motrix', was a forerunner of gravitation, developed by Newton nearly a century later.

Another theory suggested by Kepler and set out in his *Cosmographical Mystery,* was the relationship between the planets' orbits and the five regular solids. The reasoning for this was that, if the five solids are packed one inside the other, then spheres carrying the planets' orbits can be interposed between the solids. In practice, this would involve the following arrangement — the sphere of Saturn encloses the cube, that of Jupiter encloses the tetrahedron, that of Mars encloses the dodecahedron, that of the Earth encloses the icosahedron, that of Venus encloses the octahedron, and the octahedron encloses the sphere of Mercury. In each case, the corners of the solids join the surfaces of the spheres. Although the planets' orbits are elliptical, this ellipticity is sufficiently small to be accommodated in each case by the five solids. Kepler did not accept the possibility of planets beyond Saturn, as this would conflict with his theories.

Galileo Galilei (1564-1642) supported the heliocentric theory by his discoveries of the Galilean moons (four satellites of Jupiter) using the newly-invented telescope. His observations proved that other planets were capable of attracting celestial bodies. Galileo's discoveries completely overturned the old Earth-centred theories. These findings included the rugged, mountainous nature of the Moon's surface, the phases of Venus, the satellites of Jupiter, and the fact that the Milky Way consists of thousands of faint stars. From the shadows cast by the Moon's mountains, he could calculate their height, and found that they were comparable with those of Earth. On the Sun's surface, he found sunspots. All these observations inferred that the Universe was far from being the changeless, perfectly formed place the ancients imagined it to be, but rather it was more like the Earth. Also, it was far larger than previously envisaged. The fact that the satellites of Jupiter were seen to revolve around the planet, once every few days, proved that the Universe had more than one centre of rotation. The sunspots disproved the idea of an unblemished Sun. The phases of Venus proved that it travelled around the Sun, not around the Earth. The vast increase in the number of stars that the telescope revealed, both in the Milky Way and in other parts of the sky, threw doubt on the idea that they were all fixed to a sphere, all at the same distance from the Earth, and suggested that instead they might be other suns all at different distances from the Earth. Such notions had first been expressed in the previous century, before the invention of the telescope, by the mathematicians and astronomers, John Dee, Thomas Digges and Giordano Bruno. There was an innumerable number of stars, they said, and some of them might even be larger than the Sun, but they only appear tiny because of their immense distances. Digges described the region beyond the planets as 'this orb of stars fixed infinitely up extends itself in altitude spherically' (1576). Dee observed the supernova of 1572, and concluded that it was a real star and that it faded away, because it moved away through space in a straight line from the Earth.

The Renaissance — the Great Revival of Learning — called into question the ideas and teachings of the ancients. The great astronomers of the period, Brahe, Copernicus, Kepler and Galileo had, in their different ways, laid the foundations for constructing a comprehensive scheme for the new knowledge. The questioning of the old concepts prompted Descartes, a renowned mathematician, to reason about the Universe, and seek to explain the nature of the physical world in the light of the new discoveries. His *Discourse on Method* is probably one of the most influential books on the philosophy of science. The ideas and speculations of Descartes were a major influence, but it was Isaac Newton (1642-1727) who finally confirmed, by brilliant mathematical analyses, the motion of bodies in orbit and the Law of Gravitation. In this, he was building upon the foundations as formulated by Descartes and the Renaissance astronomers.

2.
THE DEVELOPMENT OF MODERN ASTRONOMY

During the seventeenth century, a revolution was taking place in astronomy. Old ideas and concepts, based on philosophical speculation, concerning the structure of the Universe, were being replaced by new ones founded on observation, logical reasoning and deduction. The theories which were prevalent in ancient times and in the Middle Ages were principally those of the philosophers of classical Greece, particularly Aristotle, Archimedes and Ptolemy. The challenges of the Renaissance resulted in a rejection of the old concepts and teachings concerning an Earth-centred Universe, and although the findings of Brahe, Kepler, Copernicus and Galileo laid the foundations for the new knowledge, it was Newton's discoveries which extended and consolidated the 'new astronomy'.

In 1687, Newton published his monumental work *Principia Mathematica,* in which he explained and described his new theory of universal gravitation; this could be applied to the Solar system in order to explain the motions of the planets. The true scale of the Solar system was established by Dominique Cassini (1625-1712) when he measured the distances to the Sun and Mars (1671), and by Kepler's laws, it was then possible to calculate the distances of the other planets. Newton used Kepler's laws in his theory of gravitation and was able to compute the mass of each planet. Prior to this, the real nature of the planets was unknown, and they were assumed to be attached to revolving transparent spheres; the observations of Galileo and others and the theories of Newton showed the planets to be spheres of material like our Earth and in free orbit around the Sun.

The primary use of astronomy in the seventeenth century was in the field of navigation; mariners needed to know the longitude at sea. A number of different methods were adopted, including the drawing up of lines of equal magnetic declination on ocean charts, and the compilation of tables of eclipses of Jupiter's satellites, but none of these methods proved to be practicable or sufficiently accurate. The only way of solving the navigation problem involved either making extremely accurate observations of the Moon's position over a long period of time, so that a proper theory of the Moon's motion could be derived, or by drawing up accurate star charts. The best star chart available in the seventeenth century was that compiled by Tycho Brahe, but this was not accurate enough. In 1675, the Royal Greenwich Observatory was founded and under its succession of Astronomers Royal, produced increasingly accurate star charts, and also observations of the Moon's motion and position which Newton used in his theory of gravitation. With the invention of the marine chronometer by John Harrison (1693-1776), the problem of time at sea and the finding of longitude was overcome.

This was a period when there was a growing interest in theoretical astronomy and, with the new theories of the Universe now firmly established, new facts became apparent. One of these concerned the positions of stars relative to one another; from ancient times, the stars were considered to be fixed in space attached to some transparent sphere or, all at the same distance from Earth. In 1718, the second Astronomer Royal, Edmond Halley (1656-1742) found that the positions of a few stars had altered over the past 1500 years, and he concluded that stars could not be fixed but moved in space relative to one another. This relative movement of individual stars is known as *proper motion*. It was slowly becoming apparent to astronomers, that not only were the stars like our Sun — bodies of hot luminous gas — but that the Sun itself was no more than an ordinary star. This had been suggested by Dee, Digges and Bruno as early as the late sixteenth century. It was also becoming apparent that the stars are not confined to a thin shell of space some distance beyond the orbit of Saturn but are scattered at random throughout an immense volume of space.

Many of the new developments in astronomy during this time and subsequently were made possible by the improved telescopes which were being constructed. Galileo's telescopes of 1610 were primitive by modern-day standards, consisting as they did of two small lenses in a tube and giving only low magnifications and images of poor quality. In 1668, Newton built a telescope which collected its light by means of a *parabolic* mirror instead of a lens; this type of telescope is called a *reflector,* while those which collect light with a lens are called *refractors.* The early refractors suffered from what is known as *chromatic aberration;* a failure to refract all colours equally, so that the image is surrounded by a colour halo. The optician, John Dollond (1706-1761) overcame this difficulty in 1754 by constructing a lens made in two parts cemented together, called an *achromatic.* Prior to this, all refractors had to be of great length, some 30 to 40 feet, in order to reduce the aberration, but now they could be made far shorter. Nearly all telescopes built before the end of the eighteenth century were quite small — their lenses or mirrors were usually less than 12 inches or so in diameter. Larger instruments were not constructed, because astronomers were mainly involved with positional astronomy, measuring positions of stars and compiling charts for navigational purposes — for which fairly small instruments were adequate — than with the more theoretical aspects of the subject. However, this was gradually changing, and one of the first astronomers who carried out proper research into 'pure' (as opposed to applied) astronomy was Sir William Herschel (1738-1822). He observed mainly with a 20 inch reflector which he built around 1780, but a few years later, he built a giant reflector of 48 inches aperture and also a number of smaller telescopes. With these, Herschel carried out 'surveys of the heavens' — star counts in each of several thousand small areas of the northern sky. He also catalogued many thousands of star clusters and *nebulae* (clouds of dust and gas in outer space). After an analysis of his observations which were made over a period of many years, Herschel concluded that stars are distributed at random throughout space, but also that they form a vast galaxy, shaped like a lens or a box with the longest side aligned along the plane of the Milky Way.

The Milky Way appears as a faint luminous band circling the entire sky, but which is in fact composed of millions of faint distant stars. The Sun was assumed to be somewhere near the centre of this galaxy. Herschel did not know how far away the stars were, but in his attempts to solve this, he found that some stars are double and revolve around one another — so proving that Newton's laws of universal gravitation are indeed universal. Another theory advanced by Herschel was the evolution of stars; because of the time taken for light to travel across space (the speed of light had already been established — at 186,000 miles per second — over a century earlier), the more distant stars ought to be, as a general rule, at an earlier stage in their evolution than the nearer stars. As we shall see presently, this rule does in fact hold for the galaxies. While carrying out his observations, Herschel in 1781 discovered the planet Uranus, the first planet to be discovered in modern times. In 1846, two mathematicians, John Adams (1819-1892) and Urbain LeVerrier (1811-1877) discovered Neptune, and the calculations of Percival Lowell (1855-1916) led to the discovery of Pluto by Clyde Tombaugh in 1930.

National observatories had also been established on the Continent, the first being at Paris (founded 1671) and, as with Greenwich, their main purpose was to compile sufficiently accurate star charts for navigational use. But in the nineteenth century, their work expanded into other fields also. In 1838, the first distance to a star was measured by the astronomer Friedrich Bessel (1784-1846). These measurements were made by the method known as *trigonometrical parallax* by which the position of a star, relative to the background of more distant stars, is measured when the Earth is at opposite points in its orbit (in January and July for example). The nearest star, Proxima Centauri, was found to be 25 million million miles away (4.3 light years). In the years after 1838, the distances of many more stars were found by this parallax method. However, the *parallactic shifts* of all stars are extremely small, in all cases being less than one second of arc, so that they are very difficult to measure accurately, and the parallax method can be used only for the nearest stars out to a distance of 1,000 million million miles. Due to the vast distances in space, astronomers use the more convenient unit of measurement: the *light year* (the distance travelled by a light ray in one year, which is 6 million million miles). Once more, it became clear that the scale of space is vast. But probably the greatest advances in astronomy during the second half of the nineteenth century resulted from two newly developed techniques which could be applied to astronomy — *spectroscopy and photography*.

The story of spectroscopy began in 1666, when Newton passed sunlight through a prism which split the light up into its component colours (the rainbow or spectrum). Then in 1814, the optician Joseph von Fraunhofer (1787-1826) showed that the Sun's spectrum is crossed by a large number of dark lines; he mapped the positions of some 500 of these lines. Subsequent work by other scientists, notably the physicist Gustav Kirchoff (1824-1887) and the chemist Robert Bunsen (1811-1899) showed that each chemical compound and element have their own unique set of spectral lines, and that those lines in the Sun's spectrum could tell astronomers what elements and compounds were present in the Sun. It was quite a different matter however, to obtain a spectrum from a star, the brightest of which are thousands of millions of times fainter than the Sun. In 1860, the problem was studied by William Huggins (1824-1910), an amateur astronomer who, with some difficulty at first, eventually succeeded in obtaining spectra of some stars, comparing them with the spectra of chemical compounds, and deducing what compounds those stars contained. In this way, he was able to show that the Sun and stars all contain basically the same material (i.e., hydrogen and a few other elements and compounds in smaller quantities). Huggins was also able to prove that nebulae were not aggregations of stars, as some astronomers had maintained, but clouds of luminous gas.

Photography was invented in 1835 and was soon applied to astronomy, the first astronomical photograph taken being one of the Moon in 1840. As techniques improved, so photography could be extended to cover other branches of astronomy, and it was used in the late nineteenth century to record spectra of stars and also to compile star charts. This quickly replaced the old visual methods of observation which were subject to bias from different observers, although the visual methods did remain in planetary work, as they were, and still are, the better of the two ways of recording details on the planets' surfaces. An image of a planet is distorted by currents of air, and therefore the details are rather blurred on a photograph (except on those taken with a large telescope), but the observer's eye can pick out the fine detail in those brief moments when air currents quieten down.

In the field of planetary astronomy, much of the work has been done by amateur astronomers using fairly modest equipment. Considerable work has been done by amateurs in observations of the Sun, Moon, meteors, comets and the planets. The amateur astronomers and their associations have played a large part in this field, because the objects in the Solar system do not, in general, require large telescopes in order to observe them properly. Also, the professional astronomers were, and still are, usually too busy concentrating on the stars, nebulae and galaxies, which only they, with their large instruments, are able to study extensively. The early amateurs did pioneering work, for example Heinrich Schwabe, who observed the Sun regularly and in 1852, announced that the size and number of sunspots vary in an eleven-year cycle; William Lassell who discovered, in the mid-nineteenth century, many of the satellites which orbit around the planets; Beer and Madler who drew up a large map of the Moon around 1830; James Nasmyth who also observed the Moon and theorized in 1874 about its geology; and W. F. Denning who did much important work on meteors around the turn of this century. Other amateurs made very large numbers of observations of the planets over the years; the planet Mars was extensively observed from 1877 onwards by the astronomers Giovanni Schiaparelli, Percival Lowell, E. M. Antoniadi and others (although some of these were professionals).

The national observatories were not slow to make use of the new tools of photography and spectroscopy and, during the second half of the nineteenth century, they were employed in research programmes. In 1872, Greenwich commenced spectroscopic observations of stars to determine their actual motions and velocities through space. The principle behind these observations is the *Doppler effect* — which can be illustrated by sound rather than light — the pitch of a car horn or a train whistle will fall as it passes the observer. The same principle applies to light waves when the lines in a star's spectrum will be shifted to the blue end of the spectrum if the star is approaching, and shifted to the red end if it is receding.

A 26-inch refractor telescope was acquired by Greenwich in 1894, and a few years later still larger telescopes with which the spectroscopic work was continued. They were also used to measure position-angles of double stars. Regular observations of the Sun commenced in 1883. At the same time, large observatories were being built, particularly in America, for research alone rather than for the compilation of star charts. These observatories were usually attached to universities, and were built on high mountains where the air was very clear and where the skies were normally free of cloud, smoke and the glare of town lights. The principal task of these observatories was to establish the real nature and composition of the stars and nebulae, and in order to do this, they had complex equipment such as spectroscopes, photometers and blink comparators. With these, the astronomers could calculate a star's chemical composition, its brightness and its proper motion, and, using the laws of physics (many of which were newly developed at the time), could then proceed to calculate other properties of a star, for example its mass and its surface temperature. The situation was a vast improvement on that of only fifty years earlier when astronomers, possessing only telescopes, could only observe the brightness and distribution of the stars in the sky.

In 1913 two astronomers, Ejnar Hertzsprung (1873) and Henry Russell (1877) plotted the luminosity of a large number of stars against their respective surface temperatures (indicated by their spectra). They obtained an interesting result — the hotter a star is, the more luminous it is, and that this was true for the majority of stars, including the Sun. Stars which obey this 'temperature-luminosity' law are said to lie in a band called the *Main Sequence*. Those at the hot, bright end are also very large and are known as *Blue Giants*, while those at the cool, dim end are very small stars and are known as *Red Dwarfs*. Stars which are not on the Main Sequence normally fall into one of two categories, being either *Red Giants* or *White Dwarfs*. The graph of 'luminosity against surface temperature' for stars is known as the *Hertzsprung-Russell diagram*.

Astronomers had realized for a long time that the stars were similar to our own Sun, but it was not known exactly how they shine. The gas laws of physics, discovered from about 1670 onwards, were applied to astronomy. In 1853, the physicist Hermann von Helmholtz (1821-1894) suggested that the Sun and stars are steadily contracting (although at an extremely slow rate) under their own weight, and that this potential energy of contraction is converted continuously into light and heat energy. Calculations showed that, if this were indeed the case, the Sun, Earth and the rest of the solar system could be no more than 18 million years old. At the time, this seemed reasonable enough, but later investigations in biology and geology showed that the Earth at least must be about 4,700 million years old. It was not until 1939, that the real source of radiation from the Sun and stars was found, namely *nuclear fusion*, by the physicist Hans Bethe (1906-). This involved the conversion of hydrogen into helium, both of which were known to exist in the Sun and stars, and in this fusion process, a small quantity of matter is annihilated as it is converted into energy. This energy is radiated in the form of light, infra-red (heat) and energy of other wavelengths. In this way, the Sun loses 4 million tons of its mass every second. Conversion of matter into energy was first postulated in 1905 by the physicist Albert Einstein (1879-1955) in his 'Theory of Relativity'.

Theories were also advanced to explain the evolution and formation of stars, using the Hertzsprung-Russell diagram. An early theory held that stars were initially Blue Giants, and then cooled continuously during their lifetimes 'sliding down' the Main Sequence, and finally becoming Red Dwarfs when they had little available hydrogen fuel left. Later theories were completely different, stating that the position occupied by a star in the Main Sequence depends upon its original mass — the greater the mass, the hotter and brighter the star. Stars also remain fairly stable and do not change appreciably in size, mass, luminosity, surface temperature or any other property during most of their lifetime. When they cannot burn away any more hydrogen fuel, stars either swell into Red Giants and then collapse into White Dwarfs, or they explode as novae.

Astronomers were also interested in the clouds of dust and gas, *the nebulae*, which lay in certain regions between the stars. In the late eighteenth century, Herschel had studied these objects, and at about the same time, the astronomer Charles Messier (1730-1817) drew up a catalogue of about one hundred of them. A more detailed catalogue, the 'New General', was drawn up in the 1880's from the observations which had been made by John Herschel (1792-1871) — the son of Sir William Herschel — and by John Dreyer (1852-1926); this listed several thousand of the nebulae. These nebulae were found to occur in several different forms; some were associated with groups of hot young stars and were composed of hot glowing gas, while others were dark, blocking out the light from stars behind them.

In 1845, Lord Rosse (1800-1867) built a giant 72-inch reflector in the grounds of his home in Ireland; his telescope was then the largest in the world. When he examined the nebulae over the next few years, he found that some of them had a spiral structure. Opinions differed as to the nature of these spiral nebulae. The philosopher Immanuel Kant (1724-1804) had suggested as early as 1755 that the Great Nebula in Andromeda (known then to have a spiral structure) was a vast collection of stars — an 'island universe' in effect. When Rosse found other spiral nebulae, some astronomers stated that they were also collections of stars lying at enormous distances from us. Other astronomers disagreed and stated that they were rotating clouds of gas quite near to the Earth, and probably were other solar systems in the early stages of formation. The problem was resolved in 1899 when a spectrogram was obtained of the Andromeda Nebula which showed it to be a collection of stars and not a cloud of gas. Spectrograms of other spiral nebulae showed that they were also collections of stars.

The problem of the nebulae had been solved, but their distances could not be established until a suitable method had been found. The solution of this began in 1912, when the astronomer Henrietta Leavitt (1868-1921) observed a certain type of variable star (a star which periodically varies in brightness) known as a *Cepheid,* and noted that each Cepheid had a period directly proportional to its brightness; these stars were among those in the bright patch of light in the southern sky called the Small Magellanic Cloud. In the next few years, the astronomer Harlow Shapley (1885-) found more of these Cepheids in globular star clusters and, from their period-luminosity law, he could calculate the relative distances of these Cepheids and globulars. From an analysis of their real velocities through space (the resultant of their transverse proper motions across the sky), and their radial line-of-sight motions, Shapley could calculate the real distance of the Cepheids, globular clusters, and hence the size of our Galaxy.

Early in this century, the astronomer Jacobus Kapteyn (1851-1922) carried out star counts for each magnitude (brightness) and, from his results, stated that our Galaxy is shaped like a lens; in 1920, he estimated its diameter as 55,000 light years and the thickness as 11,000 light years, and these results were in fairly good agreement with Shapley's. The work of Kapteyn was similar to that of Herschel a century earlier, but Kapteyn went further than Herschel and found, after an analysis of the proper motions of many stars, that these stars were moving *en masse* in two directions, one set of stars going one way and the other set moving in the opposite direction. The astronomer Jan Oort (1900-) did a more detailed study of the motions of the stars and, in 1925, he was able to show that the Galaxy as a whole is rotating in a period of 225 million years. The centre of the Galaxy is 30,000 light years distant in the constellation of Sagittarius, with the Sun about two-thirds this distance out from the centre of the Galaxy. The total number of stars in our Galaxy is estimated to be 100,000 million. Oort also showed that the Galaxy possesses spiral arms growing out of a central nucleus; the Sun lies in one of these spiral arms.

When the astronomer Edwin Hubble (1889-1953) examined the

Great Spiral Nebula in the constellation of Andromeda, he found a number of Cepheids among its constituent stars, and was therefore able to calculate its distance. When this was done in 1923, it became obvious that it lies far outside our Galaxy, and is in fact an independent galaxy in its own right and similar to our own. This galaxy is now known to be 2,200,000 light years distant with a diameter of about 180,000 light years. Our Galaxy has a diameter of 100,000 light years, so the earlier estimates of Kapteyn are somewhat in error. Large reflectors of 60, 100 and 200-inch aperture were built in America in 1908, 1917 and 1948 respectively, and with them, astronomers could observe ever further out into space. The distances of the nearer galaxies were measured by taking into account the brightness of the brightest stars in them, while for those more distant galaxies, which are too far away to be resolved into individual stars, the brightness of each galaxy is assumed to be inversely proportional to the square of its distance, and so astronomers can tell how far away they are. Hubble also found, in 1929, that every galaxy except the nearest few are receding from our Galaxy, and that this velocity of recession is directly proportional to the distance. This is known because the lines in a galaxy's spectrum are all shifted toward the red end, and hence the term *red shift* has come into general use in measurements of galactic velocities.

The constant of proportionality, linking recessional velocities and distances of the galaxies, is known as 'Hubble's constant' and has been revised several times since 1929; the present best estimate is about 180 miles per second for every 10 million light years. This means that a galaxy, at a distance of 100 million light years, must be rushing away from us at about 1,800 miles per second. Hubble made an extensive survey of the galaxies and found that about 80 per cent are spirals like our own, about 17 per cent are elliptical or spherical in shape, and the remaining 3 per cent or so have no particular form and are called 'irregular galaxies'. The range of sizes of galaxies vary, with the smallest being about 10,000 light years across, while the largest have diameters of up to 200,000 light years.

Just as our own Sun had been 'removed' from the centre of the Universe in the eighteenth century when astronomers realized that it was only an ordinary star, so likewise astronomers were realizing that our Galaxy is only an ordinary one and is not at the centre of the Universe. The recession of the galaxies from our Galaxy (and obviously, from every other galaxy) implied that the galaxies must have been huddled together as an extremely compact mass when the Universe came into being, and that this mass exploded sending material flying in all directions, which later was to form into stars and galaxies. The birth of the Universe as the result of a gigantic explosion is now an accepted fact, and one of the first to advance this theory was the priest Georges Lemaitre (1894-1966) in 1927. This theory was subsequently more fully developed in the late 1940s by the theoretical astronomers George Gamow (1904-1968), Thomas Gold (1920-), Hermann Bondi (1919-), Raymond Lyttleton, and Fred Hoyle (1915-), who took into account Einstein's theories of relativity.

There are two theories of relativity which were derived by Einstein, the 'Special Theory' in 1905 which dealt with non-accelerating systems, and the 'General Theory' in 1916 which dealt with accelerating systems and therefore had to include the factor of force in the equations. The Special Theory predicted that the speed of an object in space can only be measured relative to another object and that there are no absolute speeds, and it also predicted that an object, which moved at a speed approaching that of light (relative to the observer), would appear to that observer to have increased in mass and contracted in length. In fact, it was clear that nothing could travel as fast as, or faster than, light, because its mass would become infinite and, at the same time, its length would have shrunk to zero. Now the theories of relativity became relevant to the new branches of astronomy called *cosmology* and *cosmogony* (which deal respectively with the structure of the Universe as a whole and with its evolution), because the most distant galaxies were found to be moving at speeds of an appreciable fraction of the speed of light. The theory of the origin of the Universe, which states that it came into being as an exploding mass is known as the *Big Bang* theory. Subsequently, another theory was advanced by Hoyle, known as the *Steady State* theory. This basically states that new matter is being continuously created out of space left between receding galaxies, in a Universe which has no beginning and no end in time. This second theory was found to be unsound and was abandoned by all astronomers, even Hoyle by 1965, and today, the Big Bang theory is universally accepted.

By the 1940s, other branches of astronomy were being developed and in the following years, rapid advances were made. The first of these was *radio astronomy*, which began when the radio engineer,

Karl Jansky (1905-50), discovered by accident in 1931, radio waves coming from outer space. After the Second World War, radio astronomy assumed great importance, and special observatories were constructed in many parts of the world. In Britain, the two main observatories devoted to radio astronomy are at Jodrell Bank in Cheshire and the Radio Astronomy Observatory of Cambridge University. Many of these observatories have produced extensive and detailed maps of the 'radio sky' which, of course, looks quite different from the ordinary 'optical sky'. This is because stars, nebulae and other objects in space do not radiate light alone, but also energy of different wavelengths from light; radio waves are one such type of electromagnetic radiation. Also, the colour of a star is determined from where on the electromagnetic spectrum the maximum amount of radiation is being emitted; for example, the Sun appears yellow, because its maximum output lies in the yellow part of the spectrum. The Sun and other stars radiate radio waves as well, but those objects which are powerful radio emitters are not, in general, the brighter stars. The powerful radio emitters tend to be rather unusual objects like the Crab Nebula (remnant of a supernova), a star which was seen to explode in A.D. 1054, and the recently discovered *quasars* (*quasi-stellar* objects) and *pulsars*. The quasars were first found in 1963, and their counterparts in the optical sky looked like faint blue stars. When their red shifts were measured, however, they were found to be extremely remote objects, being up to 8,000 million light years distant (the most distant optical galaxy is 5,000 million light years away). Pulsars were first discovered by the Cambridge Radio Observatory in 1967 and are very small, very rapidly spinning stars; they are at the end of their lifetimes, and send out very regular pulses of radio waves at the rate of several every second; hence their name. Some of them are just ten miles in diameter, and yet they can be seen optically in large telescopes; they are inside our Galaxy.

In the 1960s, astronomers began to investigate the other parts of the electromagnetic spectrum, of which visible light and radio waves form only a small part. In these investigations, they encountered problems, because the Earth's atmosphere allows only light and short radio waves to pass through it (in the so-called optical and radio 'windows'), but blocks out the other radiations (longer radio waves, ultra-violet, X-rays, gamma rays and cosmic rays). Consequently, any examination of these other radiations must be carried out from above the atmosphere. In the early days, the investigations were done by sending up instruments in balloons or rockets, but in the last few years or so, satellites have been put into orbit, which contain instruments and equipment capable of making regular observations at these wavelengths and transmitting them back to receiving stations on Earth.

Rocketry first began in 1910, when Konstantin Tsiolkovsky put forward the principle of the liquid-fuelled rocket (as opposed to gunpowder rockets which had been in use for centuries). The first successful liquid-fuelled rocket was launched by Robert Goddard in 1926 and travelled 184 feet. Better rockets were developed and used toward the end of the last war, but it was not until October 1957, that the artificial Earth satellite, Sputnik I, was launched. Many more satellites were launched during the following years for use in communications (relaying radio and television signals from one part of the world to another), weather forecasting, and carrying out observations in certain parts of the electromagnetic spectrum.

The first person to go into space was Yuri Gagarin in April 1961. More astronauts went into space in the following years, and unmanned space-craft were also sent to the Moon to take close-up photographs of its surface. Finally, in July 1969, the first men (Neil Armstrong and Edwin Aldrin) stepped out onto the Moon's surface during the Apollo 11 mission (see Appendix IV). There were further Apollo flights to the Moon during the period 1969-1972, and the astronauts carried out experiments on the lunar surface and brought back samples of lunar rocks. Space-craft were also sent to the planets from 1962 onwards; to Mars and Venus in the 1960s (bypassing or orbiting, but not actually landing upon those planets) and then in the 1970s, out to the more distant planets Jupiter and Saturn. These space-craft took close-up photographs of the surfaces of the planets. In 1976, two space-craft named Viking I and II landed on the surface of Mars and transmitted pictures of the surface back to Earth, as well as taking measurements of its atmospheric pressure, temperature, seismic activity, etc.

In recent years, one of the major discoveries has been that of the *black hole*. Black holes were predicted as long ago as the eighteenth century by the mathematician Simon de Laplace (1749-1827), but it is only during the last few years that there has been any evidence of their actual existence in space. A black hole orginates from a star which has a sufficiently high mass and which, when it has reached the White Dwarf stage in its evolution, continues to collapse in on itself still further until all of its matter has been crushed out of existence. This process is, as yet, not properly understood. The 'black hole' is the region of space where this collapse occurs and is not a material object. This region of space, which is sometimes less than one inch in diameter, exerts so much gravitational attraction that nothing, not even light, can escape. Any star or object, which happens to approach to within a certain distance of a black hole, is sucked into it and is torn apart by the tremendous tidal forces which operate there, so that it suffers the same fate as the original star which created the black hole in the first place. No black hole can be seen with any telescope (optical, radio or other), but they can be detected, because they exert gravitational force upon any star or other object which happens to be close to them.

One such object is the powerful source of X-rays known as Cygnus X-I which shows up in optical telescopes as a very hot, blue super giant star; it appears that there is a black hole in its vicinity which is continuously sucking matter away from the star. Quasars, whose real nature remained unknown for many years, are now considered to be entire galaxies which are falling into black holes.

The last three centuries have seen astronomy developing slowly at first, and then in conjunction with the other sciences, particularly physics and chemistry, at an ever-increasing rate. The advent of the computer and with it the application of sophisticated mathematical techniques, has enabled the space scientists to explore, analyse and record many aspects of astronomy which have hitherto remained unknown. Speculations concerning the Universe and its workings have undergone dramatic and revolutionary changes and, as one piece of the jigsaw falls into place, a further step forward is made, and the ever-questing spirit of man pushes onward to new and exciting discoveries.

3.
EARTH AND SKY: LINES, CIRCLES AND PROJECTIONS

The Earth
The Earth is one of the smallest of the nine planets revolving about the Sun and, is similar to several other planets. It orbits a minor star (the Sun), some 30,000 light years from the centre of a galaxy known as the Milky Way. The average radius of its orbit is 93 million miles, and it takes one year to complete its elliptical journey round the Sun.

In the course of one sidereal day, the Earth completes one revolution about its axis, but its motion is complex, and all observations relating to the Earth need to be corrected. This motion involves the combination of several factors such as:

The daily rotation about its axis.
The yearly revolution around the Sun.
Precession and Nutation.
The whole movement of the Solar system in space.

The true motion of the Earth is not directly observable. What can be observed is an apparent motion, as indicated by the apparent rotation of the Celestial sphere, with the heavenly bodies rising on the eastern horizon and setting on the western horizon. The rotation of the Earth results in every place on Earth experiencing day and night. Due to the inclination of the Earth's axis to its orbit, its axis points at all times to the Pole Star, and it also precesses (see Precession) tracing out a small circle in the sky. There is a flattening at the Poles, probably due to the spinning of the Earth when its surface was still molten, and this flattening — 'oblate spheroid' — describes the shape of the Earth.

Latitude and Longitude
In order to locate any place on Earth, we use two sets of geographic co-ordinates and these imaginary circles are termed *Meridians of Longitude* and *Parallels of Latitude*.

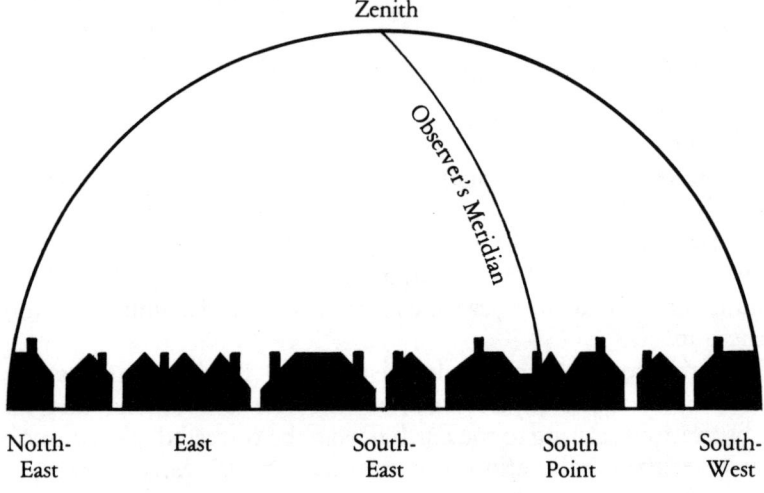

Figure 1. The Observer's Meridian

The great circle which divides the Earth into two hemispheres (north and south) is the Equator (halfway between the two Poles), and measurement along this circle is termed longitude, whilst measurement either north or south of the Equator from 0°-90° is termed latitude. Meridians of Longitude are imaginary circles running along the Earth's surface from the North to the South Pole, lying everywhere exactly in a north-south direction. Our meridian is then our north-south line running through our particular location. At any moment in time, the Sun is on one of these meridians, and for those located at that particular meridian, it is noon. Everywhere east of that meridian, it is afternoon (p.m.) and everywhere west of it, it is still morning (a.m.). The Prime Meridian runs through Greenwich, and all longitudes are measured by their angular distances from this standard meridian (longitude 0°), either east or west from 0°-180°.

In the course of 24 hours, the Sun makes one complete circuit of the heavens, passing over 360° of longitude. Therefore each hour, it covers 15° of longitude or 1° every 4 minutes. If for example, two places on Earth differ in longitude by, say, 30°, i.e., their terrestrial meridians are 30° apart, the difference between their local times, whether sidereal or mean, is 2 hours, because the time interval between the meridian passages of the First Point of Aries at the two places is two sidereal hours, and the time interval between the meridian passages of the mean Sun is two mean-time hours. Likewise, a difference of 150° longitude would give a time difference of 10 hours.

Longitude Equivalent in Time
From the previous discussions, we know that the Mean Sun transits the meridian at noon and that the Local Mean time of any place corresponds to its longitude either east or west. Each degree of longitude is equivalent to 4 minutes of time (24 ÷ 360) = 4 minutes or 15° per hour. To find the longitude equivalent in time of any place, we merely convert the longitude into time by dividing by 15. For example, 120° 45′ west over 15 = 8 hours 3 minutes, or if the longitude is 60° 10′ east, the equivalent is 4 hours 00 minutes 40 seconds. When the place is *west* of Greenwich, the time equivalent is *deducted*, and when it is *east*, the equivalent is *added* to the Greenwich time, and the result is the Local Mean time of the place. The Local Mean at any place is the Hour Angle of the Mean Sun measured from the meridian of that place. Greenwich Mean time is the Local Mean time kept on the meridian of Greenwich. At all places east of Greenwich, the Mean Sun transits the meridian earlier than at Greenwich, and at all places west, the transit occurs later, hence the addition for east longitude and the deduction for west longitude. Tables to facilitate the conversion of longitude into time are included under Appendix III. See also Chapter 5.

The International Date Line
With the adoption of Greenwich as the Prime Meridian for longitude

42   ASTRONOMY FOR ASTROLOGERS

	WEST												GREENWICH NOON	EAST											
	SLOW ON GREENWICH													FAST ON GREENWICH											
					A.M.														P.M.						
Degs. of Long.	180	165	150	135	120	105	90	75	60	45	30	15	0	15	30	45	60	75	90	105	120	135	150	165	180
Long. Equiv. Hours	12	11	10	9	8	7	6	5	4	3	2	1	0	1	2	3	4	5	6	7	8	9	10	11	12
Standard Time	Mid-Night	1	2	3	4	5	6	7	8	9	10	11	Noon	1	2	3	4	5	6	7	8	9	10	11	Mid-Night

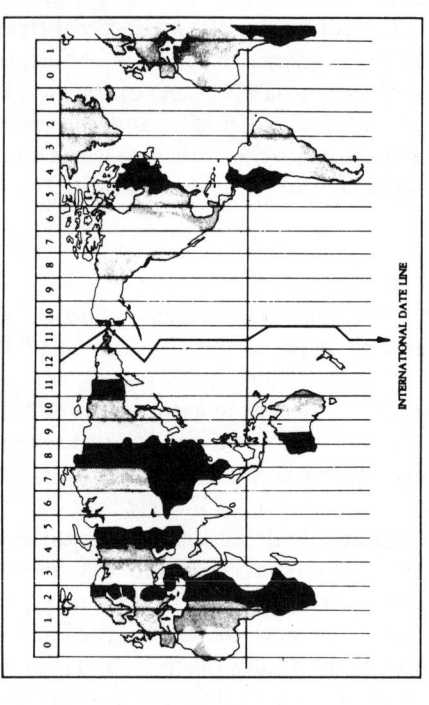

Figure 2. The International Date Line

and time, it was decided that the 180th meridian would be designated as the International Date Line.

Due to the Earth's rotation once every 24 hours, the Sun will transit the meridian of different places at different times. When it is noon at Greenwich, it will be midnight at 180° longitude. On either side of the Date Line, the date will be different. At one particular instant, it will be Monday to the west of that line but Sunday to the east of it. When crossing the Date Line from west to east, one loses a full day; crossing it from east to west, one gains a full day.

The problem of this change of date became known in the early days of the circumnavigation of the globe, when the survivors of Magellan's expedition (1522) reached civilization having sailed westward across the Pacific and then around the Cape of Good Hope. Not only had they practical proof that the Earth was round, but also that they had gained a day. Additional evidence during the next century or so, confirmed that there was a discrepancy as to the date around the borders of the Pacific, according to whether the voyagers came from east or west.

The Line as originally drawn, looped westward of the Hawaiian Islands to include islands which appeared on nineteenth century charts at the western end of the Hawaiian chain. These islands were subsequently proved to be non-existent, so the Date Line was 'straightened out'. The Cook Islands remain on a different side of the Date Line from New Zealand by whom they are administered. The drawing of the International Date Line was not the result of a formal international agreement but, in the words of the hydrographer of the Navy, is 'merely a method of expressing graphically — the differences of date which exist among some of the island groups in the Pacific'.

Positions in the Sky

The Celestial Sphere
To an observer on Earth, the sky appears as a vast inverted bowl, and the stars and other heavenly bodies seem to be on the inside of a large sphere with the Earth at the centre. Within this imaginary hollow sphere, half visible, half unseen, the Earth rotates upon its axis, and, as a result of this rotation, the observer's view of the celestial sphere appears exactly the same as if the Earth were stationary, and the celestial sphere rotated around the same axis at the same speed

or velocity but in an east to west direction. This apparent westward movement of the celestial sphere, causes the Sun and the other bodies to appear to rise east of, and set west of, the observer's meridian (see 'meridians of longitude', page 40).

The hypothetical concept of a celestial sphere is useful, in that the positions and motions of heavenly bodies can be observed and plotted, and by using spherical trigonometry, many problems of positional astronomy can be solved. The celestial sphere is concentric with the terrestrial one, and both spheres have a common centre, axis and equatorial plane.

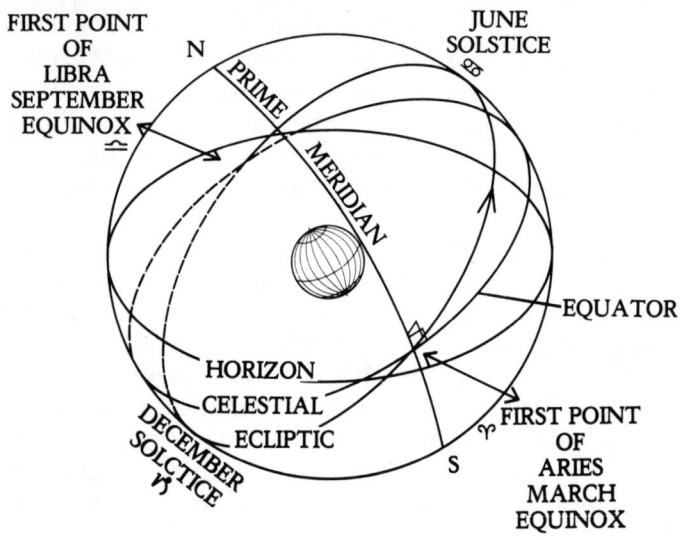

Figure 3. The Celestial Sphere

Three Great Circles

A 'great circle' is any circle whose plane (level) passes through the centre of the Earth. A 'small circle', is in contrast, a circle whose plane does not pass through the centre of the Earth. The *Horizon, Equator* and *Ecliptic* circles are the three main circles of reference for locating an object (celestial body) relative to any place on Earth. If we project the Earth's Equator onto the imaginary Celestial Sphere, we have the Celestial Equator (immediately over the Earth's Equator),

EARTH AND SKY: LINES, CIRCLES AND PROJECTIONS   45

and this imaginary line or circle extending round the heavens divides it into two apparent hemispheres, the northern and southern; in the middle of each are the imaginary points known as the *Celestial Poles*, immediately over, and corresponding to, the North and South Poles of the Earth.

The *Ecliptic*, another imaginary circle, forms an acute angle with the celestial Equator or equinoctial (as it is sometimes called). The Ecliptic represents the apparent annual path of the Sun in the heavens, or the actual path of the Earth as viewed from the Sun, and it may be considered as dividing the heavens into two hemispheres, the central points of which are called the *Poles of the Ecliptic*. The circles of the Ecliptic and the Equator intersect in opposite points of the heavens: at the commencement of the signs Aries and Libra; the First Point of Aries (Vernal Equinox) and the First Point of Libra (Autumnal Equinox). When the Sun in its annual journey reaches these two points, it is Spring (Aries) and Autumn (Libra) in the northern hemisphere. The reverse applies in southern latitudes — northern Spring is southern Autumn and northern Autumn is southern Spring. At this time of the year, there is equal duration of day and night all over the Earth, hence the term Equinox.

The highest points of the Ecliptic, that is, those farthest from the Equator, are called the *Solstices* and are the points that the Sun reaches when it enters the signs Cancer and Capricorn (Summer and Winter Solstices in June and December). When the Sun reaches either of these two points, it appears to 'stand still' — hence the term Solstice — and has acquired its greatest declination (height or distance from the Equator), before it returns again towards the opposite solstice. At the time of the June Solstice in the northern hemisphere, the vertical Sun traces out the imaginary circle known as the 'Tropic of Cancer', and at the time of the December Solstice, the imaginary circle known as the 'Tropic of Capricorn'. These tropic lines have no reference to the heavens but merely indicate the latitude (23° 27') where the Sun is directly overhead at maximum declination 23° 27', either at the June Solstice when it enters the sign Cancer, or at the December Solstice when it enters the sign Capricorn (see Seasons).

The Ecliptic is divided into twelve equal parts, called signs, with each sign containing 30°. The Equator or Equinoctial is divided into twenty-four parts called hours: an hour corresponding to 15°, which is the extent or arc of the heavens that apparently passes over us in that space of time. The circles of the Ecliptic and the Equator with their appropriate divisions and graduations are, for the purpose of locating, the precise position of any celestial body either in Right Ascension (R.A.) and Declination (Dec.), using the Equator, or in latitude and longitude, using the Ecliptic.

Astronomical Co-ordinate Systems

The Horizon System

When we refer to the horizon, we usually mean the *visible* horizon which is a small circle formed by the apparent joining of earth and sky, and which is parallel to the *Rational* horizon. The two should not be confused, for it is the *Rational or Celestial horizon* (which is a great circle on the Celestial Sphere) every point of which is 90° from the observer's *Zenith* (the point directly overhead) and which divides the Celestial Sphere into two hemispheres — upper and lower.

The apparent (visible) horizon is an imaginary plane, extending all round an observer situated upon any part of the surface of the Earth, at the utmost limits of which plane, the concave hemisphere of the heavens appears to meet the Earth's surface. The Rational horizon is a plane, parallel to the visible horizon, passing through the centre of the Earth and extending to the heavens, which it divides into two hemispheres; the central point of the heavens immediately overhead being the *Zenith* and that of the lower hemisphere being the *Nadir*. These two points are the Poles of the Horizon. The difference between the visible horizon and the rational horizon is the semi-diameter of the Earth. This difference *(the parallactic angle)* is hardly perceptible in respect of the Sun and planets, owing to their distance from the Earth, and even less so for the fixed stars. The Moon, however, being nearer the Earth, disappears below the visible horizon a few minutes before it passes the rational horizon, and likewise, in rising prevents it appearing above the visible horizon until a few minutes after it has passed the rational horizon. The circle where the Earth appears to meet the sky (visible horizon) varies with the height of the observer's eye, therefore, the plane of reference is the celestial horizon.

The vertical circle, passing through the zenith and nadir of the observer and the north and south points of the horizon, is called the *Meridian* of the observer. Another vertical circle, passing through

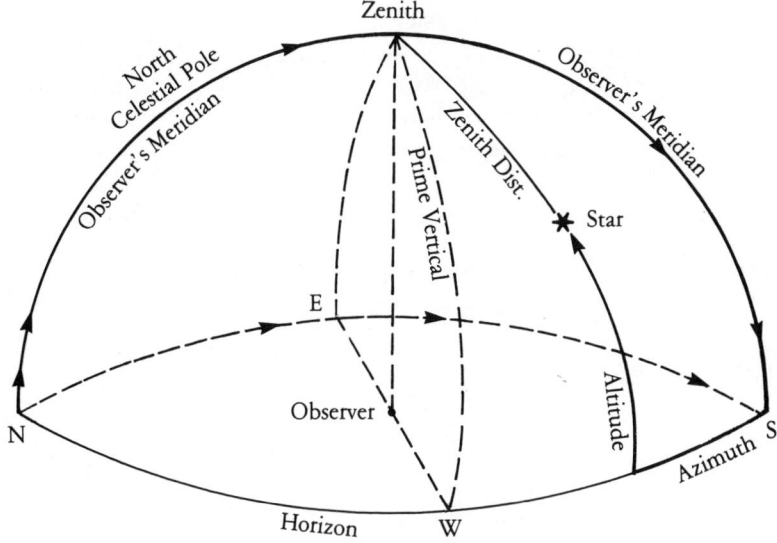

Figure 4. Horizon System Co-ordinates

the zenith and nadir of the observer and the east and west points of the horizon, is called the *Prime Vertical* (the plane of which corresponds to the points of intersection of the horizon and the Equator). All great circles passing through the observer's zenith are perpendicular to the Celestial Horizon and are termed vertical circles. All other vertical circles, which also pass through the zenith and nadir, do not pass through the east and west points of the horizon.

The Horizon system uses the co-ordinates of *Altitude* (the angular distance of an object above the horizon) and *Azimuth* (the angle between the vertical plane through the object and the observer's meridian plane). Altitude is measured as the object's vertical distance above the horizon; azimuth as the angular distance eastward around the horizon from the north point. The zenith distance is an object's angular distance from the zenith and is the complement of the object's altitude (90° less altitude = zenith distance). The *Polar Altitude or Elevation* is the term used to denote the height of the pole above the horizon at a given place, or in other words, the latitude of the place or its angular distance from the Equator.

Horizon co-ordinates are important astronomically, since they give

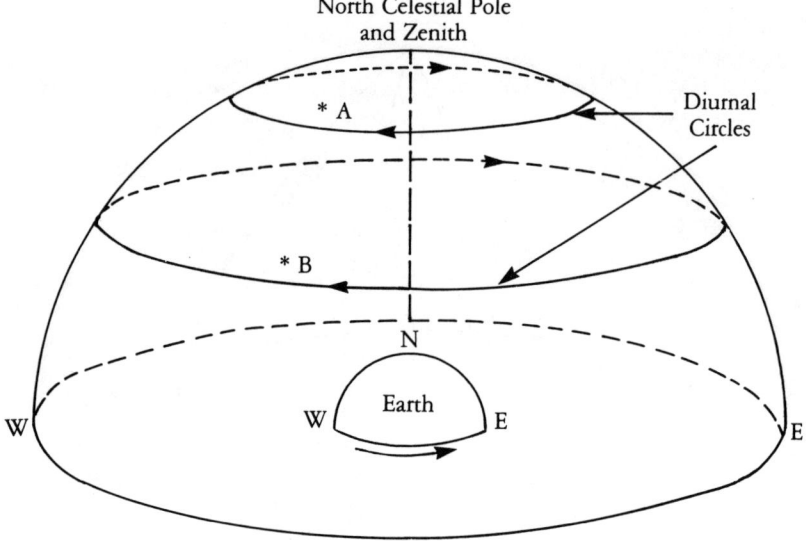

Figure 5. The Celestial Sphere: North Pole

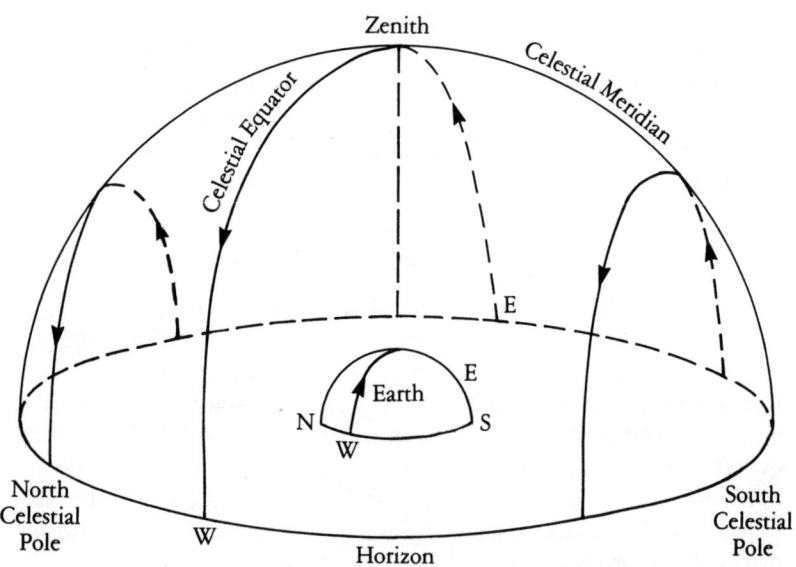

Figure 6. The Celestial Sphere: Equator

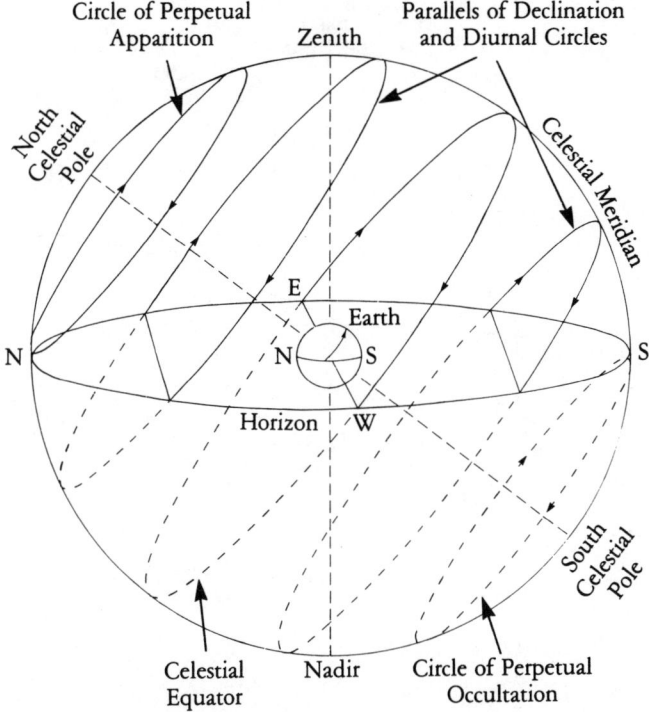

Figure 7. The Celestial Sphere: Intermediate Latitudes

a method for constructing frames of reference which are essential before any other co-ordinate system can be established. By observation, we know that the daily rotation of the Earth from west to east causes the celestial bodies to appear to move across the sky from east to west, rising in the east, ascending the heavens until they reach their highest point, then declining and setting in the west. This daily movement appears to take place in circles of the celestial sphere called *Diurnal Circles* which coincide with the parallels of declination. However, the position of the diurnal circle of a body relative to the observer's horizon varies with the observer's latitude. The altitude and azimuth of a body as observed from, say London, would be different from what would be seen from New York. As an example, let us consider an observer at three different positions on earth: the North pole, the Equator and at an intermediate latitude (see Figures 5, 6 and 7):

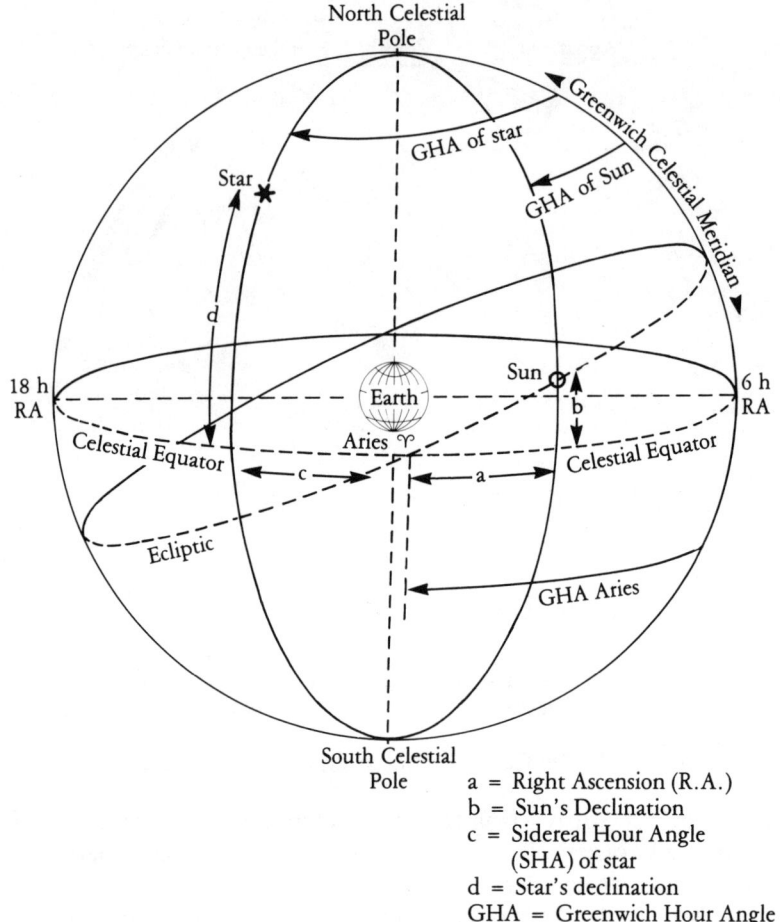

Figure 8. Equator System Co-ordinates

1. At the pole, the observer's zenith and the North pole will coincide as do the Celestial Equator and the Celestial Horizon. If we consider A and B to be fixed stars and their declinations being practically constant, each remains at the same angular distance from the Celestial Equator and therefore from the horizon as, in this case, the horizon and the Celestial Equator coincide. Thus, the diurnal circle coincides with the declination circle and altitude circle. The rotation of the Earth causes the stars to appear to move westward in diurnal circles which are

EARTH AND SKY: LINES, CIRCLES AND PROJECTIONS   51

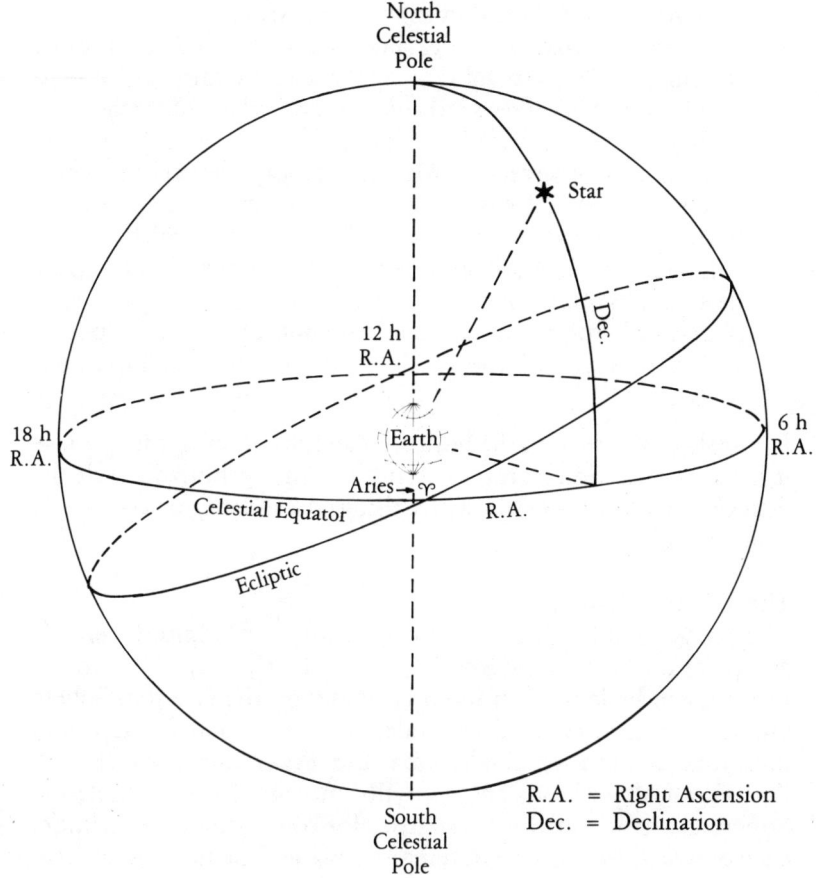

Figure 9. Equator System:
Right Ascension and Declination

parallel to the Equator and to the horizon. Therefore, the stars (A and B) remain continuously above the observer's horizon — i.e., they are circumpolar.

2. At the Earth's Equator, the zenith lies in the Celestial Equator which coincides with the Prime Vertical, and the Celestial Poles lie in the horizon. The diurnal circles of stars A and B are now perpendicular to the horizon and are half above and half below the horizon, so that the stars A and B will only be visible half of the time. At the Equator, all stars rise vertically, and no stars

are circumpolar since they all rise and set.
3. In the intermediate latitudes (between the Earth's Equator and the poles), the Celestial Pole appears at the same altitude in the sky as the observer's latitude, and the plane of the horizon is oblique to the plane of the Celestial Equator and the diurnal circles. For an observer in north latitudes, any celestial body which is north of the Celestial Equator will be above the observer's horizon for more than 12 hours, while any body which is south will be above the horizon for less than 12 hours. Bodies whose declinations places them within or north of the circumpolar circle (Circle of Perpetual Apparition) will not set. Similarly, bodies within or south of the Circle of Perpetual Occultation are invisible.

In astrological charting, the horizon is an important factor, because it is the intersection of the eastern point of the horizon with the Ecliptic that determines the degree rising (Ascendant) for a particular time and place.

The Equator System
The two geographical co-ordinates (latitude and longitude) enable any place on Earth to be located, and similarly, any object in the heavens can be located, if its co-ordinates on the Celestial Sphere are known. The celestial equivalents of terrestrial latitude and longitude are termed *Declination* and *Right Ascension* (R.A.). Astronomical positions are normally measured on the Celestial Sphere using one of three systems, Horizon, Equator or Ecliptic, each of which has a different reference plane. The Equator system, as the name suggests, uses the great circle of the Equator as its principal frame of reference. The Celestial Equator, otherwise termed the Equinoctial, is a great circle and is a projection of the Earth's Equator onto the Celestial Sphere. The Celestial Poles are the poles of rotation of the Celestial Sphere and are directly overhead at the terrestrial poles. The Celestial Equator has, as its zero point, the First Point of Aries (Vernal Equinox) and this point, which is like a 'celestial Greenwich', is the point of intersection at any moment of the celestial Equator and the Ecliptic. Right Ascension is the angle between the *Hour Circle* (great circle passing through a celestial body and the celestial poles), through the object and the First Point of Aries. The measurement of R.A. is made eastward along the celestial

equator from the Equinox (First Point of Aries), sometimes in arc (0°-360°), but more usually in sidereal time, one hour being equivalent to 15°. Right Ascension is, in effect, the interval in sidereal time between the transit of the Equinox and that of the object concerned. The angle between the hour circle through the object and the observer's meridian is sometimes used as an alternative and termed the *Hour Angle* (the difference between R.A. of the object and the R.A. circle on the meridian at the time of observation), and measured westward from the meridian.

Declination, the other co-ordinate of the Equator system, is the angular distance of an object or body either north or south of the Celestial Equator. It corresponds to latitude on Earth and is measured from 0°-90°. Some reference works indicate north declination by the symbol + (positive), and south declination by — (negative). Normally, the astrologer is not concerned with measurement in Right Ascension, except for some methods of progressions or directions, or for finding the time of rising and setting of planets (see Appendix II).

A knowledge of this system is important since, from these co-ordinates, the positions of the Sun, Moon and planets are converted into celestial longitude (see Ecliptic system), which is the co-ordinate listed in most ephemerides.

The Ecliptic System

The Ecliptic represents the yearly path of the Sun's centre on the Celestial Sphere as seen from the Earth, or the Earth as seen from the Sun. The Circle of the Ecliptic is an important great circle, and its intersection with the celestial Equator marks the zero point (First Point of Aries) for measurement of *Celestial Longitude.*

The Ecliptic Poles — points on the Celestial Sphere — are 90° from the Ecliptic, (about 23½° from the terrestrial poles) and for all practical purposes, the Ecliptic and its Poles can be considered as fixed on the celestial sphere. The plane of the Ecliptic is not coincident with that of the Celestial Equator, and the angle between the two planes is 23½° and known as the *Obliquity of the Ecliptic.* This represents the maximum angular distance of the Sun north or south of the Celestial Equator at the *Solstices.*

Celestial Longitude is the angular distance along the Ecliptic between the plane through the object and the First Point of Aries. This co-

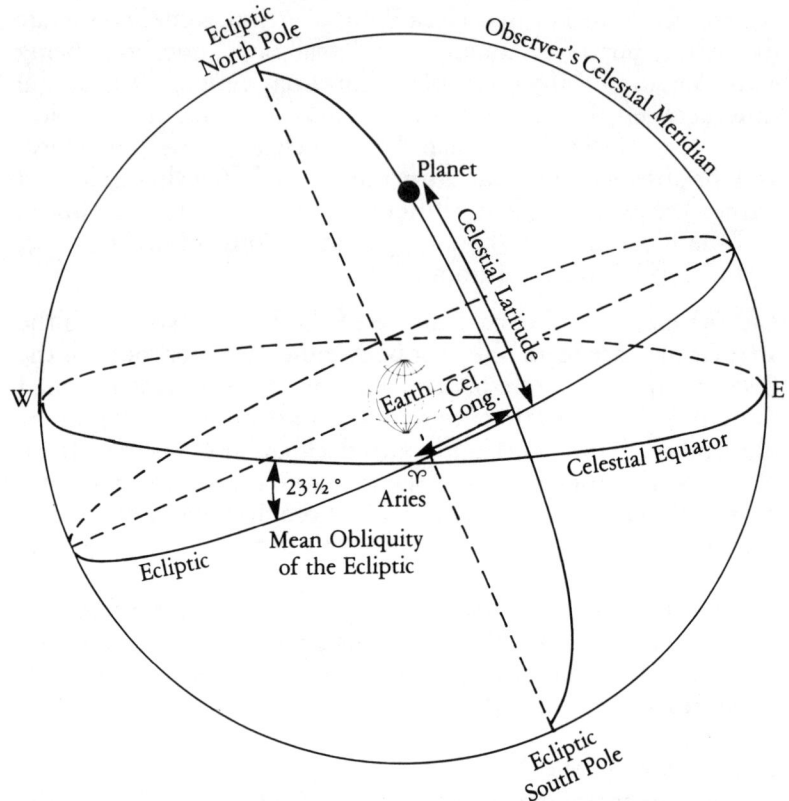

Figure 10. Ecliptic System Co-ordinates

ordinate is measured in degrees and minutes of arc eastward from the First Point of Aries, and is used to determine the position of a planet. If for example, the Sun is 50° eastward from the intersection of the Ecliptic and the Equator (First Point of Aries) we know that its longitude is 20° Taurus, (30° Aries + 20° Taurus).

Celestial Latitude the other co-ordinate of the Ecliptic system, is the perpendicular distance of an object from the Ecliptic in angular measure, or in other words, the angular distance between the Ecliptic and a celestial body measured in degrees and minutes, either north or south of the Ecliptic. It should not be confused with terrestrial latitude which is, of course, measured from the Earth's equator. A planet is exactly on the Ecliptic, when its latitude is zero. Normally, astrologers are not concerned with celestial latitude, except when calculating the times of rising and setting of planets or for certain types of progressions and directions (see Appendix II).

The Zodiac

On either side of the Ecliptic and extending for approximately 8°-9° north and south, there is a band or belt termed the Zodiac (Circle of Animals) within which the Sun, Moon and planets always remain, the only exception being Pluto, whose inclination to the Ecliptic is as much as 17° measured in celestial latitude.

This imaginary belt is divided into twelve signs of 30°, each sign bearing the name of a constellation (star group), although, due to precession, the signs and constellations no longer coincide. During the last thirty years or so, considerable controversy and argument have existed concerning the relative merits of the tropical and Sidereal zodiac. The term 'zodiacs' is misleading, for there is only one circle of the zodiac and, whether we call it tropical or Sidereal, will depend solely on the point from which it is measured.

The Tropical cycle is the cycle of the seasons corresponding to the Sun's yearly return each March to the First Point of Aries (Vernal Equinox), and the solar monthly progress is measured through the signs along the Ecliptic in degrees of longitude. The Sidereal (Fixed or Starry) zodiac is measured from a fixed reference point on the same Ecliptic circle which locates the fixed star Spica (Alpha Virginis) permanently in 29° Virgo. The Sidereal cycle is that of the retrogression of the Vernal Point through the twelve zodiacal constellations (at present from Pisces to Aquarius) during an era of 25,800 years.

Many critics of astrology argue that it is a pseudo-science, because its advocates neglect to take into account precession, and consequently, when the Sun 'enters' Aries at the Vernal Equinox it is, in fact, in the constellation Pisces, the difference between 0° Aries tropical and 0° Aries sidereal being approximately 24°.

The First Point of Aries is important astronomically as well as astrologically, for it is from this point that astronomers check movements and determine positions on the Celestial Sphere. In contrast to the Tropical zodiac, the sidereal zodiac of the constellations is non-moving and non-precessional, being permanently aligned to the fixed stars. The acceptance or rejection of a particular zodiac depends on which cycle is considered to have greater significance.

A considerable amount of pioneering work concerning the sidereal zodiac was done by Cyril Fagan and others during the 1950s and 1960s. Many of their findings were published in various journals, but often their advocacy of a fixed zodiac met with determined opposition from 'entrenched' tropicalists, many of whom rejected the idea that a sidereal zodiac could have value. Others, seeking a compromise, expunged the precession from their tropical charts to make them non-precessional, but used the 'new found' longitudes in terms of the tropical zodiac, either not realizing or ignoring the implications of this erroneous procedure. Fortunately for astrology, other researchers, more tolerant and imaginative in their outlook, have continued the investigations into the sidereal techniques in an endeavour to discover whether, in fact, the sidereal zodiac has significance or not.

House Division
It is beyond the scope of this work to deal with the whole question of house division, but a brief outline of some of the fundamentals may prove useful.

There appear to be some misconceptions concerning house division, and it has become one of the most contentious problems in astrology. The methods that have been devised are many and varied, but many of them do not stand critical analysis. What the innovators of the various systems fail to realize is that the Zodiac cannot be 'draped' on the cusps of the twelve mundane houses. If the Earth were not inclined to the Ecliptic, all would be well, but due to the Obliquity of the Ecliptic, the Signs of the Zodiac are intercepted according to the angle of the obliquity and the system employed. The interception or lack of it, is no criterion that the validity of a particular system is correct. The basic fundamentals of those house systems worthy of serious consideration are quite simple, but as with all things astrological, need to be approached realistically.

Looking at the sky, we see that it meets the Earth, and this is the great circle of the *Horizon*. Immediately overhead is the *Zenith* with the opposite point, the *Nadir*, immediately beneath our feet. If we look due south, we have due east on the left, with due west on the right. Now, if we imagine a great circle passing from the east point of the horizon, cutting through the zenith and passing down through the west point and continuing to rise once more at the east point, we have the great circle of the *Prime Vertical*.

Again, if we imagine another great circle rising at the north point of the horizon, cutting through the Prime Vertical at right angles to the zenith, and descending at the south point of the horizon and continuing around under the Earth, we have the *Meridian Circle.*

These three great circles of the sphere, (Horizon, Prime Vertical and Meridian), are the basis for house systems that have some claim for consideration. One of these systems is the *Campanus* system, of which the Prime Vertical is employed as the foundation circle. If the Prime Vertical is divided into twelve equal parts, with six great circles of the sphere from the north or south points of the horizon passing through the dividing points on the Prime Vertical, we obtain the cusps of the twelve Campanus houses. This division gives the six houses above the horizontal plane and six below which appear like lunes, and in which all the bodies must be contained. As every place on Earth has its own horizon, zenith and nadir, so it has its own Campanian lunes. The method of Campanus is free from any suggestion of either zodiacal or mundane motion, since the Prime Vertical is the basic circle. In this system, the horizon circle is one of the boundaries of the first and seventh houses.

By knowing the Right Ascension of the Midheaven (R.A.M.C.), and the co-ordinates of the place of observation, we can construct the twelve houses. The position of a celestial body is determined by its equatorial co-ordinates, and these must be known before we can locate it in any of the astrological houses (lunes). In locating a planet's position, its latitude has to be known, for while it may appear to be in one house, bodily, it may be in a different one altogether.

The house system which is frequently used, and for which Tables of Houses are given in *Raphael's Ephemeris,* is the Placidean system. It may be useful to explain the basis of these tables. The Semi-Arc system of Placidus was introduced into Britain during the seventeenth century and was rejected by most of the leading astrologers of the day, such as Lilly, Gadbury, Coley and others. However, an astrologer named Partridge supported it, and eventually the tables were published and became easily available for use.

The Placidean system is based on the tri-section of the semi-arc of each degree of the Ecliptic. It does not divide time, nor does it divide the space between the horizon and meridian in a simple way. Basically, the system consists of taking the time for any degree to move from the ascendant to the midheaven, and to equally tri-sect this time to ascertain the time at which this degree will become the cusps of the 12th and 11th houses. Likewise, the semi-nocturnal arc from the lower meridian (I.C.) to the ascendant is tri-sected, and the times are those at which the same degree will become the cusps of the 2nd and 3rd houses. The following example illustrates the method:

At London — Latitude 51° 32′ north.

			Sidereal Time		
				Hr.	Min.
M.C.	=	4° Gemini		4	08
I.C.	=	4° Sagittarius		16	08
Asc.	=	4° Gemini		20	13
Therefore semi-diurnal arc			=	4	08
Less				20	13
				7	55 ÷ 3
			=	2	38
and semi-nocturnal arc			=	20	13
Less				16	08
				4	05 ÷ 3
			=	1	22
M.C.	=	4° Gemini at		4	08
11th cusp	=	4 08 less 2 38		1	30
12th cusp	=	1 30 less 2 38		22	52
Ascendant at				20	13
2nd cusp	=	20 13 less 1 22		18	51
3rd cusp	=	18 51 less 1 22		17	29

The above example shows that, although the time that a degree may spend in a particular quadrant may be unequal, the motion is uniform due to the apparent rotation of the Celestial Sphere. It therefore reaches the points of tri-section (I.C.-Asc. and Asc.-M.C.) at precisely one-third of the time which is required to complete the total arc of the particular quadrant. Any degree of the Ecliptic makes a complete revolution in one Sidereal day, and the time at which it reaches those points on the semi-diurnal and semi-nocturnal arcs

EARTH AND SKY: LINES, CIRCLES AND PROJECTIONS   59

which tri-sect them, is the time at which the degree becomes the cusp of the particular house.

As with all methods of house division which use the Ascendant as the zero point, distortion occurs in high latitudes, and at the polar circle latitude (66½°), a degree of the Ecliptic will become circumpolar for the first time. Above the polar circle, certain degrees will not rise and therefore systems, such as the Placidean whose basis is the tri-section of semi-arcs, present problems. However, it is not advisable to either accept or reject any system without studying it in relation to one's own personal experiences.

Tables of Houses
The Placidean tables listed in *Raphael's Ephemeris* are for London, Liverpool and New York and are serviceable for latitudes between 39°-55° north. They can also be used for places in southern latitudes by applying a simple procedure.

The purpose of these tables is to determine the Ascendant (Rising sign), Midheaven (M.C.) and the cusps of the intermediate houses for a specified Sidereal time and place. With this system, the size of the houses can vary, that is, some houses contain more than thirty degrees, and a sign which does not 'cut' the cusp of a particular house is termed an *intercepted sign*. When a sign is intercepted in a particular house, the opposite sign will also be intercepted in the opposite house.

When precision is required, interpolation of the listings in the tables will need to be made, as the local Sidereal time is unlikely to correspond exactly with any Sidereal time shown in the tables.

Due to the Earth's rotation, all signs rise and set every 24 hours, the average time for the 30° of a sign to rise being about two hours, except at the polar latitudes where certain signs neither rise nor set. At the Equator, the signs rise 'evenly', but in the intermediate latitudes, and as we approach the poles, the signs do not rise uniformly, due to the angle which the Ecliptic makes with the Equator. Signs which take longer than average to ascend are termed 'signs of long ascension', while those that ascend quickly are known as 'signs of short ascension'. In the northern hemisphere at intermediate latitudes, the signs Cancer to Sagittarius are signs of long ascension; the short ascension signs are Capricorn to Gemini. In southern latitudes, the reverse applies.

4.
THE CALENDAR

Early Forms of Reckoning
The Calendar, so called from the Roman Calends or Kalends, is a method of distributing time into certain periods adapted to the purposes of civil life such as hours, days, weeks, months and years.

In the myths and legends of many nations, the primitive division of time and the invention of the calendar is associated with celestial deities. In Babylonia, the 'tablets of fate' were in the special care of the god Nebo, whose function was to inscribe thereon the destinies of the coming year. The Egyptians appear to have begun with a lunar calendar, although there is no contemporary evidence to support this, but the importance of the monthly and half-monthly festivals in later times and the adoption of the month as a unit in later calendars, appears to confirm the use of a lunar calendar. As with Babylonian mythology, so the Egyptians had their divine scribe, Thoth, and the Egyptian obelisk was a symbol of the sun god, Ra. At a very early date, the Egyptians began to observe the heliacal rising of the star Sirius, the rising of which corresponded closely with the inundation by the Nile and upon which, the Egyptian agriculture and economy depended. The pre-Columbian civilizations of America had calendars which were complex, but which had an admirable symmetrical completeness, in that the various rules acted as a check on each other. The astronomical attainments of the Maya were remarkable, and their ability to make a close approximation of the true length of the lunar month, the solar year and the synodic period of Venus indicate their knowledge of precise time-reckoning.

The Julian (Old Style calendar) was introduced by Julius Caesar in 45 B.C. This replaced the old local calendar of Rome which was based on the lunar year and covered a period of 355 days, with an additional period of 22 or 23 days inserted whenever the Pontifices (priests) thought it necessary. The working of the calendar was the responsibility of the pontifices, and the Pontifex Maximus (high priest), would every month, proclaim the sighting of the new moon, and name the festivals that would occur during that month. The first day of the month, the day of proclamation, was called 'calendae', or callings, from which the word calendar is derived. This calendar consisted of 12 lunar months but was primitive and probably dated from the time of the Etruscan dynasty or even earlier. Martius (March) was the first month of the Roman year, but in 153 B.C., Januarius (January 1) ousted March 1 as the official New Year's Day. Over the years, the Roman calendar became completely confused and had moved ahead of the seasons by almost three months. In order to restore some semblance of order to what had become a chaotic and useless record, Julius Caesar extended the year 46 B.C. from 355 days to 445 days, (the so-called 'Year of Confusion') by adding 23 days to February and inserting 67 days between November and December, thus bringing the civil year in line with the natural year. This new calendar (Julian-Old Style), lasted, subject to minor modifications, until the introduction of the Gregorian calendar (New Style) in 1582. The amended Roman calendar was a modified version of the ancient Egyptian calendar which had been in use for about 3,000 years.

The Egyptian calendar was based on 360 days, divided into 12 months of 30 days, followed at the end of one year and the commencement of the next, by five additional days which were not allocated to any one month, but celebrated as Feast Days. This calendar had the defect of being based on a uniform year of 365 days, and was therefore approximately almost one quarter of a day shorter than the solar year. Every four years, Sothis (Sirius) rose a day later, with the result that the calendar did not correspond with the solar year and consequently with the seasons, to the extent of one day every four years. This error became greater until eventually, after 1460 (365 × 4) solar years, known as the Sothic Period, the calendrical New Year's Day had worked right round the seasons and returned to its correct place again. It is strange that the Egyptians seemed unaware of this anomaly, and it was only in later times that they sought to correct the error by the insertion of an extra day every four years.

The Julian calendar had a four-year cycle, in which the first three years (common years) had 365 days and the fourth year (leap year) had 366 days. The additional day every fourth year was included in February, immediately after the Feast of Terminalia which fell on the 23rd of that month. February 24 was, according to the Roman calendar, the sixth day before the Kalends of March, and the intercalcated day was regarded as a continuation of the 24th. This duplication was termed 'bissextilis' meaning doubled sixth.

Due to misunderstandings during the first 36 years of the Julian calendar (45-10 B.C. inclusive), every third year instead of every fourth, was treated as a leap year, with the result that twelve leap years had occurred instead of nine. This error was corrected by reckoning the next twelve years (9 B.C.-A.D. 3) as common years, which made A.D. 4 the first leap year of the Christian Era. Thereafter under the Julian calendar, all years that were exactly divisible by 4, (including centurial years ending in '00') were reckoned as leap years. The addition of an extra day every fourth year was based on the erroneous assumption that the length of the solar year was 365.25 days, whereas it is in fact 365.2422 days or 365 days, 5 hours, 48 minutes, 46 seconds. This error resulted in an over-estimation of the true length of the year by 0.0078 days (11 minutes 14 seconds) and this, in the course of 128 years, made a cumulative error of approximately one whole day.

The number seven has always had a special significance. To the early civilizations, the importance of this number would be apparent, particularly when they could relate the number to the Sun, Moon and the five planets. It would also have significance when related to certain constellations containing visible stars of seven or so, such as the Pleiades, Ursa Major and Ursa Minor. The seven-day periods probably owe their origins to the phases of the Moon, and the Babylonians are thought to have divided up the month (moonth) according to the Moon's phases. The seven-day week was not part of the Julian calendar. According to legend, the Romans until Constantine's conversion to Christianity in A.D. 312, determined the intervals contained within a month, by market days which were spaced either seven or eight days apart, depending upon the number of days in the month. With Constantine's conversion, the seven-day week of the Christians, (which they had acquired from the Jews) became legal throughout the Roman world.

From the earliest times, the days have been named according to the seven planets (Sun and Moon being considered planets). Not only were the days named according to the planets, but the hours of each day were related to a particular planet. Saturn, for example, ruled the first hour of the first day, so that day was called 'dies Saturnie' (Saturn's day). Jupiter ruled the second hour, Mars the third, and so on in recurring sequence until the twenty-fourth hour of the first day was given to Mars. The first hour of the second day was ruled by the Sun, and the recurring pattern continued, so that ensuing days in order were Moon's day, Mars' day, Mercury's day, Jove's day (Jupiter), Venus' day. The old names derived from Roman or Norse mythology have continued to be used, despite the opposition of the early Church.

The schematism of temporary hours probably owes its origin to the Persian astrologers (Magi), for it seems unlikely to have been invented by the Babylonians, Assyrians or Egyptians as these nations commenced their day at sunset. Nor is it of Roman invention as the Roman day commenced at midnight. If these schemes of temporary hours have any validity, then the newly discovered planets, (Uranus, Neptune and Pluto) should be included. But to include them would upset the names of the days, the number of days in the week and the length of the month.

Easter is the chief festival of the Christian Year, and occurs about the same time as the ancient Roman celebration of the Vernal Equinox. The date for the celebration of Easter was settled by the first Council of the Christian Churches at Nicea in Asia Minor in A.D. 325. The Council decided that Easter would be observed on the first Sunday following the 14th day of the Paschal Moon, referred to as the Paschal Full Moon. This moon is the first moon whose 14th day comes on or after 21 March. If the Paschal Full Moon falls on a Sunday, then Easter is the following Sunday. The earliest date on which Easter can fall is 22 March, and the latest possible date is 25 April. The date of the Vernal Equinox adopted by the Council was 21 March, and this date was in accordance with the Alexandrian reckoning (Alexandria then being the centre of astronomical learning). Thus the Ecclesiastical Calendar governs the formation of the civil calendar of today. Apart from the determination of Easter and the various feast days dependent upon this date, today's calendar is based on three main factors:

1. The Tropical Year (365.24219 days)
2. The Synodic Month (29.530588 days)
3. The Solar Day of 24 hours grouped in 7-day weeks.

Due to the mistake in the assumed length of the solar year under the Julian calendar, the date of the Vernal Equinox had, by A.D. 730, moved back from 21 March to 18 March, and although attention was drawn to this fact, nothing was done to correct the discrepancy. By the year A.D. 1582, the date of the Vernal Equinox had moved further back to 11 March — earlier by ten days than 21 March, the date agreed upon by the Council at Nicea.

Calendar Reform
The 'Old Style' calendar introduced by Julius Caesar in 46 B.C. on the advice of the Alexandrian astronomer Sosigenes, continued for more than sixteen centuries despite its ever increasing error. In 1577, a commission consisting of astronomers, mathematicians and clergy was appointed by Pope Gregory to study the problems of calendar reform, and eventually a 'New Style' calendar came into being in 1582. The person chiefly responsible for the ingenious reforms that were subsequently incorporated into the new calendar was Luigi Lilio, a physician with an interest in astronomy. Plans for the reform of the calendar were not new. The Venerable Bede, an Anglo-Saxon monk and scholar (A.D. 730), had drawn attention to the need for calendar reform, and during the ensuring centuries, scholars devised methods for reform, none of which were adopted. The reforms and changes of 1582 abolished the Julian calendar and brought into effect the following amendments:

1. Ten days were dropped from the Julian calendar; Thursday 4 October (Old Style) was called Friday, 15 October. This restored the Vernal Equinox to 21 March.
2. The length of the solar year was corrected to 365 days, 5 hours, 49 minutes, 12 seconds. This arrangement is not quite correct, as the average length of the solar year, as determined by Simon Newcomb, an American astronomer, for the epoch 1900, is 365.2422 days. The average length of the calendar year is 365.2425 days, so that there is still a slight discrepancy of 26 seconds amounting to an error of one day in 3,323 years. This is nothing much to worry about, as the error will eventually be

corrected, making the Gregorian calendar correct to within one day in 20,000 years.
3. January 1 was adopted as the first day of the year and not 25 March as had been the practice.
4. The length of the months was fixed as they are at present. Three of every four centesimal years (ending in '00') were made common years, with an additional day every fourth year, except the century years which were to be leap years, only if divisible by 400. Thus 1600 was a leap year, but 1700, 1800 and 1900 were not, but 2000 will be.

The Gregorian calendar was not immediately adopted by all European nations. The late sixteenth century was a period of religious unrest and persecution, and the Protestant countries of Europe were in no mood to accept the dictates of Rome. In the various Italian states, Spain and Portugal the calendar was adopted according to the mandate, on 15 October (New Style). France and Lorraine followed suit in December 1582. Holland, Prussia and the Catholic region of Germany, Switzerland, and the Netherlands made the change with Friday, 21 December, 1582 being immediately followed by Saturday, 1 January 1583. Poland made the change three years later, with Tuesday, 21 December, 1585 being immediately followed by Wednesday, 1 January, 1586. In Hungary, the change took place in 1587.

In the Protestant countries of Europe, apart from Holland, there was strong opposition to the introduction of the New calendar, as to everything else of a Catholic origin. In some places where Protestants and Catholics were living together, the use of two different calendars caused considerable confusion. At Augsburg the quarrels lasted several years and were known as the 'Kalenderstreit' (calendar quarrels). Denmark and the German Protestant States abandoned the Julian calendar and adopted the New Style in 1700 with Sunday, 18 February being immediately followed by Monday, 1 March; the Protestant Cantons of Switzerland in 1701 with Tuesday 31 December 1700 being followed by Wednesday, 12 January, 1701. The remaining Protestant provinces of the Netherlands changed to the New Style on various dates in 1700-1701.

In England, resistance to calendar reform persisted for nearly two centuries, and it was not until 25th February, 1751, when Lord Chesterfield introduced a Bill into the House of Lords, that the matter

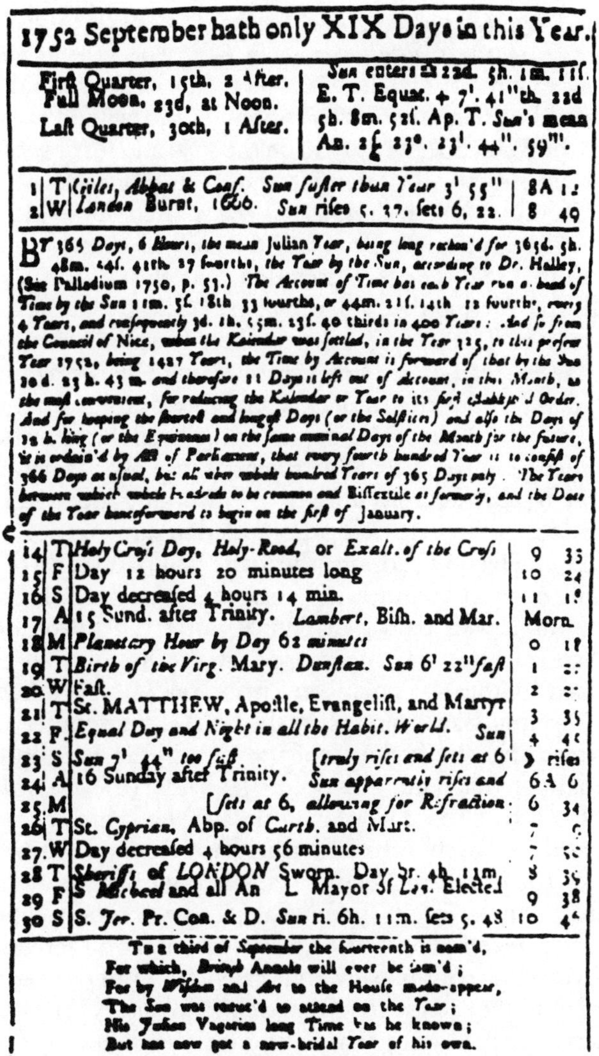

Figure 11. Calendar Change September 1752. Extract from *The Ladies Diary or Woman's Almanack* showing the 'loss of eleven days'.

Reproduced from *Sky & Telescope* with acknowledgements.

was given serious consideration. Chesterfield's Bill, had the imposing title *An Act for Regulating the Commencement of the Year and for Correcting the Calendar now in Use.* The year at that time commenced on 25 March. George Parker, the Second Earl of Macclesfield was an amateur astronomer, and he had presented a paper to the Royal Society in 1750 on the solar and lunar years, which acted as an impetus for calendar reform in England.

The Calendar (New Style) Act was passed in 1751, and its provisions became law in Britain and its colonies (including North America) in 1752. The Act provided that eleven days should be omitted after Wednesday, 2 September, 1752, so that the following day should be Thursday, 14 September. It was necessary to omit eleven days instead of ten because 1700 was a leap year under the Julian calendar, but not under the Gregorian; for similar reasons, it was necessary to omit twelve days after 1800 and thirteen after 1900.

The change to the New Style calendar provoked much hostility and dissent, particularly among the working population who imagined that they were being defrauded in some way of time and wages. In an election cartoon, the artist William Hogarth depicts a drinking party at an inn, with a banner bearing the slogan 'Give us back our eleven days'. In France, after the Revolution, the Gregorian calendar was superseded by the Republican calendar introduced by the National Convention on 24 November, 1793. As the Republic had been established on 22 September, 1792, it was decreed that the first year of the Republican Era commenced at midnight on that date. This decimal calendar (the seven-day week was replaced by a ten-day week or decade) had three decades in a month and twelve months in a year. Each day had ten hours and each hour 100 minutes. Needless, to say, this calendar was not very successful, only lasting thirteen years, and was finally abandoned when France reverted to the Gregorian calendar on 1 January 1806.

The acceptance of the New Style calendar by all nations was not achieved until the early years of the twentieth century. The reluctance of certain nations to adopt the calendar caused not only confusion regarding dates, but also resulted in practical difficulties. In 1867, the United States purchased Alaska from Russia, and as the Alaskan population used the Russian calendar (Julian-Old Style), the dates were then twelve days behind the Gregorian calendar as used by the United States. Normally, the transition from one calendar to another can be accomplished with little difficulty. However, in the

Alaskan changeover, an additional complication arose because, before the acquisition, Alaskan week-day names were those of the Eastern Hemisphere dated in accordance with the Julian calendar, but after the acquisition, the week-day names had to be the same as those of the Western Hemisphere, dated in accordance with the Gregorian calendar. On being acquired by the United States, Alaska had 'crossed' the 180th meridian, (the International Date Line) from East to West, and had thereby moved back one day. It was, therefore, necessary to omit only eleven days from the Alaskan calendar, but to have an eight-day week containing two days of the same name when the change over was made. In 1873, Japan adopted the Gregorian calendar, and in China, it was introduced by Sun Yet Sen in 1912. Many parts of China retained the old traditional lunar calendars, but in 1929, the New Style calendar became the official calendar.

Russia had used the Julian calendar since 1 January, 1700, when it had been introduced by Peter the Great, but by a decree of the Soviet of People's Commissars, dated 26 January, 1918, Russia changed over to the New Style, with Wednesday, 31 January being followed by Thursday, 14 February. However, the Russian Orthodox Church still adhered to the old Julian calendar, although the government had officially adopted the New Style. In 1923, it was decided to abolish the New Style calendar which had been in use for five years and introduce a new calendar. On 6 October, a new Soviet calendar came into operation, and this calendar consisted of five days to the week and six weeks to the month, so that the year contained twelve months of thirty days, plus five national holiday days, with an extra day for leap year. In 1931, after eight years trial, this calendar was modified to allow six days to the week. On 27 June, 1940, Russia resumed using the New Style calendar with its seven day week. Russian calendar changes are complex, and astrologers need to be aware of the difficulties associated with Russian dates.

In Eastern Europe, the use of the Julian calendar was gradually phased out, with Albania changing over in 1912; Bulgaria in 1916; Yugo-Slavia and Roumania in 1919; Greece in 1923. The Eastern Orthodox Churches in Russia, Greece, Serbia and Roumania did not accept the Gregorian calendar until May 1923. The last European nation to officially adopt the Gregorian calendar was Turkey and, although the New calendar was in semi-official use from 1917 onwards, it was not until 1 January, 1926, after the proclamation of the Republic, that it was officially adopted.

The Gregorian and Julian calendars continued in use together until 1925, by which time most nations had adopted the Gregorian calendar. From its inception in 1582, it had taken nearly 350 years for the New Style calendar to be universally accepted.

Errors connected with the differences between the two calendars can be avoided by converting the Julian (Old Style) date to the corresponding Gregorian (New Style) date or vice versa.

To Convert Julian to Gregorian Date	Days + Add
Julian Date (Old Style)	
October 5 1582 — 29 February 1700	10
March 1 1700 — 29 February 1800	11
March 1 1800 — 29 February 1900	12
March 1 1900 — 31 December 1925	13

The years 1700, 1800 and 1900 were not leap years under the Gregorian calendar. Thus 22 February 1600 (Julian) becomes, by adding 10: '32' February 1600 Gregorian which is equivalent to 3 March, since 1600 was a leap year in the New Style calendar. But 22 February 1800 (Julian) becomes by adding 11: '33' February 1800 Gregorian, which is equivalent to 5 March, since 1800 was not a leap year in the New Style calendar (see also Julian Day Number).

To Convert Gregorian to Julian Date	Days — Deduct
Gregorian Date (New Style)	
October 15 1582 — 11 March 1700	10
March 12 1700 — 12 March 1800	11
March 13 1800 — 13 March 1900	12
March 14 1900 — 31 December 1925	13

When converting a date in March 1700, 1800 or 1900, it has to be borne in mind, that these were leap years under the Julian calendar.

The historical dating of the Christian Era is related to the birth of Christ, and despite the statements and the speculative birth charts that appear from time to time in astrological journals, there is no firm evidence for the actual date and even less for the birth time. The traditional date, 25 December, has connotations with the December Solstice, while the date of the Annunciation, 25 March, is very close to the date of the Vernal Equinox, 21 March. These dates have always been of astronomical significance, and it seems probable that the early Church adopted these dates, along with the 'pagan shrines', when it sought to establish Christianity.

The commencement of the year has varied during the centuries, and several dates were in use in different countries until well into the Middle Ages. In 1582, Pope Gregory decreed that 1 January should in future be taken as the commencement of the year for all purposes. In the same way that the adoption of the New Style calendar varied from country to country, so also did the adoption of 1 January as New Year's Day. In England, prior to 1752, the Legal Year commenced on 25 March, and the Historical Year on 1 January. This practice of having 'different' years leads to problems, particularly with dates between 1 January and 24 March inclusive, since the year quoted will depend upon the method of expression (Historical or Legal). Although Great Britain adopted 1 January as New Year's Day for all purposes in 1752, it did not alter the commencement of its financial year, which commenced on the 25 March, a date which had been regarded as New Year's Day for the preceding 450 years. To have altered the date of the financial year to 1 January would have resulted in an incomplete year (25 March-31 December 1752). This, in conjunction with the 'lost eleven days' due to the introduction of the Gregorian calendar, would, it was thought, cause trouble and confusion, so the financial year was preserved by adding the 'lost eleven days' to 24 March, so making the financial year commence thereafter on the 5 April.

If the Julian calendar had been in use, 1800 would have been a leap year, so in order to compensate for this loss, the commencement of the financial year was fixed as 6 April, and thus it has been ever since.

During the present century, various proposals for calendar reform have been made, including suggestions for a perpetual calendar. No serious consideration has been given to the various proposals, and the world is now united in the secular use of the Gregorian calendar dates.

The Julian Date

It is sometimes necessary to determine dates either in the future or in the past, and it is useful to have some way of denoting astronomical days. The Julian period (not to be confused with the Julian calendar) was devised in 1582 by Joseph Scaliger (1540-1609) and named after his father Julius. It was made up of the product of the 28 year solar cycle, the 19 year lunar cycle and the 15 year cycle of indiction. This product 28 × 19 × 15 = 7980 years. The Julian Day began at noon, 1 January 4713 B.C. (Julian Day Number 0), the most recent period that three major chronological cycles began on the same day; (a) the 28 year solar cycle after which dates in the Julian calendar return to the same days of the week; (b) the 19 year lunar cycle after which the phases of the Moon return to the same dates of the year; (c) the 15 year cycle of Indiction used in ancient Rome to regulate taxes.

The use of the Julian Day Number permits the determination of the precise number of days that have elapsed between one epoch and another, provided that both are expressed in terms of the Julian Day. Because Julian Date runs from mid-day to mid-day, no change of Day Number occurs at night. The Julian Day Number is tabulated from 1 January 1900, in the *American Ephemeris for the twentieth century,* and in greater detail in the tables by Tuckerman, and by Stahlman and Gingerich.

With the assistance of tables such as these, the Julian Date is easily found. If, however, no such references are available, we can still obtain the Julian Date by using a simple procedure. As an example, let us assume that we require the Julian Date for 12 September 1983. The first step in the calculation is to find the number of years which have elapsed since 1 January 4713 B.C. If the year is A.D., add the year number to *4712* and the total is the number of years elapsed. Therefore 4712 + 1983 = 6695 × 365.25 = 2445348.75. We take 2445348, ignoring fractions.

When the year in question is a leap year, the result of the multiplication will be a full number of days with no fraction, but all other years will contain a fraction or decimal part. In leap years, one day is subtracted from the result and the remainder is the Julian Date of January 0 of the year. In common years, the total remaining after dropping the fraction of the result is the number of January 0 of the year, always for Greenwich Mean Noon.

This procedure holds good for all dates in the Julian calendar, but when using the Gregorian (New Style) calendar, some complications are introduced. When calculating the Julian Date of any date after 4 October, 1582 in the New Style calendar, we must deduct 11 days for a leap year and 10 days for a common year, bearing in mind that century years not equally divisible by four are not leap years, i.e., 1700, 1800 and 1900. For the years after 1700, an additional one day must be deducted; after 1800, two days; after 1900, three days. Thus, beginning with 1901, the deduction is 14 days for a leap year and 13 days for common years.

Returning to our example, we have a figure of 2445348, from which we deduct 13 days as 1983 is a common year. This gives 2445335 = Julian Date 0 January, 1983. From 1 January to 12 September, we have 255 days which, added to 2445335 gives 2445590 = Julian Date 12 September 1983 as required. In making the corrections, one must be sure that the date in question is expressed in the Gregorian (New Style) calendar.

Days, Months and Years

The Day

The natural units of the calendar are: the *Day* based on the period of rotation of the Earth, the *Month* based on the period of revolution of the Moon about the Earth, and the *Year* based on the period of revolution of the Earth around the Sun.

The Day may be measured with respect to (a) The Sun — the *True or Apparent Sun* (an Apparent Solar Day), or the *Mean Sun* (Mean Solar Day), or (b) The *Stars* or more particularly the *First Point of Aries* — a Sidereal Day.

The solar day is the period of the Earth's rotation with respect to the Sun. The Sidereal day is the time required for the Earth to make a complete rotation with respect to a point in space, (the Vernal Equinox-First Point of Aries) where the Sun in its apparent path (Ecliptic) crosses the celestial equator from south to north. The term 'sidereal day' is not quite accurate, because the Vernal Equinox slowly shifts its position due to Precession. This shift is, however, so slow that a Sidereal day is, for all practical purposes, compatible with the true period of rotation of the Earth with respect to the stars. A solar day is slightly longer than a Sidereal day or one complete rotation of the Earth.

The daily motion of the Earth in its orbit is about 1° (365 days in a year and 360 degrees in a circle). This 1° angle is nearly the same as the additional angle over and above 360° through which the Earth must turn to complete a solar day. As it takes the Earth about 4 minutes to turn through 1°, a solar day is, therefore, about 4 minutes longer than a Sidereal day. The Apparent solar day, like the Sidereal day, is measured through exactly 24 hours, but a unit of solar time is longer than the corresponding unit of Sidereal time by about 1 ÷ 365.

One Sidereal day of 24 hours Sidereal time is equal to 23 hours, 56 minutes, 4.091 seconds of mean solar time. Due to this difference, of 3 minutes 56 seconds, which has to be corrected when dealing with astrological charting, (see Mean time correction), the stars rise and set earlier each successive day. In the course of one year, the number of Sidereal days exceeds that of mean solar days by exactly one day.

The Sidereal Day begins at Sidereal noon — 0 h, 0 m, 0 s — Sidereal time when the Vernal Equinox — First Point of Aries — is on the observer's meridian. It would be highly impractical to use Sidereal time for regulating everyday affairs, due to the fact that a Sidereal day can commence at any moment of civil time, depending on the locality and the time of year. We, therefore, use Mean Solar time based on the motion of the fictitious Mean Sun, which provides a uniform measurement of 'clock time'. Sidereal time is of the utmost importance to astrologers, because it is the measure of time that they constantly use when calculating charts (see examples under Time — Sidereal time).

The Month

When we refer to a month, we usually mean the calendar month which is a one-twelfth division of a year and which is not based on lunar motion. The word month is derived from 'moonth' and is reputed to have Babylonian origins because these people, along with many ancient civilizations, adopted the Moon's phases as a basis for time reckoning. Although this form of reckoning served the ancient societies reasonably well, it is totally unsuitable for modern needs, because the Moon's phases cannot be reconciled with the Earth's rotation (day), or the Earth's revolution around the Sun (year). Apart from the calendar month, there are several other 'kinds of month', chiefly used by astronomers, such as the *Synodical Month; Sidereal Month; Anomalistic Month;* and *Nodical Month*.

The Synodical Month

This is the interval between two successive 'New Moons'. New Moon occurs when the longitude of the Sun and Moon are the same, as seen from the Earth. The average value of this month is 29.5306 mean solar days (29 days, 12 hours, 44 minutes, 2.7 seconds). This period from New Moon to New Moon is often termed a *Lunation*. As a tropical year has 365.2422 days, the number of lunations in a tropical year is 12.3683 (365.2422 ÷ 29.5306).

The Sidereal Month

As the name suggests, is the Moon's complete period of revolution relative to the stars as seen from Earth; its mean value is 27.3217 mean solar days (27 days, 7 hours, 43 minutes, 11.5 seconds). The number of Sidereal months in a Sidereal year is exactly one greater than the number of synodic (New Moon to New Moon), (365.2564 ÷ 27.3217) = 13.3687.

The Anomalistic Month

Due to perturbations, the direction of perigee (nearest to the Earth) is altering, and the interval required by the Moon to move in its path around the Earth from perigee to perigee is termed the anomalistic month; its value is 27.5546 mean solar days (27 days, 13 hours, 18 minutes, 37.5 seconds).

The Nodical Month

The Moon's ascending node (a point in the Moon's orbit where it cuts the plane of the Ecliptic) has a backward movement along the Ecliptic due to perturbations. The longitude of the node decreases at the rate of nearly 20° per year, and in 18.6 years, the Moon's node completes a circuit of the Ecliptic. The Nodical month is the interval between two successive passages of the Moon through the ascending node; its value is 27.2122 mean solar days. Another name for this month is the *Draconic* which is derived from the mythological belief that, at the time of eclipses (which can only occur when the Sun and Moon are at or near one of the Moon's nodes, at New or Full Moon), a dragon or similar fire-eating beast swallowed the Sun.

The Week

The week is an independent unit of seven days, and probably its length may have been based on the interval between the quarter phases of the Moon. The days of the week are named from the Sun, Moon and the planets known to the ancients, or from pagan deities (see Calendar).

The Year

The year as we normally understand it, is the period of twelve months that are used for civil reckoning. There are, however, several kinds of year, two of which have special significance for astronomers and astrologers: the *Sidereal Year* and the *Tropical Year*.

The Sidereal Year is the interval between two successive returns of the Earth to the same point among the stars as viewed from the Sun. Or, if we consider the Sun moving in its apparent orbit, then a Sidereal year is the interval between two successive returns of the Sun to the same point among the stars, as viewed from the Earth. This period of revolution of the Earth about the Sun with respect to the stars is the Sidereal year which equals 365 days, 6 hours, 9 minutes, 9.5 seconds (365.25636 mean solar days). The Sidereal year is the true year and is just over 20 minutes longer than the tropical year.

The Tropical Year is defined as the interval between two successive passages of the Sun through the Vernal Equinox (First Point of Aries), which is the intersection of the Ecliptic and the Equator. The tropical year is, in fact, the period of revolution of the Earth with respect to the Vernal Equinox, and is sometimes referred to as the *Equinoctial Year*. The Vernal Equinox is not a fixed point on the Ecliptic due to precession, and consequently, the tropical year differs in length from the Sidereal year. Whereas the length of the Sidereal year is 365.2564 mean solar days, that of the tropical year is 365.2422 mean solar days, giving a difference of just over 20 minutes longer for the Sidereal year. If the First Point of Aries were a fixed point amongst the stars, the Sidereal and tropical years would be identical, but as it has an annual retrograde motion of about 50 seconds relative to the stars, the tropical year is shorter than the Sidereal. The tropical year is sometimes referred to as the *Seasonal year,* because it marks the beginning of the various seasons. Other terms for it are the *Astronomical year* and the *Natural year*.

The Anomalistic Year is the interval between two successive perihelion passages of the Earth — or the interval between two successive passages of the Sun in the apparent orbit through perigee. Its length is 365 days, 6 hours, 13 minutes, 53 seconds (365.2596 mean solar days). It differs from a Sidereal year, because the major axis of the Earth's orbit slowly shifts in the plane of the Earth's orbital revolution due to perturbations by the other planets.

The Eclipse Year is the interval between successive returns of the Sun to the same node of the Moon's orbit, this interval being 346.6203 days. Nineteen eclipse years are 6585.78 days, and as the average value of the synodic month or lunation is 29.5306 days, 223 lunations are equivalent to 6585.3 days, and these 223 lunations equal 19 revolutions of the Sun with respect to a node: 18 years 11 days approximately. This 18 years 11 days is called the *Saros*, named by the Chaldean astronomers who discovered this cycle. Another interesting relationship concerning lunations is that 235 lunations equal 19 years of 365¼ days (19 × 365¼ = 6939.75 days), (235 × 29.5306 = 6939.69 days). This is the *Metonic cycle*. After a period of 19 years, the phases of the Moon will recur on the same calendar date and within two hours of the same time. The discovery of this cycle was made by Meton of Athens in 432 B.C.

The Besselian Year is used to define the instant, according to civil reckoning, at which the tropical year is assumed to commence. It is the general astronomical practice to define the beginning of the tropical year (solar year) as the instant when the right ascension of the mean sun is exactly 18 hours 40 minutes. This instant falls near the beginning of the civil year, and the year defined in this way is the Besselian year, named after the German astronomer Bessel who first introduced it into astronomical practice. The year defined in this way is used in deriving precessional and other corrections relating to the heavenly bodies. It is customary to denote the beginning of any Besselian year by the notation '0', as for example 1980.0, 1981.0, and so on.

5.
TIME

Introduction

Time is an elusive entity which seems to defy analysis. We experience time through a succession of changes, events and occurrences, and although we may sometimes wish to disassociate ourselves from time and its relentless march, we are nevertheless always conscious of its presence. Modern man lives by the clock; he has no alternative. To ignore time and its implications, even if we could, would result in an unreal if not chaotic existence. We need time, not only for regulating the practical everyday affairs of life, but also as a means for establishing the more profound relationships with a world beyond our immediate environment.

At any instant of time, we are observing the immediate present, and this fleeting instant which was formerly the future, and will shortly become the past, has all the qualities of that moment of time. Yesterday, today and tomorrow are inexorably linked. The philosophical implications of time are complex, but in the study of time, we can seek to understand reality even though we may only arrive at limited conclusions.

Broadly speaking, there is a distinction between time viewed as an endless flowing stream, and time consciously observed, i.e., the immediate present. Although by the very nature of things, we are subjected to 'artificial time systems', our responses are also governed by our 'internal clocks'. The cosmic connection which affects all creation manifests in man and animals via the biological and circadian rhythms. Early man, being more attuned to his environment, responded more naturally and instinctively to external forces and his own internal time rhythms. Modern man has the same natural responses but these are overlaid, so to speak, by the needs and technicalities of modern living. If we could live more in conformity with our own individual 'time systems' — no easy task — we might alleviate the pressures and tensions of modern life. We become disturbed when we are out of step with time.

The Development of Time-Keeping
From remote antiquity, man has regulated his activities by the Sun. Initially, the division of the day depended upon day and night (light and dark). This division, although adequate as a primary measurement, needed to be more definable and, eventually, the day was divided into hours, sometimes unequal, based on daylight and darkness, or equal hours which divided up the whole day. Later, it became necessary to divide the hours into portions, half, quarter, and later still into minutes.

The earliest time-recording devices were probably sun dials of one kind or another, the most simple of which was the gnomon, consisting of a rod or stick whose shadow indicated the hour. The disadvantage with sun dials, (although it mattered little in earlier times) is that they indicate apparent solar time which is not uniform and which varies by about 16 minutes on either side of the mean during the course of a year. This method of time-keeping was quite adequate for most communities, and it was only toward the end of the eighteenth century that apparent time was replaced by mean time. Even so, except for special purposes, the time kept was still local time based on the meridian of the place or locality (see Local Time).

The mechanical clock (Latin — *clocca* — bell) was invented in the latter decades of the thirteenth century, and was used principally for sounding the hours for religious and secular purposes. The early clocks were primitive instruments, but significant contributions to horology were made during the next few centuries, and by the seventeenth century, the pendulum clock and the balance spring for watches had been developed. These inventions were fundamental in solving the problem of time-keeping at sea, which was so essential for determining longitude and for navigation in general. The invention of the pendulum clock, based on designs by Galileo, is generally attributed to the Dutch astronomer Huygens (1629-95).

The problem of longitude and its accurate determination was finally solved with the invention of the marine chronometer by John Harrison (1693-1776).

Prior to the invention of the electric telegraph (1836), the time determined at an astronomical observatory could be known elsewhere only by transportation of timepieces or by visible or audible signals such as the dropping of a time ball, ringing of bells or blowing of whistles.

With the coming of the railways from the 1830s onward, the inconsistencies of using local time became obvious. Even in the late eighteenth century, the running of the mail coaches to a strict timetable presented difficulties. The coachman and the mail guard were responsible not only for the safety of passengers and goods, but also had to ensure that the coach kept to time. The guard who carried a timepiece regulated it to 'gain about 15 minutes in 24 hours', so that when travelling eastward, it might accord with real time. In the opposite direction, a corresponding allowance was made. This mail coach tradition of carrying a timepiece was continued by the railway guards, although without the allowance for 'easting and westing'.

The expansion in communications which occurred from the 1830s-1850s, changed people's attitude towards time and timekeeping. Whereas previously it has been sufficient to know the time (local) to within reasonable limits, it now became important for a 'travelling population' using the 'new railways' to comply with time and time-tables. Although local time served the purposes of local communities, it was inconvenient for use by the railway companies. By the 1840s, at least three organizations, the Post Office, the railways and the telegraph companies were pressing for a uniform time system throughout Great Britain. In 1840, as the *Illustrated London News* reported, the Post Office suggested that all post office clocks in the Kingdom be regulated by means of time brought from London by the mail coach chronometers. It was, however, the railways who eventually obtained a uniformity of time, insofar as their services were concerned.

In November 1840, The Great Western Railway ordered that London time should be kept at all its stations and in its time-tables; other railways followed suit during the next few years. A few complications arose, as when the late running of a train was attributed to the fact that London time was kept on the line between Rugby

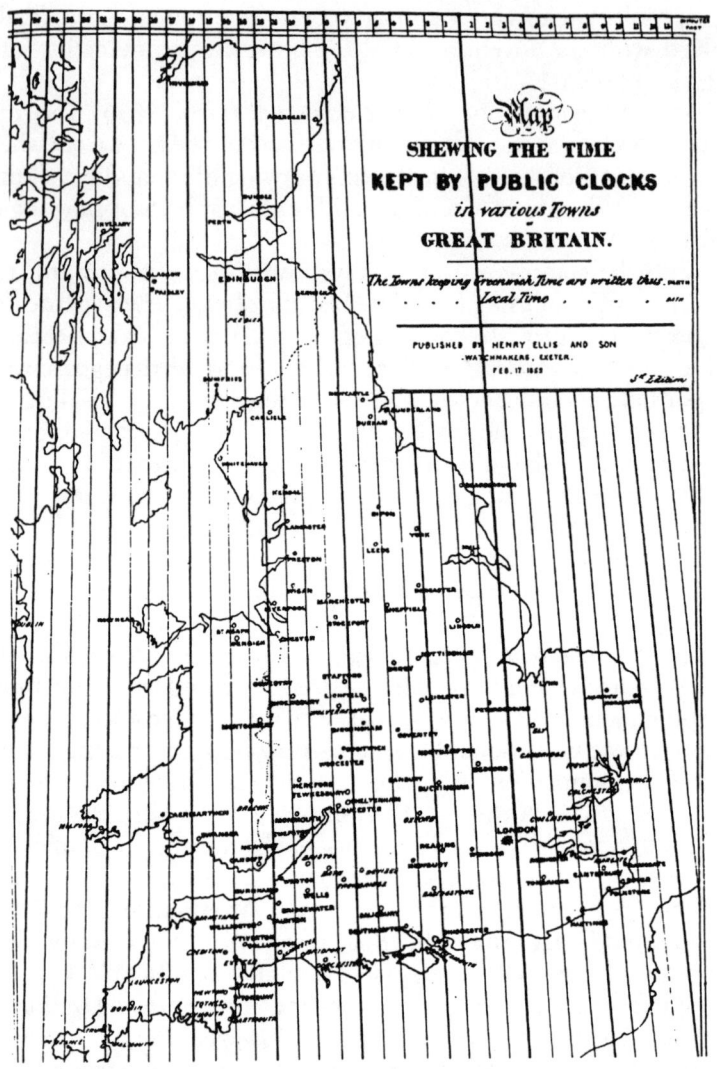

Figure 12. Towns (in italic) in Great Britain still keeping local time in February 1852. The scale along the top shows the number of minutes' difference between local and Greenwich time. From the edition of a map published by Henry Ellis & Son, Exeter, in February 1852 (RGO MSS. 1168/149).
(Reproduced by courtesy of the Royal Greenwich Observatory.)

and York (run by the Midland Railway), whereas local Rugby time was kept at Rugby station (run by the North Western Railway). Other anomalies occurred with the population as a whole keeping a different time from that used by the railways. Early morning in London could still be the late hours of the previous day in places such as west Wales or Cornwall. The notification of an event occurring in London in the early morning, could be received in Dublin the previous evening!

It is sometimes stated that birth times in Great Britain prior to 1880 (the legal date for the adoption of Greenwich time) are given in local time. This is a misleading assumption, for by 1855, the majority of public clocks in Great Britain were set to Greenwich Mean time. It is therefore reasonable to suppose that the local population would set their clocks according to the town clocks. In February 1852, Henry Ellis and Son, of Exeter, published a map showing the towns in Great Britain still keeping local time and those keeping Greenwich time. This map is highly instructive and shows clearly that many towns had abandoned local time, and had in fact commenced using Greenwich time. A letter in the *London Times* dated 2 October 1851, confirms that Greenwich time had been adopted in many places in the Kingdom, although some towns of consequence, notably in the east and west of England, still held out against the use of Greenwich time. Gradually, Greenwich time became the accepted standard and with the adoption of the Greenwich meridian as the Prime meridian, time-keeping entered a more stable phase. Subsequently, the modern technology of the twentieth century produced inventions that enabled time-keeping to be co-ordinated to a degree of sophistication undreamed of by previous generations.

Kinds of Time

Apparent Solar Time
The natural basis for the measurement of time is the apparent movement of the Sun around the Earth. While there have been many philosophical reflections on the nature of time, all that is required in astronomical practice is an accurate system of time measurement.

The rotation of the Earth about its axis in a west to east direction, and its orbit around the Sun, are reflected in the apparent motion of the Sun and stars across the sky. In the course of a year, the Sun as seen from the Earth appears to describe a great circle of the heavens, i.e., its annual journey along the Ecliptic. The rotation of the Earth about its axis from west to east is readily appreciated, because we can see the Sun in its daily path rising in the east, culminating in the south (the north in southern latitudes), and setting in the west. However, it is less obvious to an observer that the Earth is moving round the Sun, and the only visible indications of this are the changing seasons.

The solar day, i.e., the day measured by the Sun, is affected by the inclination of the Ecliptic, and by the actual angular velocity of the Earth about the Sun which is not uniform, so that the Sun's velocity is also not uniform. An apparent solar day can be defined as the period of time which elapses between two successive transits of the Sun across any one particular meridian (the north-south line through the particular place or location). As the Earth rotates about its axis at a uniform speed, it is also moving on its orbit around the Sun. Each day, the Sun will transit the meridian, but the Earth will have rotated on its axis more than 360° in space during the period of an apparent solar day. The apparent movement of the Sun is not uniform, and even if it were, the fact that the Ecliptic is inclined to the Equator, would result in the movement of the Sun being variable. The intervals between successive meridian passages of the Sun are not equal, and this variation in the length of apparent solar days is not conducive for accurate time-keeping by the apparent or *True Sun*.

Mean Time
To overcome the vagaries of the Apparent or True Sun in its journey along the Ecliptic, an allowance has to be made, so that a convenient and regular method of time-keeping can be achieved. Accordingly, an imaginary Sun, called the *Mean Sun* is introduced, having a uniform motion in Right Ascension (see Circles and Projections) equal to the mean motion of the True Sun in Right Ascension. The relationship between the 'two suns' is fixed by another imaginary sun, called the *Dynamical Mean Sun,* moving at a constant speed in the Ecliptic, its rate of movement being the mean or average rate of the apparent sun's rate of movement. Let us imagine that we have 'two suns', the Apparent and the Dynamical in the same position on the Ecliptic at say, 1 January. The Apparent Sun is moving faster than the Dynamical Sun at this period, and will gradually widen the distance between the two suns. At a later period, the distance between them will decrease when the Apparent Sun

is moving slower, until eventually the two suns will be in identical positions, after which the Apparent Sun will slowly lag behind. The object of having this imaginary Dynamical mean sun is to establish the position of the astronomical mean sun, usually referred to as the *Mean Sun*. At the instant when the Dynamical sun passes through the First Point of Aries, the Mean Sun is assumed to be starting off from Aries along the celestial Equator with the same angular velocity as the Dynamical Sun. The motion of the Mean Sun in Right Ascension is therefore uniform, and the intervals between successive meridian passages are equal. The Mean Sun moves round the Celestial Equator in a manner in which its Right Ascension is always equal to the longitude of the Dynamical Sun.

Mean Solar time is defined by the astronomical mean sun and is measured by the hour angle of the Mean Sun. When the Mean Sun crosses the meridian above the horizon at any place, it is local mean noon for that place or local mean time 12.00.

When the Apparent or True Sun is on the meridian of any place, it is local apparent noon of that place, and the hour angle of the True Sun, measured westward from the meridian, gives local apparent time.

Equation of Time

Due to the non-uniform motion of the Earth relative to the Sun, and to the fact that the True Sun moves along the Ecliptic, whereas the Mean Sun moves along the Celestial Equator, Apparent solar time and Mean time differ from each other. This difference expressed in minutes and seconds, is termed the *Equation of Time*. In all observations of the Sun this equation, which varies throughout the year, has to be applied. The equation is, in effect, the difference between the hour angles of the True Sun and of the Mean Sun. In astrological charting, we normally use Mean time, and therefore are not concerned with corrections involving this equation.

Local Time

The term Local time is subject to a certain amount of ambiguity. Normally, the term denotes the clock time in use at a particular locality. However, this clock time may be recording the Standard time of the zone or area, or it may show Daylight Saving time, but the term Local time may still be used.

Local (Mean Solar) Time is the mean solar time for a definite meridian and differs by four minutes for every one degree of longitude, but Standard time is the Zone time of a definite area or locality based on the Local Mean time of a particular standard meridian which has been adopted for standard time purposes. For example, New York uses the standard meridian of 75° west, and all clocks are 5 hours slow on Greenwich. New York, however, is not exactly on the 75th meridian but 73° 57' west of Greenwich, so that this longitude when expressed in time is 73° 57' over 15 which equals 4 hours 55 minutes 48 seconds. When it is noon G.M.T. at London, the New York clocks show 7.00 a.m. Eastern Standard time, but the Local (Mean Solar) time of New York is 12.00 less 4 hours 55 minutes 48 seconds, which equals 7 hours 4 minutes 12 seconds a.m. Local Mean Solar time. The difference of 4 minutes 12 seconds between the Standard time and the Local mean solar time is the difference expressed in time of the actual New York meridian (73° 57') and the Standard meridian which has been adopted for New York Standard time (E.S.T. 75° West). Unless information is given to the contrary, it can be assumed that the term 'local time', when given for chart calculations, is the clock time of the particular locality. When Daylight Saving time is in operation (see Table for British Summer Times), then the clock time given must be *reduced* by the amount of the advance, normally 1 hour.

Greenwich Mean Time
This is the local mean time of the meridian of Greenwich. The difference between Greenwich Mean Time and Local Mean Time at any instant of time, is the longitude expressed in time. Many of the principal ephemerides used by astrologers are Greenwich based, with the positions given for 12.00 G.M.T. When using these ephemerides, it is essential that the clock time of birth is converted into the equivalent Greenwich time and date. Unless the conversion is done correctly, the time and, in some cases, the date will be in error.

Example No. 1
Find the equivalent G.M.T. when it is 8.00 p.m. Pacific Standard Time. 31.12.80.

Working:
As P.S.T. is based on the 120th meridian west, the Standard difference is 8 hours slow on Greenwich.

TIME

P.S.T. 8.00 p.m.	=	20 00	
Add difference		8 00	
		28 00	
	−	24 00	= 4.00 a.m.
			G.M.T. 1.1.81

Example No. 2
Find the equivalent G.M.T. when it is 3.00 a.m. Indian Standard Time 1.1.81.

Working:
As I.S.T. is 5½ hours in advance of Greenwich we deduct the Standard difference.

I.S.T. 1.1.81	03 00	
	+ 24 00	for ease of deduction
	27 00	
Less difference	05 30	= 21.30 = 9.30 p.m.
		G.M.T. 31.12.80

The Greenwich time and date at any locality can always be found, provided we know what Standard or Zone time is in use.

When Daylight Saving time is in use, then the clock time must be corrected before finding the equivalent Greenwich time.

Example No. 3
Find the equivalent G.M.T. when it is Noon P.D.S.T. 1.1.81.

Noon P.D.S.T.	12 00	
Less 1 hour	01 00	
Pacific Standard time	11 00	a.m.
Add Standard time difference	08 00	
	19 00	= 7.00 p.m. G.M.T. 1.1.81

Standard Time
To avoid the confusion which would result from the use of the Local Mean Time of a large number of places, the world has been divided into a number of Standard Time zones, and these standards are based

upon a central meridian reckoned either east or west from the Prime meridian of Greenwich. Places east of Greenwich will have standard times that are in advance of the Greenwich time, while those places west of Greenwich will have standard times which are slow on Greenwich time. There are, however, a few exceptions to this rule, for instance, parts of Western Spain and France bordering the Atlantic are to the west of Greenwich, but their standard times are based on Central European Standard time (1 hour in advance). Details concerning the various Standard times in operation in the principal countries of the world can be found in the *Nautical Almanac* and other similar publications (also see References).

Standard time, is in effect, the local mean time of the meridian that has been adopted for a definite zone or area. New York, as already stated, uses the 75th meridian west, which is 5 hours slow on Greenwich; Tokyo uses the 135th meridian east, so compared with Greenwich, Japanese standard time is 9 hours in advance. When it is noon in Japan, it is 3.00 a.m. G.M.T. In large countries such as the United States, Canada or Russia, several time zones are in operation and these range from 3½-8 hours in North America, and from 3-13 hours in the Soviet Socialist Republics. Since the inception of standard time zones at the end of the last century, many countries have altered or amended their original standards, and it is therefore essential to consult appropriate references for the place and year required.

It is often assumed that, prior to the official adoption of a standard time, a country used local time. In some cases this was so, but not always. Great Britain kept Greenwich time from 13 January 1848, although some localities still adhered to local time. Sweden used the 15th meridian (1 hour fast on Greenwich) from 1 January 1879. The date of legalization of a particular standard time was often many years subsequent to its adoption and use, and although railway communities generally adopted the standard as used by the railways, some areas still retained the use of local time. By 1905, most of the major countries were using standard times with the exception of France, Portugal, Holland, Greece, Turkey, Russia, Ireland and most of Central America except Chile. Of the thirty-six nations then using standard times, twenty had adopted Greenwich as the basis of their systems. When using a Greenwich based ephemeris, the clock time of birth is converted into Greenwich time by *adding* the standard difference for west longitude and *deducting* for east longitude. If

Daylight Saving time applies, then the equivalent advance has to be deducted from the clock time given.

Daylight Saving Time / Summer Time / War Time
These terms are identical and relate to advancing the clock for certain periods during the year. The amount of the advance is normally one hour, commencing in the early Spring and ending in the Autumn. However, variations do occur, not only in the amount of the advance, but also in the duration. The amount of the advance must always be *deducted* from the given clock time, in order to arrive at the Standard time of the country or state. During the Second World War, Daylight Saving time, known as War time, was observed uniformly nationwide in North America from 2 February 1942-30 September 1945. In Great Britain, Double Summer time was used (+ 2 hours in advance of G.M.T.).

An experiment with British Standard time was introduced on the 18 February 1968, and continued until the 31 October 1971, whereby all clocks were advanced one hour ahead of G.M.T. All clock times quoted for this period should have one hour deducted to arrive at the Greenwich time. From 1972, British Summer time was re-introduced, and all clocks are now advanced by one hour from March to October each year. In Europe, the question of Daylight Saving time was more or less resolved when, at 00.59 G.M.T. 6 April 1980, fourteen countries in continental Europe, except Switzerland, from the Atlantic to the Urals switched simultaneously to summer time. Prior to this time, the position concerning summer time in Europe was confusing if not chaotic, but some uniformity has at last been achieved. (See *Daily Telegraph* 17.7.80 and 4.4.77; *Sunday Times,* 29.2.76 and 6.4.80.)

Universal Time
This term is synonymous with Greenwich Mean Time and is used in scientific notation, astronomical data, etc. It is reckoned from 0-24 hours, e.g., 21.00 = 9 p.m.

Universal time in principle is determined by the average rate of the apparent diurnal motion of the Sun relative to the meridian of Greenwich; but in practice, the numerical measure of Universal Time at any instant is formally computed from its relation to the measure of time defined by the diurnal motion of the Vernal Equinox (First Point of Aries) otherwise known as Sidereal Time.

Ephemeris Time

Because the Earth is not a perfect time-keeper, it is essential to have a uniform measure of time. Ephemeris Time is a system with a constant rate defined by reference to the motion of the Sun, Moon and planets. In practice, it is the motion of the Moon which can be most readily determined with accuracy, and Ephemeris Time refers to the dynamical theory of the motion of the Moon. Owing to the irregularity of the Earth's rotation, it does not provide a satisfactory basis for astronomical time systems and for tables compiled from the gravitation theories of the Sun, Moon and planets. The value of Ephemeris Time changes annually and is listed in the ephemerides. Up to and including 1959, *Raphael's Ephemeris* was based on Greenwich Mean Time. From 1960 to 1982, the times and tabulations in the ephemeris were in Ephemeris Time (E.T.) but, commencing with the issue for 1983, all listings, unless otherwise stated, are based on Greenwich time. To all intents and purposes, the use of Ephemeris Time can be disregarded, but if precision is required, the Greenwich time should be converted to Ephemeris Time before finding the position of the Sun or Moon from the tables.

Sidereal Time

As Sidereal time is a very important factor in astrological charting, it may be useful to consider it in some detail, and give examples of how to calculate the Sidereal time for various times and places.

The circle of the Celestial Equator which lies in the same plane as the Earth's Equator, always rises due east, crosses the upper meridian at a point from the zenith of the observer equal to the latitude of the observer, and sets due west. It has as its starting point the First Point of Aries (Vernal Equinoctial Point), which is the point where it intersects the circle of the Ecliptic. This equinoctial point perpetually slides backwards along the circle of the Ecliptic at the rate of 1° in about 72 years (see Precession). The degrees of the Celestial Equator, measured from this shifting point, are known as degrees of Right Ascension (R.A.), and it is usual for astronomers to measure such distances in terms of time, rather than arc where 360° = 24 hours.

A Sidereal Day may be defined as the interval between successive upper transits or culminations of any star on the observer's meridian. This definition of a sidereal day assumes that the Earth rotates at a constant rate. It also assumes that the Equator and the Ecliptic are fixed planes. However, because of the effects of precession and nutation, this is not the case. The Vernal Equinox, due to precession moves westward, and because of this westward motion of the Vernal Equinox, the interval between two successive transits of the moving equinox will be 0.008 seconds less than the interval between two successive transits of the fixed Equinox. The interval between successive transits of the moving Equinox is defined as a Sidereal day of 24 hours. The instant of transit of the Equinox is Sidereal noon, and the interval between successive transits of the fixed Equinox is the period of the Earth's rotation.

Sidereal time, at any instant, is the hour angle of the Vernal Equinox expressed in time, or in other words, the angle between an observer's meridian and a body or point measured westward from the meridian in a direction parallel to the Celestial Equator. There is a distinction to be made between Apparent Sidereal time and Mean Sidereal time. Apparent Sidereal time refers to the true Equinox of date, that is, the true Equinox of date found by making allowance for precession and nutation. Mean Sidereal time refers to the Mean Equinox of date — by making allowance only for precession. The difference between apparent and mean Sidereal time is termed the equation of the Equinoxes, formerly called nutation in right ascension.

Apparent Sidereal time is determined by the observation of stars, and is corrected by allowing for nutation, thus giving Mean Sidereal time. Sidereal clocks are adjusted to keep Mean Sidereal time. During the course of a Sidereal day, the Earth rotates on its axis in a period of 23 hours 56 minutes 04 seconds of Mean time (Civil time) and, for an observer located at a particular longitude, the Sidereal Day is equivalent to the apparent rotation period of the Celestial Sphere. This rotation period can be determined by measuring the interval between two successive upper transits of the First Point of Aries or of a given star across the meridian. Some time during the course of 24 hours, the First Point of Aries will be on the meridian, and the time of day when this occurs will depend upon the longitude of the observer and the time of year. When the First Point of Aries is on the meridian, its hour angle is zero and the Sidereal time zero hours. The constant rotation of the Celestial Sphere increases this angle and at say, 45°, 3 hours have elapsed, and the Sidereal time is 3 hours. At 90°, it will be 6 hours Sidereal time, and so on, until after 24 hours, the First Point of Aries once again returns to the meridian.

Sidereal time is synonymous with the Right Ascension of the Meridian (R.A.M.C.). The difference between Local Sidereal time (L.S.T.) and Greenwich Sidereal time (G.S.T.) corresponds to the longitude of the observer expressed in time, one hour being equivalent to 15°, since the Earth rotates through 15° per hour. Places on the same meridian always have the same Local Sidereal time. Sidereal time at Greenwich is local for the Greenwich meridian and for all places on that meridian irrespective of latitude. Other places on Earth, not on the Greenwich meridian, would have a Local Sidereal time differing from the Greenwich Sidereal time, and this difference would depend on the longitude of the place either east or west of Greenwich. Sidereal time is, therefore always *local*, it cannot be otherwise.

In determining the Local Sidereal time for a given time and place, we can ascertain the culminating degree of the Ecliptic, either from Tables of Houses or from Tables of Right Ascension. From the tables of houses for the appropriate latitude, we can obtain the rising degree (Ascendant) and the other factors associated with house division (mundane position). The finding of the correct Sidereal time is not difficult, but it is a very important procedure in astrological charting. Unless the Local Sidereal time is correct, the chart will be in error. Much controversy surrounds house division, but house position is important, being the only factor which alters in a short space of time.

Sidereal time is always given only for the time for which the ephemeris is computed, e.g., noon or midnight, so certain corrections are necessary in order to obtain the local Sidereal time for a time and place other than the time and meridian for which the ephemeris is calculated. *Raphael's Ephemeris* gives the Sidereal time for noon at Greenwich, other ephemerides may give it for a meridian other than Greenwich and/or for a time other than noon, such as 0 hours (the commencement of a civil day).

There are several methods for ascertaining the Sidereal time for a specified time and place, some easier than others. Some formulae use the Local Mean time of the locality, but this is an unnecessary complication and can cause confusion. The easiest method is to convert the time given to the time for which the ephemeris is computed, as for example Greenwich time if using *Raphael's* or the *American Ephemeris.*

The fictitious Mean sun crosses the meridian either earlier or later depending upon the longitude of the place either east or west, and therefore the Sidereal time will not be the same as for the meridian

TIME

for which the ephemeris is calculated. By taking the difference in longitude between the birthplace and the 'ephemeris meridian', the necessary adjustment can be made to determine the correct Sidereal time for any time and place. In the calculation of charts, it is desirable to be as accurate as possible, but there is little point in trying to achieve precision with birth times which are only approximate. When the data given are exact and reliable, then the chart should be calculated precisely using simple and straightforward methods. From the ephemeris, it will be seen that the Sidereal time as tabulated, appears to increase from day to day by about 3 minutes 56 seconds due to the fact that, in one mean solar day (24 hours of clock time), the rotating Earth turns through 24 hours 3 minutes 56½ seconds of Sidereal time, to keep pace with the average daily motion of the fictitious Mean sun. The difference between Mean time and Sidereal time has to be allowed for, and to do this, we apply a correction (Mean time correction) of 9.856 seconds per Mean time hour. As Sidereal time is always local for a definite place and time, an adjustment has to be made for the difference in longitude between the place for which the chart is required, and the meridian for which the ephemeris is calculated. The following examples illustrate the various methods that can be employed in finding the Local Sidereal time of birth.

Example No. 1:
Find the L.S.T. at 135° 33′ East longitude at 7.00 p.m. Standard time 1.1.80. The Standard in use at this longitude is 9 hours in advance of Greenwich, so the equivalent G.M.T. is 10.00 a.m. 1.1.80.

Working:
Using a Greenwich based ephemeris for Noon:

	H	M	S
S.T. at Noon 1.1.80	18	41	13
Less interval to noon (12-10)	2	00	00
	16	41	13
Less Mean time correction 2 × 9.86 secs.	00	00	20
	16	40	53
Add difference in longitude 135° 33′ / 15	9	02	12
Local Sidereal time as required	1	43	05

Example No. 2
Using an ephemeris based on the 75th meridian West for 0 hours Eastern Standard Time: Data as for example No. 1.

Working:

	H	M	S
S.T. at 0 hours E.S.T. 1.1.80	6	40	04
Add interval 5.00 a.m. E.S.T.	5	00	00
Add Mean time correction 5 × 9.86 secs.	0	00	49
Add difference in longitude (75° + 135° 33′ = 210° 33′) / 15	14	02	12
Local Sidereal time as required	1	43	05

Example No. 3
This example uses the Local Mean time of birth to arrive at the Sidereal time required, but the method is cumbersome and can cause confusion.

Working:

	H	M	S
S.T. at Noon G.M.T. 1.1.80	18	41	13
*Less correction for 9 hours 02 mins. 12 secs. (135° 33′ East × 9.86 secs.) / 15	00	01	29
S.T. at 135° 33′ East, Noon L.M.T.	18	39	44
Add interval of L.M.T.	7	02	12
Add correction 7.02.12 × 9.86 secs.	0	01	09
S.T. as required	1	43	05

*This correction of 9.86 secs. per 15° of longitude or 0.657 seconds per 1°, is to adjust the Sidereal time between the birthplace and the meridian for which the ephemeris is calculated. For places, *West* the correction is *added*, and for places *East* it is *deducted*.

TIME

Example No. 4
Checking the above examples using the Nautical Almanac:

		Degs.	Mins.
Greenwich Hour Angle — Aries at 10 a.m.			
G.M.T. 1.1.80		250	13
Add East longitude 135° 33'		135	33
		385	46
Convert into time 25° 46' / 15	less circle	360	00
= 1 hour 43 mins. 05 secs. as required		25	46

Example No. 5
Find the L.S.T. at 75° West Longitude at 3.00 p.m. E.S.T. 1.1.80. The Standard in use is 5 hours slow on Greenwich, so the equivalent Greenwich time is 8.00 p.m. 1.1.80.

Working:
Using a Greenwich based ephemeris for Noon:

	H	M	S
S.T. at Noon 1.1.80	18	41	13
Add G.M.T. interval	8	00	00
Add Mean time correction	00	1	19
	26	42	32
Less Long. Equiv. West 75 / 15	5	00	00
S.T. as required	21	42	32

Example No. 6
Using an ephemeris based on 75th meridian West for midnight E.S.T.

	H	M	S
S.T. at 0 hours 75° West 1.1.80	6	40	04
Add time elapsed (3.00 p.m.)	15	00	00
Add Mean time correction	00	02	28
S.T. as required	21	42	32

Example No. 7
Using Nautical Almanac:

	Degs.	Mins.
Greenwich Hour Angle — Aries at 8.00 p.m. (3.00 p.m. E.S.T.)	40	38
Add for ease of deduction	360	00
	400	38
Less 75° West Longitude	75	00
	325	38

Convert into time $\dfrac{325°\ 38'}{15}$

$= \dfrac{\text{H M S}}{21\ 42\ 32}$

Example No. 8
Find the L.S.T. at 122° 26′ West Longitude at 10.30 p.m. Pacific Standard time, 25.1.80 = 6.30 a.m. Greenwich Mean Time 26.1.80.

Working:
Using Greenwich based ephemeris for Noon G.M.T.

	H	M	S
S.T. at Noon G.M.T. 26.1.80	20	19	47
Less interval to noon (12.00-6.30)	5	30	00
	14	49	47
Less Mean time correction	00	00	54
	14	48	53
Less Long. Equiv. West $\dfrac{122°\ 26'}{15}$	8	09	44
S.T. as required	6	39	09

Example No. 9
Using ephemeris based on 75th meridian West for Noon E.S.T.

	H	M	S
S.T. at Noon 75° West 25.1.80	20	16	40
Add interval (10.30 p.m. P.S.T. = 1.30 a.m. E.S.T.)	13	30	00
Add Mean time correction	00	02	13
	33	48	53
Less Long. Equiv. West (Difference between 122° 26' and 75°) = 47° 26' / 15	3	09	44
	30	39	09
Less	24	00	00
S.T. as required	6	39	09

Example No. 10
Using an ephemeris based on 75th meridian West for midnight E.S.T.

	H	M	S
S.T. at 0 hours 75° West 26.1.80	8	18	38
Add interval (10.30 p.m. P.S.T. = 1.30 a.m. E.S.T.)	1	30	00
Add Mean time correction	0	00	15
	9	48	53
Less Long. Equiv. West (Difference between 122° 26' and 75°) = 47° 26' / 15	3	09	44
S.T. as required	6	39	09

Example No. 11
Using Nautical Almanac:

	Degs.	Mins.
Greenwich Hour Angle — Aries at 6.30 a.m. G.M.T. 26.1.80	222	13
Less Long. West 122° 26'	122	26
	99	47

Convert into time $\dfrac{99° \ 47'}{15}$

$= \dfrac{\text{H M S}}{6 \ 39 \ 09}$

6.
THE ASTROLOGICAL EPHEMERIS

An ephemeris is an indispensable publication for all astrological calculations. There are several types of ephemerides available, one of the most reliable being *Raphael's* which is published annually. As the ephemeris is an essential 'tool' for the astrologer, it may be useful to discuss some of its contents and listings. Up to and including 1959, *Raphael's Ephemeris* was calculated for noon G.M.T., but from 1960 until 1982, it was calculated for Ephemeris Time. The practice of using Ephemeris Time has now been discontinued and, commencing with the issue for 1983, it has reverted to Noon G.M.T. Unless the birth data are precise, the value of Ephemeris Time can be ignored and the information contained in the ephemeris treated as for Greenwich Mean Time.

If we refer to an ephemeris for 1980 (pages 2 and 3), we can see that there is a column headed 'Sidereal Time'. This Sidereal time or Right Ascension of the Mean Sun, is the Sidereal time at noon for the Greenwich meridian. Each day, this time increases by an average of 3 minutes 56 seconds, hence the necessity for a Mean time correction of 9.86 seconds per hour. Even though the Sidereal time, as shown in the ephemeris, for noon increases by 3 minutes 56 seconds, the Earth has, in a period of 24 hours clock time, turned a full 24 hours plus the additional 3 minutes 56 seconds. For places other than Greenwich and for times other than noon, examples are given under 'Time-Sidereal Time'.

The symbols at the top of each page in the ephemeris refer to the 'Sun, Moon planets and long.' indicating their positions in celestial longitude for each day of the month. This longitude is, in effect, the position expressed in degrees and minutes of the signs of the zodiac which the body occupies at noon on a particular day.

The symbol of the zodiacal sign is listed for the first day of the month and again for the last day. When a planet changes signs, the symbol is shown against the day when the change occurred. In calculating the planets' positions for a time other than noon, care is needed to note the sign occupied and not merely taking the sign shown at the top of the page for the first day of the month.

The symbol 'R' which appears in the planets' position column (page 3) indicates that the planet has turned retrograde on that day, whilst the symbol 'D' indicates direct, that is, the planet is going from retrograde to forward motion (see 'Retrograde'). In the column next to the Sun's longitude, there is a heading 'Sun Dec.' (declination), and this relates to the distance that the Sun has above or below the Equator. The measurement is in degrees and minutes either north or south of the Equator. The position of the Earth in relation to the Sun determines the Sun's declination. From the ephemeris, we note that the Sun's declination on 1 January is 23° 03′S, which tells us that the Sun is 23° 03′ south of the Equator. Each day, the declination decreases and will continue to do so until about 20 March when, with zero declination, the Sun crosses the Equator going from south to north at the Vernal Equinox. Its declination will then be north and increasing until it reaches its maximum declination 23° 26′ at the June Solstice, on or about 21 June.

The Moon, owing to her fast motion, moves on average about 13° per day and passes through all the 12 signs of the zodiac in about 27½ days. When the Moon changes signs, the sign is listed in the ephemeris, but only if the change occurred before noon. For example, on 1 January, the Moon at noon is shown in 29° 43′ Gemini, but at 12.30 p.m., it entered Cancer. As with the Sun, the actual time of entering a sign is shown on page 39 of the ephemeris. The easiest way to obtain the daily motions of the planets, is to refer to the table on page 26 and 27 of the ephemeris. For the slower moving planets, motions are not given in the table, but simple proportion will give their longitude for a given time.

The heading 'Moon Lat.' refers to the Moon's latitude, which is a measurement in degrees and minutes of its distance north or south of the Ecliptic. The Sun has no latitude being always on the Ecliptic.

The Moon's orbit relative to the Ecliptic is tilted, the mean tilt being 5° 8′, and the listings in the ephemeris show the Moon's latitude for each day, and indicates how its orbit is tilted relative to the Ecliptic. Normally, latitude is not required for ordinary chart calculations but it is for more advanced procedures. (see 'Rising and Setting of Planets'). The Moon's Declination shown in the ephemeris for both noon and midnight, increases or decreases either north or south during each month. When the Moon's declination is zero, it is then on the Equator. Its maximum declination varies from month to month and from year to year. During a period of 19 years, this variation is from about 28½° to about 18°, and this phenomenon is termed the 'regression of the nodes', which is a retrograde motion along the Ecliptic. The ascending node is where the Moon crosses the Ecliptic from south to north, and the descending node is where it crosses going from north to south. Astronomically, the line joining these two points is referred to as the Nodal Line, which is the line of intersection of the plane of the Earth's path and that of the Moon's path.

Aspects

An aspect is the angular distance measured along the Ecliptic in Celestial Longitude as viewed from the Earth. The table on page 3 ('Lunar Aspects') lists all the aspects made by the Moon, and the table on the lower half of the page gives the Mutual aspects which are aspects between Sun and planet and/or planet and planet. In this table, if a planet makes more than one aspect on a given day, the planet's symbol is not repeated, but each aspect is separated by a comma, e.g., 15 January, Sun sesqiquadrate Jupiter, sextile Uranus. Many aspects are considered important in astrology, but the major configurations have the most significance. Of these the conjunction, square (quadrature) and opposition are the principal aspects.

The Conjunction — symbol ☌

A conjunction occurs when a planet is in line with the Sun and the Earth. A conjunction may be either superior or inferior. When a superior conjunction occurs, the planet is in line with the Sun and with the Earth and is located on the far side of the Sun. An inferior conjunction is one that occurs when a planet is in line with the Sun and the Earth and is on the near side of the Sun, (between Sun and

Earth). As the term suggests, inferior conjunctions can only occur with Mercury and Venus (the inferior planets) whose orbits lie closer into the Sun than the orbit of the Earth. The time interval between successive conjunctions is known as the planet's synodic period.

The term 'syzygy' relates to the Moon when in conjunction or opposition, i.e., New or Full.

Opposition — Symbol ☍ 180°
A superior planet is in conjunction when it is in line with the Sun and the Earth and located on the far side of the Sun. The opposite point in its orbit, when it is again in line with the Earth and Sun but with the Earth this time between the Sun and the planet, is termed an opposition. At opposition, the planet is closer to the Earth than at conjunction. Mercury and Venus (the inferior planets) cannot be opposition to the Sun.

Quadrature (Square) — Symbol □ 90°
The quadrature aspect occurs when the Sun-planet-Earth angle is exactly 90°. Planets whose orbits are larger than the Earth's (i.e., the superior planets) can form this aspect, but the inferior planets (Mercury and Venus), whose distance from the Sun cannot exceed 28° and 48° respectively, cannot. The Moon in its orbit of the Earth will, during its monthly course, form all aspects with the Sun and the planets.

Phenomena

Greatest Elongation East and West
Elongation is the angle between the Sun and a celestial body when observed from the Earth. The maximum elongation that Mercury and Venus can attain is 28° for Mercury and 48° for Venus. All other planets can reach a maximum elongation of 180°. When a planet is located east of the Sun, it is at eastern elongation, and as it sets after the Sun, it is termed an 'evening star', whereas a planet located west of the Sun rises before the Sun and has western elongation, and is termed a 'morning star'. Greatest elongation east always follows the planet's superior conjunction with the Sun, whilst greatest elongation west always follows the planet's inferior conjunction with the Sun.

Perihelion and Aphelion

These terms relate to the closest (perhihelion) and farthest (aphelion) approach to the Sun in the orbit of a planet. From the table 'Phenomena' on page 29 of *Raphael's Ephemeris*, we can see that, on 3 January, the Earth is closest to the Sun (⊕ in Perihelion), and on 5 July (⊕ in Aphelion), it is farthest away. As the Earth's orbit is elliptical, the Earth's distance from the Sun varies day by day. In January each year, the Earth reaches its closest point to the Sun. By July each year, the Earth has reached its farthest point from the Sun. Periodically, the planets are at perihelion and aphelion, and the date and time when this occurs are listed in the Ephemeris table of 'Phenomena'.

Perigee and Apogee

A planet or the Moon is at perigee when at the point closest to the Earth, and at apogee when farthest from the Earth. As the Moon's apparent orbit of the Earth describes an ellipse, the Moon's distance from the Earth and the speed in its orbit varies daily. At perigee, the Moon's motion is fastest, while at apogee, it is slowest. In astrological charting, the moon's longitude is found by interpolating its twenty-four hour average motion, and this is normally sufficient for birth chart calculations. For research purposes using precise data, the interpolation should be more exact by using non-linear techniques, i.e. correcting for second and third differences.

Nodes of the Planets

The nodes of a planet's orbit are the points where the orbit intersects the plane of the Ecliptic. The point where the planet crosses from south to north is the ascending node (☊), and the point where it crosses from north to south is the descending node (☋). Celestial latitude is the measurement either north or south of the Ecliptic, and when a planet is at its node, its latitude is zero and it is exactly on the Ecliptic. The period between two consecutive north and south nodes is equal to the planet's Sidereal period. For example, Mercury is in its ascending node on 14 February and again on 12 May, corresponding with its Sidereal period of 88 days.

Distances apart of all Conjunctions and Oppositions

One of the most useful tables in *Raphael's Ephemeris* is the one dealing with conjunctions and oppositions. With the aid of this table, every conjunction and opposition occurring during the year can be ascertained. This table gives the date; aspect, the time when the aspect occurs and the distance apart of the two planets in degrees and minutes of declination. The time given in the ephemeris is in Ephemeris Time (1960-82). If the time is required for a place other than Greenwich, then the time given in the ephemeris will need to be converted for the meridian required. Declination is the distance of a celestial body either north or south of the Celestial Equator. When two bodies are within a 1° orb or so of the same degree, either on the same side of the Equator or opposite sides, they are in parallel aspect. The closer the bodies are in terms of declination when forming a conjunction or opposition, the more significant the aspect. Conjunctions and oppositions are always of the utmost importance, and it is highly probable that the distance apart in declination may also have some bearing in charts for mundane events such as earthquakes, mine disasters and the like.

The 'blacked in' symbol for the Sun indicates that the conjunction is also a solar eclipse. In 1980, for example, 16 February was the date of a solar eclipse as indicated in the table by 'Moon ☌ ●'; likewise 10 August.

Certain conjunctions in the table are shown 'blacked out', and this indicates an occultation which is caused by the Moon being in the same degree of longitude and declination as a planet, and the Moon will, for a short time, 'eclipse or hide' the planet.

There are many useful tables in *Raphael's Ephemeris,* many of which are self-explanatory. A proper use of the ephemeris enables the astrologer to study the various astronomical phenomena and endeavour to relate it to everyday affairs.

7.
THE SOLAR SYSTEM: THE PLANETS

The Sun
The Sun is at the centre of the Solar System and is the source of heat and light for the Earth. In ancient times, it was thought that the Sun was either a ball of fire or a red-hot stone, perhaps just two feet across. The true size and distance of the Sun were unknown until a few centuries ago, and although it is the most important body in the Solar System, and life as we know it could not exist without it, nevertheless, it is merely one star among thousands of millions and is nothing out of the ordinary.

The Sun is an enormous sphere of extremely hot incandescent gas, with a diameter of 864,000 miles, and at an average distance from Earth of 93 million miles. Such is its diameter that 109 Earths, stretched out like beads on a string, would be needed to cross it from side to side. Its enormous volume could contain over a million Earth-sized globes.

The Sun consists principally of hydrogen and helium, but about 1 per cent of it is made of heavier elements, such as sodium, magnesium, iron and calcium, and there are smaller quantities of about sixty other substances, all in gaseous form. These substances are identified by the dark 'Fraunhofer lines' which cross the bright rainbow spectrum of the Sun. Although the Sun is composed of gas, its average density is 1.41 times greater than that of water.

Because of the Sun's enormous bulk and mass (330,000 times greater than the Earth's mass), the pressure at the centre is extremely high, as is the density (twelve times that of lead), and the temperature

Planet	Mercury	Venus	Earth	Mars	Jupiter	Saturn	Uranus	Neptune	Pluto
Distance (mean) from Sun (millions of miles)	36	67.2	93	141.6	484.3	886.1	1783	2793	3660
Period of revolution about Sun (sidereal)	87.9 days	224.7 days	365.25 days	686.98 days	11.86 years	29.46 years	84.01 years	164.79 years	247.70 years
Diameter (miles)	3000	7700	7927	4219	88700	75100	29300	31200	3700
Period of rotation about axis (sidereal)	58.5 days	243 days	23 Hrs 56 Min	24 Hrs 37 Min	9 Hrs 51 Min	10 Hrs 14 Min	10 Hrs 48 Min	14 Hrs	6 days 9 Hrs
Inclination of orbit to Ecliptic	7° 0'	3° 24'	0° 0'	1° 51'	1° 18'	2° 29'	0° 46'	1° 46'	17° 10'
Eccentricity of orbit	0.206	0.007	0.017	0.093	0.048	0.056	0.047	0.009	0.246
Mass (Earth = 1)	0.05	0.81	1.00	0.11	318	95	15	17	?
Density (Water = 1)	5.4	4.99	5.52	4.12	1.3	0.7	1.65	2.0	?

Figure 13. The Solar System: Planetary Data

THE SOLAR SYSTEM: THE PLANETS

there is no less than fifteen million degrees Centigrade. Under these conditions, the atoms are moving about so rapidly and colliding with one another so violently, that they have been smashed into their component particles; sub-atomic protons, alpha particles and electrons. In the Sun's core, four protons (which are nuclei of hydrogen atoms) are forced together into one alpha particle (a nucleus of a helium atom) and in this process, which is called nuclear fusion, a small amount of mass from these particles is converted into energy. The core of the Sun is therefore similar to a vast thermonuclear furnace in which billions and billions of such particles are continually being fused, with the result that four million tons of solar material are converted into energy every second. This energy radiates outward from the core, and it is then transported through the Sun's outer layer to the surface by three tiers of convection currents. At the surface of the Sun, called the photosphere, this energy bursts forth continuously at the rate of about 300,000 million watts through every acre of solar surface, not only in the form of light and heat, but also as radio waves, ultra-violet light, X-rays and gamma rays. This colossal energy pours away into space, and the Earth intercepts only one two-thousand-millionth of it.

The Sun maintains its stable equilibrium under the opposing action of two gigantic forces: the gravitational force pulling inward and the pressure of gas pushing outward; these exactly balance each other. In this way, the Sun's violent power is held in check. As a 'middle-aged' star, the Sun has been shining for 5,000 million years, and it has sufficient hydrogen 'fuel' to convert to helium and supply it with energy for another 8,000 million years.

Directly above the photosphere is a layer of gas called the chromosphere, and above this is the corona — the Sun's atmosphere — which may be seen at the time of a total solar eclipse. The corona consists of very thin but extremely hot gas of over one million degrees Centigrade which extends more than one million miles above the Sun's surface, gradually thinning out into space.

Since 1611, it has been known that dark blemishes, called sunspots, appear on the Sun's visible surface from time to time. A sunspot normally consists of a dark central region (umbra) surrounded by a lighter grey area (penumbra), although the smallest spots called pores (which are only a few hundred miles across) do not have penumbrae. The largest spots are far larger even than the Earth and are often irregular in shape. Sunspots occur singly or in groups. Because the Sun is composed of gas, it does not rotate as a solid body would, but differentially, that is, the equatorial regions rotate more rapidly than do those nearer the poles. As the rotation periods are 26 days and 37 days respectively, it is possible to observe sunspots drifting across the Sun's face from day to day at different speeds according to their solar latitude. The lifetime of sunspots lasts for between a few hours and many weeks. Sunspots are relatively cool regions in the photosphere, about 2,000°C cooler than their surroundings (the surface of the Sun has a temperature of 6,000°C), which explains their dark colour since, if they could be seen on their own, they would actually be brighter, displaying a prominent illumination. Sunspots are also localized areas of very powerful magnetic fields, while the Sun has a general magnetic field which is much weaker. The number of sunspots increases and decreases in an eleven-year cycle, with maxima in recent decades occurring in 1947, 1958, 1969, and 1981, but around minimum periods of sunspot activity, there are often no spots visible at all. The astrological significance of sunspots is discussed under 'Cosmic Cycles'.

Other manifestations of solar activity include prominences, plages and flares. Prominences are visible at a total eclipse of the Sun and are clouds of hot gas, some of which surge violently upwards, occasionally to more than 100,000 miles above the photosphere. Plages are masses of incandescent gas in the chromosphere and are heated by strong magnetic fields. A solar flare is a sudden, local explosion occurring in a particular region of the Sun's atmosphere, visible in hydrogen light as a brilliant flash lasting between a few seconds and one hour, and caused by local, powerful and unstable magnetic fields. Flares cause violent shock waves to travel through the Sun's surface at more than 1,000 miles an hour, and they also release intense bursts of energy in the form of X-rays, ultraviolet light, radio waves and energetic charged particles. When sunspot activity increases every 11 years, so do these other aspects of solar activity, and there are noticeable effects on the Earth and its environs. The X-rays streaming out from a solar flare interfere with short-wave radio communications on Earth, causing temporary disruptions and fade-outs. A constant stream of electrons from the Sun is responsible for the Aurorae. The Aurora Borealis ('northern lights') and Aurora Australis ('southern lights') are caused by energetic electrons from the Sun striking the Earth's upper atmosphere, causing it to glow or fluoresce in places. The aurorae are visible mainly in high latitudes, because the electrons are guided by the Earth's magnetic field down towards the magnetic poles. In appearance, aurorae look like enormous luminous curtains hanging in the sky, and sometimes, there are rays and arcs with many different colours.

As solar activity increases, so do flare disruptions and aurorae. A constant stream of electrically charged sub-atomic particles is radiated in all directions from the Sun. This is known as the solar wind, with one million tons of solar wind material leaving the Sun's vicinity every second. Flares add particles to the solar wind, resulting in sudden surges. The solar wind affects the magnetic field of the Earth and of other planets, bending the flux lines round to form a 'magnetosphere' for each planet.

The Moon

The Moon is our nearest neighbour in space and orbits the Earth at an average distance of 238,840 miles once every 27 days, 7 hours, 43 minutes, 11 seconds. Its diameter is 2,158 miles, just over one quarter of the Earth's diameter.

It shines by reflecting sunlight, and its constantly changing position with respect to the Sun during each month, enables us to see differing amounts of its illuminated side. When the Moon is between the Sun and the Earth, it is 'New' and not visible, but during the next few days, it becomes a crescent which gradually increases to a half-moon or First Quarter. After this, it increases still further through its three-quarter or gibbous phase until it reaches Full. The time that elapses between New Moon and Full Moon while the Moon is waxing (increasing) is normally 14½ days. After 'Full', the Moon turns more and more of its dark side towards the Earth, passing through all its phases again but in reverse order, until it is at New once more. Because the Earth is also travelling around the Sun, the Moon has to 'catch up' with the Sun as it moves eastward against the stars by about 30° each month. For this reason, there is a difference between the time taken for the Moon to pass the same star twice in its orbit (called its sidereal period — 27⅓ days) and its synodic period of 29½ days, which is the time that elapses between one Full Moon and the next one.

The Moon rises later each night because it is moving eastwards, against the background of the stars, at an average rate of 13° 12' per day. The difference between the rising time of the Moon on one night and that on the following night is called the *retardation*,

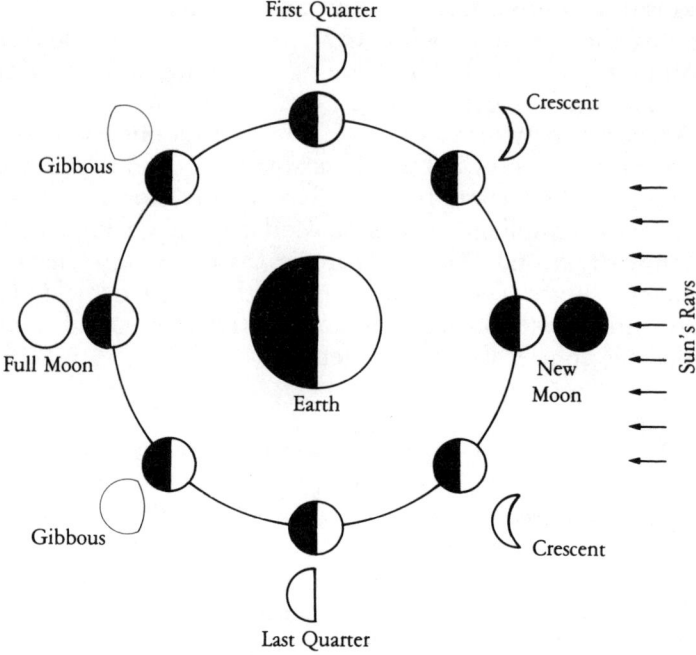

Figure 14. The Phases of the Moon

and this depends upon the angle which the Moon's orbit makes with the eastern horizon. In early autumn, the Moon's orbit around Full cuts the eastern horizon at a sharp angle, and therefore the retardation is very low, with the Moon rising only 15 minutes or so later each night (Harvest and Hunter's Moons). Six months later, the Moon's orbit around Full makes a steep angle with the eastern horizon and consequently, the retardation at this time is far longer, more than one hour. On average, the retardation is about fifty minutes.

Visibility of the Moon above the horizon is governed by its phases. A Full Moon, for instance, always rises at sunset, sets at sunrise and can be visible all night. But a First Quarter Moon sets around midnight, while at about the same time the Last Quarter rises, the exact times of rising or setting depending on the Moon's declination. As the Moon rises later each day as the month progresses, a waxing (increasing) Moon is normally visible in the afternoon, evening or early part of the night, while a waning (decreasing) Moon is likely

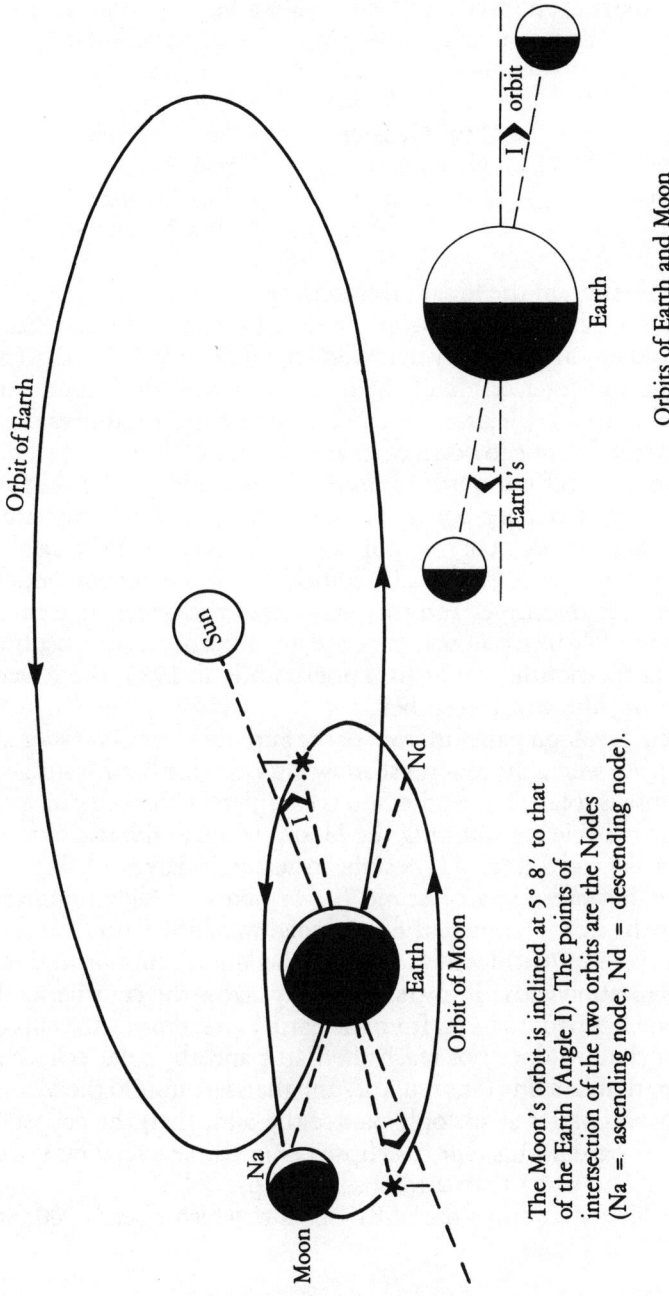

Figure 15. Orbits of the Moon and Earth.

to be seen later in the night or in the early morning. The *altitude* (height above the horizon) at which the Moon appears in any latitude depends on its phase and on the time of year, as follows:

Season	Moon High up	Moon Low down
Spring	First Quarter	Last Quarter
Summer	New Moon	Full Moon
Autumn	Last Quarter	First Quarter
Winter	Full Moon	New Moon

The inclination of the lunar orbit to the plane of the Ecliptic is 5° 8', and for this reason, eclipses of the Sun or Moon, when the Sun, Earth and Moon are exactly in line, do not occur every month. The two points of intersection of the lunar orbit with the Ecliptic are called the *Nodes,* the ascending node where the orbit moves from south of the Ecliptic to north of it, and the descending node where the orbit moves from north to south. These nodes are 180° apart and are not stationary but move slowly in a retrograde direction completing one circuit of the Ecliptic every 18½ years. When a new or full moon coincides or nearly coincides with one of the nodes, then there is an eclipse, and the positions of the nodes determine the months in which eclipses take place, with sets of eclipses occuring always at six-monthly intervals. For example, in 1983, there were eclipses in June and December.

When the Moon passes in front of the Sun, there is a *Solar eclipse.* At the place where the Moon's shadow intersects the Earth's surface, the eclipse is total, that is, the Sun is completely blocked out with its corona visible surrounding the Moon, while at the same time, both the sky and countryside become increasingly darkened. Totality does not, however, last a long time, (never more than eight minutes), because the cross-section of the lunar shadow on the Earth's surface cannot exceed 170 miles in width, and the Moon's motion and the Earth's rotation cause it to travel rapidly across the continents. If the Moon happens to be far from the Earth at the time of an eclipse, then its shadow does not reach the Earth and the solar eclipse is *annular,* that is, a ring (annulus) of sunlight is left around the Moon. If the Moon passes across only part of the Sun, then the eclipse is said to be partial, this type of eclipse being visible over a far wider region of the Earth than a total solar eclipse.

If the Moon passes into the Earth's shadow, which is nearly 900,000

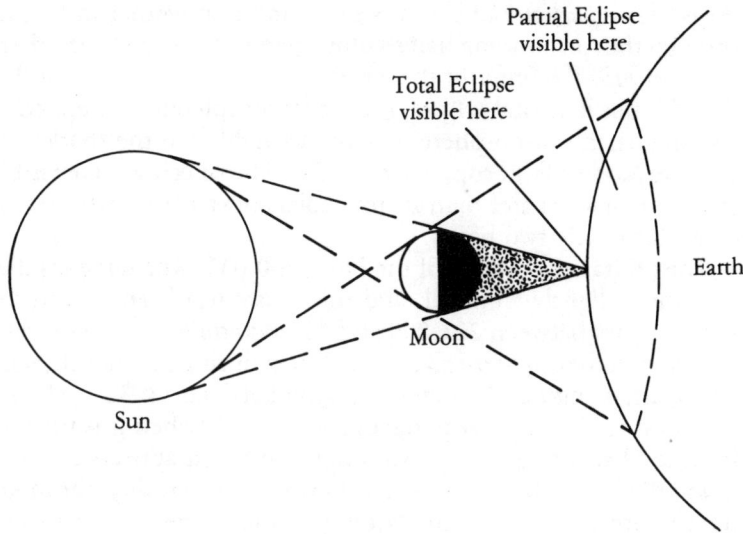

Figure 16. Solar Eclipse

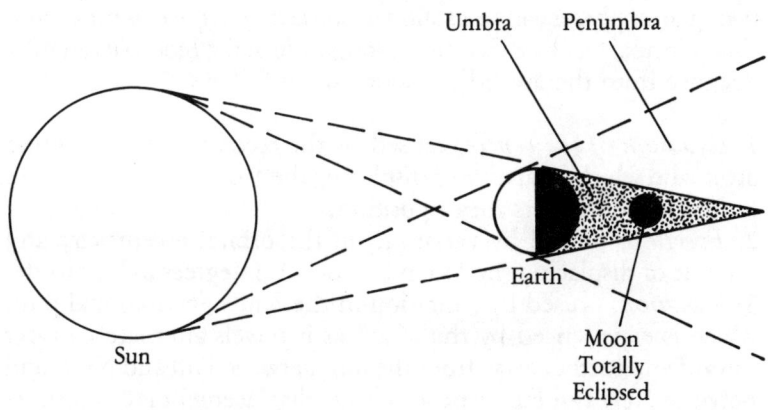

Figure 17. Lunar Eclipse

miles long, there is a *Lunar eclipse*. If it is totally immersed in the full shadow (umbra), the eclipse is total. If it is partly immersed, the eclipse is *partial*, but if it misses the umbra altogether and passes through the surrounding half shadow (penumbra) only, then there is a *penumbral eclipse*. In the latter case, the Moon is only dulled slightly, but in a total eclipse, it is either completely obliterated or else the Earth's atmosphere may refract light into the shadow to give the Moon a faint coppery glow. Total lunar eclipses are visible over a much wider area than are total solar ones and can last, in some cases, for nearly two hours.

The orbital eccentricity of the Moon is 0.055, which means that its orbit is slightly elliptical, and this causes its distance from the Earth to vary between 221,000 and 253,000 miles. It also causes a variation in the apparent size of the Moon during the month, with its apparent angular diameter changing between 33'31" (when it is nearest to the Earth at perigee) and 29'22" (when it is furthest from the Earth at apogee). Although the Moon appears to travel round the Earth, this is only an illusion because, in reality, the Moon travels with the Earth as the latter goes round the Sun. It weaves its way in and out of the Earth's orbit, alternately lagging behind and racing ahead of the Earth during every month. The overall effect then is that the Moon is seen to trace out an apparent orbit around us, in which its speed against the stars and its distance from the Earth do not change a great deal. These changes are however great enough to be measurable so, for example, the time interval between any two quarter phases can be as short as six days or as great as nine days. The principal factors affecting the longitude of the Moon (its angular distance from the ascending node) are as follows:

1. *Equation of the centre*, caused by the eccentricity of the lunar orbit, and which is capable of displacing the Moon up to 6.3 degrees in longitude from its mean position.
2. *Evection*, caused by variations in the orbital eccentricity and capable of displacing the Moon by up to 1.3 degrees in longitude.
3. *Variation*, caused by alteration in the Sun's gravitational pull, which is experienced by the Moon as it travels alternately nearer toward and further away from the Sun between Full and New, and between New and Full. The longitude displacement is 0.6 degrees maximum.
4. *Annual Equation*, caused by alterations experienced by both Earth

THE SOLAR SYSTEM: THE PLANETS

and Moon in the Sun's gravitational pull, because their distance from the sun varies by 3 million miles throughout the year. The longitude displacement in this case is 0.2 degrees at maximum.

If the above corrections are not applied, then the difference between the Moon's actual position and its mean position (assuming uniform speed around a circular orbit) can be as great as 8½°.

Tidal forces, operating over several thousands of millions of years, have slowed the Moon's axial rotation, until it is at present equal to its Sidereal period of 27 days. This type of rotation, where the rotation period of a planet or satellite is the same length as its revolution period around the primary body, is known as 'captured' or 'synchronous rotation'. The result is that the Moon appears to keep the same face turned toward the Earth. However, the slight irregularities in the Moon's motion result in variations to this rule, known as *Libration:*

1. *Libration in longitude* is caused by the Moon's rotation and revolution becoming out of step with one another, due to the variable speed of the Moon along its eccentric orbit. The effect of this is, that we can see a short distance — a few degrees — alternately around the Moon's eastern and western edges.
2. *Libration in latitude* is the result of the slight inclination of the Moon's axis (1½°) to the perpendicular of the orbital plane, with the effect that we can see a corresponding distance alternately round each of the Moon's polar regions.
3. *Diurnal Libration.* The Earth's radius is 1 ÷ 60 of the average distance between the Earth and the Moon, and when the Moon is close to rising or setting, we are able to see about 1° around the Moon's upper edge.

The overall effect of these various librations is that, from Earth, 59 per cent of the Moon's surface is visible at one time or another, with the remaining 41 per cent being permanently invisible.

Occultations

The Moon's Sidereal period of orbital revolution around the Earth is about 27 days, so that its average motion per hour is approximately half a degree. As it moves eastward with reference to the stars, it will in some instances occult or cover a star or planet depending upon its position and that of the star or planet. Because a star appears as only a point of light, when the Moon's edge crosses it, the star's disappearance or reappearance is instantaneous, but the Moon's edge can take up to several minutes to cross a planet. Occultations of bright stars or planets are quite rare.

The Appearance and Surface of the Moon

Even without a telescope, it is possible to see a few dark patches on the Moon's face, while the smallest telescope or a pair of binoculars will show much more detail including the mountain ranges and the craters. The dark regions, covering about one-third of the Moon's visible side, are bluish-grey in colour and are vast plains of solidified lava. The first observers of the Moon imagined these to be seas (marias) and gave them strange names such as: Bay of Steam, Sea of Crises, Ocean of Storms, Sea of Serenity, Sea of Tranquillity.

Water cannot exist on the Moon's surface, because there is no atmosphere and, of course, no life. The lack of an atmosphere means that the surface is exposed to various dangerous radiations from space such as cosmic rays, and also the rocks are subject to extremes of temperature from approximately $+100°C$ to $-200°C$ during each month. This is also a result of the very long days and nights, each point on the lunar surface away from the poles having 15 days of daylight followed by 15 days of night. The absence of air also means that the lunar shadows are almost jet black.

There are relatively few craters on the dark plains, and they are concentrated principally on the rugged uplands of the Moon, which cover about two-thirds of the visible surface and which are white or pale yellow in colour. The Moon's surface is sometimes called the 'regolith' and consists of rocks covered by a thin layer of dust or powder. The craters are generally named after famous scientists and astronomers of the past. These craters range in size from 180 miles in diameter to less than one mile and, on some parts of the Moon, they are packed so closely together that they frequently break up one another's walls, particularly in the south where the distribution density is highest. The total number of craters on the surface runs into thousands. In general, the floor of a crater tends to be sunk below the level of the surrounding terrain, and while craters may be over 10,000 feet deep, they are more like saucers than bowls in cross-section, and the walls are not vertical but gently sloping, often in terrace form. In fact, an observer standing inside one of the larger craters would probably not be able to see the wall at all, since they would be below the horizon which curves more steeply than the Earth's horizon on account of the Moon's smaller size. Such craters are, therefore, better described as walled plains.

Some craters (Plato, Grimaldi, Ptolemy, Alphonsus among others) have flat, dark floors of the same colour as the 'seas', while some others (Copernicus, Tycho, Kepler, Aristarchus, Proclus) are the centres of bright 'rays' many hundreds of miles in length which dominate the Moon near Full, and some craters have central mountain peaks. Small craters tend to have regular circular forms, but the larger ones are often quite irregular in appearance, with smaller craters either inside them or lying across their walls. These walls are frequently broken, fractured or uneven in places.

The mountain ranges are named after those on the Earth (Apennines, Alps, Carpathians, Caucasus, Altai for instance), and are often hundreds of miles in length with peaks rising to as much as 30,000 feet above the surrounding terrain. These mountains are generally not nearly so steep nor so rugged as those on the Earth.

The dark plains are regions of solidified lava (basalt), which occupy basins depressed below the level of their surroundings and are of various shapes and sizes, many of which are roughly circular in form and several hundred miles in width. They are mainly quite smooth but there are, in places, ridges, geological faults and rilles (clefts).

The Interior and Origin of the Moon

The interior of the Moon is similar to that of the Earth, since both have a crust which surrounds a mantle of heavier rocks and a dense core at the centre, and both worlds have hot interiors. At one time, some astronomers considered that the Moon broke away from the Earth when both were in the process of formation many millions of years ago, but this idea is no longer held to be mathematically viable. Instead, it is now thought that the Moon was either an independent planet which was captured by the Earth, or that it was formed at the same time and in the same part of space as the Earth. About 4,500 million years ago, the lunar crust cooled to form the upland regions, and the plains a few hundred million years later, when lava flooded up from the interior, later cooling and solidifying. The craters have originated from two main causes, some of them having been formed by meteors (lumps of rocks) crashing onto the lunar surface, while others are extinct volcanoes or calderas.

Mercury

Mercury is the nearest planet to the Sun with a mean distance from it of 36 million miles, although the high eccentricity (0.21) of the planet's orbit causes this distance to vary between 29 and 43 million miles. Consequently, Mercury's maximum distance from the Sun (elongation) is never more than 27° and can be as small as 18°, so the planet is difficult to observe and never appears in a dark sky in Britain. The best time to look for it is, either on spring evenings or autumn mornings, when the Ecliptic makes a steep angle with the horizon. On spring evenings, it can be seen just after sunset low down in the west or south-west, when it is close to western elongation; while on autumn mornings, it is visible just before sunrise low down in the east or south-east, when close to eastern elongation. It is unlikely to be seen at more than ten degrees or so above the horizon, and care must be taken to avoid looking at the Sun.

It is the Solar System's smallest planet, with a diameter of 3,000 miles, an orbital revolution period of 88 days (its year) and a rotation period of 59 days (its day). There is no appreciable atmosphere and certainly no life, since the planet's proximity to the Sun produces temperatures in excess of 400°C during the long days. Telescopes show only a few markings on the planet's surface, but spacecraft flying past have shown a world very similar to the Moon, with craters and smooth plains of which the largest, called Caloris Basin, is 800 miles across.

Mercury is the second hottest planet and the smallest in size and mass; it has the shortest Sidereal period and has been known from remote antiquity.

Venus

Unlike Mercury, Venus may be seen in a dark sky in Britain, because its maximum angular distance or elongation from the Sun is 48°. Also, it is visible for weeks or months at a time, whereas Mercury's visibility is confined to a few days either side of its elongation. Venus is visible in the west or south-west after sunset (evening star) or in the east or south-east before sunrise (morning star), often at a considerable altitude above the horizon.

Venus and Mercury are known as inferior planets, because their orbits lie inside that of the Earth, and as they orbit the Sun, they pass successively through inferior conjunction, western (morning) elongation, superior conjunction, eastern (evening) elongation,

THE SOLAR SYSTEM: THE PLANETS

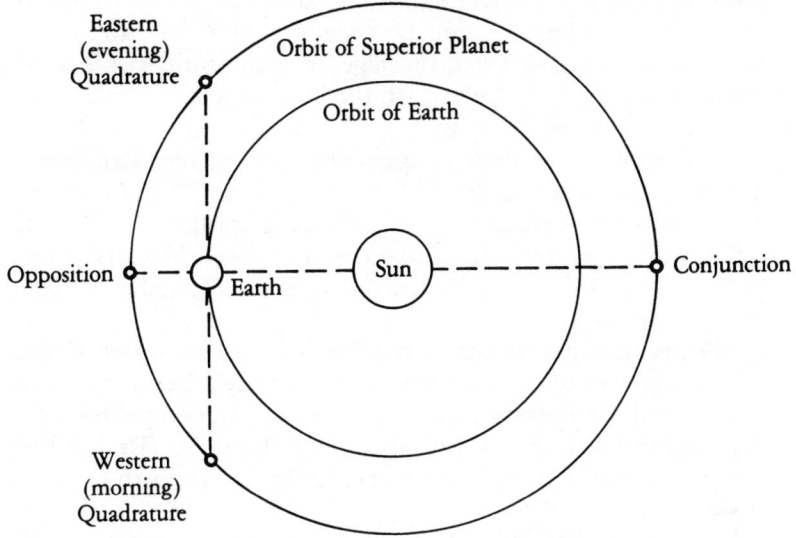

Figure 18. Planetary Configurations: Superior Planets

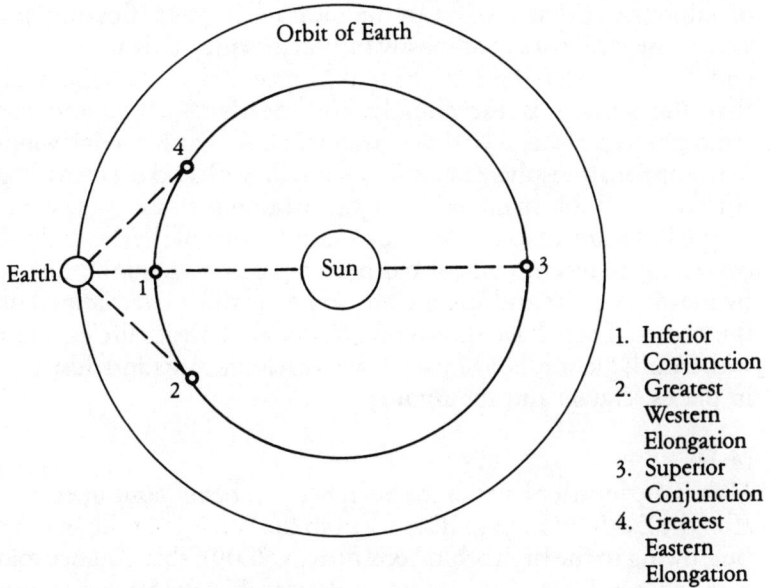

Figure 19. Planetary Configurations: Inferior Planets

finally returning to inferior conjunction, as Figure 19 shows. Mercury passes through inferior conjunction once every 116 days, and Venus does so once every 584 days on average, these intervals of time being known as the 'synodic period' of the two planets.

In a small telescope, Venus shows phases like those of the Moon, and so does Mercury although, appearing much smaller than Venus, its phases are much more difficult to observe. Because of the inclination of these planets' orbits to the Ecliptic, transits of Mercury and Venus across the Sun's disc occur only rarely (Mercury: 1960, 1970, 1973, 1986, 1993; Venus: 1761, 1769, 1874, 1882, 2004, 2012).

The distance of Venus from the Sun is 67 million miles, and its orbit is closer to being circular than that of any other planet. The orbital revolution period is 225 days, the axial rotation period is 243 days and the diameter of this planet is 7,700 miles. The farthest that Venus can be from the Sun as seen from the Earth is 48° at elongation.

Venus is the brightest of the planets and often appears really brilliant, because it is covered in thick white clouds which are an excellent reflector of sunlight. These clouds are composed of a mixture of sulphuric acid and water in the form of droplets, floating in a very dense atmosphere of mostly carbon dioxide. This atmosphere and the clouds trap the Sun's heat like a greenhouse, with the result that the surface is exceedingly hot (nearly 500°C), and the atmospheric pressure is 90 times greater than the Earth's. High winds in the upper atmosphere cause the clouds to swirl, and these swirling patterns are visible in ultraviolet light. Astronomers using telescopes on the Earth are unable to see the surface because of the dense cloud cover, but in recent years, it has been possible to map the surface by means of radar and space-craft, some of which have landed on the planet. These have shown that Venus is a hostile, lifeless place with a dull, gloomy landscape strewn with loose rocks and dust and, in places, craters and mountains.

Mars
Mars is the fourth planet in the Solar System, being positioned next after the Earth. Its average distance from the Sun is 142 million miles but, owing to the high orbital eccentricity (0.09), this distance may vary between 129 and 154 million miles. It orbits the Sun once every 687 days, and comes to opposition once every two years two months

on average, but the high orbital eccentricity causes its distance from the Earth to vary from one opposition to the next. When Mars is at perihelion and in opposition to the Sun at the same time, it is said to be 'at perihelic opposition', and its distance from the Earth is then only 35 million miles, while its apparent angular diameter is 25 seconds. This happens once every 15 or 17 years (1909, 1924, 1939, 1956, 1971 and 1988) and the planet is then, for a few weeks, very favourably placed for observation. If Mars is near aphelion at its opposition, however, it is 60 million miles from us and has an angular diameter of only 14 seconds. After each opposition, the planet recedes rapidly from the Earth to reach superior conjunction with the Sun about one year later, when its distance from us has increased to 235 million miles, while its angular diameter has shrunk to less than 4 seconds.

Being a superior planet (outside the Earth's orbit), Mars may be seen at any time of the night and at its brightest, it outshines every other planet except Venus. Mars is rather a small world, with a diameter of 4,200 miles, and an axial rotation period of 24 hours 37 minutes, and its colour is orange-red, with some darker markings visible which have been carefully mapped. These darker regions were once considered to be areas of vegetation, but in the 1960s this idea was disproved, when the surface conditions were found to be hostile to life, particularly with its thin carbon dioxide atmosphere (surface pressure is less than one-hundredth that of the Earth). It is also a distinctly cold, though not frozen, world with the temperature not normally exceeding $+20°C$ (even on the equator at midday), while during the nights, it falls rapidly to around $-70°C$. At the poles, there are white caps composed of a mixture of water, ice and solid carbon dioxide ('dry ice'), and these polar caps wax and wane with the Martian seasons (the planet's axial tilt is $25°$). The dark regions are now known to be craters, mountains, extinct volcanoes and sinuous channels. The channels are up to 1,000 miles in length and 100 miles wide, and bear a striking resemblance to dried-up river beds, which they probably are, since there may well have been a time when the planet's climate and atmosphere were fundamentally different to what they are today, and water was able to flow.

Much of the surface of Mars is covered with loose rocks and dust, and large areas are subject to severe dust storms which are whipped up by high winds, particularly when the planet is near perihelion. After the storms, the appearance of the darker regions is often changed considerably, and dust suspended in the Martian atmosphere gives a pink sky. Clouds of ice crystals and solid carbon dioxide particles are also seen from time to time.

Mars has two satellites or moons named Deimos and Phobos (Terror and Fear). Deimos orbits Mars once in 30 hours and Phobos in just 7½ hours. Each moon is less than 15 miles across. Phobos presents an interesting phenomenon in that, to an observer on Mars, it would rise in the west and set in the east three times a day.

Prior to the Space Age, much of the information concerning Mars was obtained using telescopes, but the various space probes, either flying past and taking photographs (e.g. the Mariners) or landing on the planet's surface (the two Vikings in 1976), have greatly contributed to our knowledge of the 'mysterious red planet'.

Mercury, Venus, the Earth and Mars are all predominantly solid and rocky, with relatively small volumes and high densities and, as such, are called the 'terrestrial planets'.

The next four planets, Jupiter, Saturn, Uranus and Neptune, on the other hand, have large volumes and low densities, and because of their compositions are known as the 'gas giants'.

Jupiter

Jupiter is the Solar System's largest world with a diameter through its equator of 89,000 miles, and it orbits the Sun once every 11.86 years at a mean distance of 484 million miles.

In a telescope, alternating light and dark bands of differing thicknesses traverse Jupiter's disc, parallel to the planet's equator, and there are dark caps in the polar regions. Smaller details such as spots, wisps and arches may also be seen, the most notable of which is the 'Giant Red Spot', 20,000 miles in length, which has been seen for over 300 years. The colours of these features range from white or yellow to grey and brown with reddish and bluish tinges. All of these features are the upper regions of a cloud blanket which completely covers the planet. These clouds are composed of frozen ammonia crystals in the upper layers, with crystals of ammonia hydrosulphide, water ice and water droplets probably making up the lower layers. The clouds float in a deep atmosphere of hydrogen and helium, hundreds of miles deep, below which the tremendous pressures have probably liquified the hydrogen to form vast, extremely cold oceans. Lower down still, pressures are even more intense, with the hydrogen probably being in metallic form, possibly making up the bulk of the planet and surrounding a core of iron and rock. Temperatures in the atmosphere are very low indeed, between $-120°C$ and $-170°C$, but the extreme pressures in the interior generate heat, which drives the wind and storms in the planet's atmosphere. These storms are often violent and may persist for many weeks with frequent lightning discharges.

Jupiter spins very rapidly on its axis once every 9 hours 55 minutes, and near the equator, the rate of spin is slightly faster. This rapid rotation has caused a significant flattening at the poles and bulging at the equator. It has a very powerful magnetic field, 20,000 times stronger than the Earth's, and in 1955, it was found that Jupiter sends out radio waves. This giant planet has about fifteen moons, four of which are visible in any small telescope. These moons (Ganymede, Callisto, Io, and Europa), termed the Galilean Moons, were discovered by Galileo in 1610 with the newly invented telescope. These four moons are icy worlds as large as, or larger than, our Moon. Io has active volcanoes on its surface which are caused by a combination of electro-magnetic and tidal forces pulling on the satellite. Jupiter was once thought to act in the same way as a star, giving off light and heat, although rather feebly. It is now known that this is not possible, for a true star shines and is powered by nuclear reaction in its core. The mass of Jupiter, high though it is, is not great enough to cause the enormous pressures and temperatures which are required for the hydrogen-into-helium nuclear reaction to proceed.

Saturn

Saturn orbits the Sun at a mean distance of 886 million miles, once every 29.46 years, and it is rather similar to Jupiter in general appearance, structure and composition. The equatorial diameter is 75,000 miles making it the second largest planet and, like Jupiter, it is considerably flattened at the poles because of the rapid rotation (once every 10 hours 14 minutes). This planet is completely covered with clouds arranged in bands parallel to the equator and alternately light and dark with dark polar caps. Much less detail is visible than on Jupiter, although bright spots and wisps appear from time to time.

The atmosphere is a deep one of hydrogen and helium, and the banded clouds floating in it probably consist of frozen ammonia crystals, while deeper down, the hydrogen probably becomes metallic under the great pressures, and lower down still, there is likely to be ice surrounding a rocky core. Each of these layers is several thousand miles thick. Saturn, being further from the Sun, is an even colder world than Jupiter, with temperatures in its atmosphere of around $-180°C$, although the very high pressures in its interior do generate some heat, and the unusually low density of the planet means that it could actually float on water if there existed an ocean large enough to contain it!

The most remarkable feature about Saturn is its system of rings, of which there are three main ones, all concentric with the planet and in the plane of its equator. The outermost of these is a dull white (10,000 miles in width), then a gap of 3,000 miles (called Cassini's Division) separates it from the central ring which is the brightest and widest (16,000 miles), and finally, there is a dull grey, semi-transparent ring of 10,000 miles width. These rings, of a white or yellowish-white colour, are composed of millions of lumps of ice and rock, whirling round the planet at speeds of tens of thousands of miles per hour in a great swarm, but although this ring-system is so wide (170,000 miles), it is extremely thin (10 miles). Because Saturn and its ring-system are inclined at $26½°$ to the orbital plane's perpendicular, the rings appear at different angles as the planet travels around the Sun. At two points on its orbit — at the planet's equinoxes which occur every 14 or 15 years — the rings appear edge-on to the Earth, and their thinness causes them to disappear for a while. A few other, much fainter, rings exist outside the main system, but these are not normally visible from the Earth.

When Galileo first observed Saturn in 1610, he was unable to see the rings properly, because the optics of his telescope were rather poor. The rings were first seen as such by the Dutch astronomer Huygens in 1655, who described them as 'a flat ring, which nowhere touches the body of the planet and is inclined to the Ecliptic'.

Saturn is now known to have twelve moons in orbit outside the ring system, of which the largest (Titan) is as big as Mercury and is covered in an orange fog.

Our knowledge of Saturn, as with Jupiter, has greatly increased during the last few years due to the observations and measurements taken by the Pioneer and Voyager spacecraft. In particular, a great deal has been learnt about Jupiter's satellites and Saturn's rings.

Uranus
Prior to 1781, Saturn was the outermost planet known to exist. On

13 March of that year, Uranus was accidentally discovered by William Herschel who was carrying out a survey of the sky (making star-counts in selected areas of the sky). Further observations of this bright disc enabled its orbit to be calculated, and it was found to be a new planet, moving far beyond the orbit of Saturn. Herschel originally intended to name the new planet Georgium Sidus (George's star) after the reigning monarch George III. Eventually, it was named Uranus although, in older ephemerides, the name of Herschel was listed for this planet.

Because of the remoteness of Uranus (1,784 million miles from the Sun), it is almost invisible without a telescope, hence until the invention of the telescope, it remained undiscovered. Its orbital motion is very slow, taking 84 years to complete one revolution of the Sun. Its diameter has been measured as 29,000 miles (or just under four times that of the Earth), and in a large telescope, it appears as a small greenish-white disc crossed by a few vague, darker bands.

Uranus is a very cold world with temperatures around −200°C, and its interior probably consists of a rocky core surrounded by ice. This ice, in turn, is surrounded by a deep atmosphere of hydrogen and methane, with helium and ammonia probably also present. The axial rotation period at the planet's equator is 10 hours, 48 minutes. An unusual feature of Uranus is its exceptionally high axial inclination — 98° to the perpendicular to the plane of its orbit — which means that, for long periods of its 'year', each pole points, in turn, towards the Sun. In 1977, a system of rings (like those of Saturn but much fainter) were found to be surrounding the planet. In addition, there are five satellites all less than 1,000 miles in diameter, with revolution periods of between 1½ and 13½ days.

Neptune
The discovery of Neptune in 1846, based on mathematical calculations by John Adams and Urbain Leverrier, provoked some argument as to who was entitled to the credit for its discovery. After Uranus had been observed for a few decades, it became clear that it was not moving in its predicted path, but was acting as if another, yet undiscovered, planet was affecting it gravitationally (perturbation). The calculations of Adams and Leverrier were sent to the Berlin Observatory in September 1846, where on the 23rd of that month, astronomers d'Arrest and Galle found the new planet, less than one degree away from its predicted position.

Neptune's orbital revolution period is 165 years and its distance from the Sun is 2,793 million miles. At the time of its discovery, Neptune was in the constellation of Capricornus, and it will return to this point again in the year 2011. The diameter of Neptune based on recent measurements (1969) is 31,000 miles, which is slightly larger than Uranus. The exact constitution of Neptune is unknown, but it probably has a solid core, and is known to have an atmosphere of hydrogen, helium and methane. Temperatures in the atmosphere are around − 220°C. The structure and composition of Neptune are uncertain but it is thought that this planet is similar to Uranus.

Neptune can only be seen through a telescope, since it is very faint, and even through large telescopes, it appears as only a very small bluish-white disc which is almost featureless.

Neptune and Uranus, together with Jupiter and Saturn, make up the four 'gas giants' — large planets of relatively low density with an appreciable proportion of their masses contained in their atmospheres.

Neptune has two satellites, Triton and Nereid. Triton is one of the largest moons in the Solar System and was discovered by Lassell in 1846, a few weeks after the discovery of Neptune. Nereid is much smaller (200 miles) and was found by Kuiper in 1949; it orbits Neptune once in 362 days, while Triton goes round once in 6 days.

The discovery of Neptune by mathematical analysis was a brilliant confirmation of Newton's laws concerning the mass and motion of bodies.

Pluto

The existence of Pluto was established mathematically by Percival Lowell, and it was discovered observationally by Clyde Tombaugh in 1930. As with Uranus, Neptune was also found to be wandering from its predicted orbit, and this led astronomers to suggest that there must be a ninth planet beyond it. The astronomer Lowell (who also observed 'canals' on Mars), carried out computations in order to determine the mass and position of an unknown planet which was thought to be responsible for the irregularities in the orbits of Uranus and Neptune. An extensive photographic programme by Tombaugh of Lowell's Observatory in Flagstaff, Arizona, led to the discovery of Pluto in January 1930.

Pluto is a highly eccentric planet which moves in an orbit greatly inclined to the Ecliptic (about 17°), with a mean distance from the

VOL. LXXIX....No. 26,347.

NINTH PLANET DISCOVERED ON EDGE OF SOLAR SYSTEM; FIRST FOUND IN 84 YEARS

LIES FAR BEYOND NEPTUNE

Sighted Jan. 21 After 25 Years' Search Begun by Late Percival Lowell.

SEEN AT FLAGSTAFF, ARIZ.

Observatory Staff There Spots It by Special Photo-Telescope —Makes Thorough Check.

ASTRONOMERS HAIL FINDING

The Sphere, Possibly Larger Than Jupiter and 4,000,000,000 Miles Away, Meets Predictions.

By The Associated Press.
FLAGSTAFF, Ariz., March 13.—In the little cluster of orbs which scampers across the sidereal abyss under the name of the solar system there are, be it known, nine instead of a mere eight, worlds.

New Planet Compared With Earth and Neptune

Size:
Earth—8,000 miles in diameter.
Neptune—32,000.
New Planet—8,000 or more.

Distance from Sun:
Earth—One astronomical unit.
Neptune—Thirty astronomical units.
New Planet—About fifty units.

Speed of Revolution:
Earth—19 miles a second.
Neptune—3½ miles a second.
New Planet—From 1 to 2 miles a second.

Time of Revolution:
Earth—One year.
Neptune—146 Earth-years (entire revolution not yet observed).
New Planet—Probably 300 to 600 years.

Note—These figures on the new planet are tentative, based upon computations of astronomers here on the Flagstaff announcement.

Figure 20: The *New York Times* front-page Pluto story on March 14, 1930.

© 1930 by The New York Times Company. Reprinted by permission.

Sun of 3,666 million miles and an orbital revolution period of 248 years. Owing to its highly eccentric orbit (greater than that of any other planet), Pluto at perihelion is within the orbit of Neptune, and perihelion will occur in 1989. However, owing to its unusually high inclination to the plane of the Ecliptic, there is little likelihood of a collision with Neptune.

This planet is visible only in fairly large telescopes, and no markings can be seen on its surface. It has a diameter of about 3,700 miles and rotates once every six days. Unlike the four previous planets, Pluto is solid throughout. From its surface, the Sun would appear as only a very brilliant star and would have no more illumination than the Full Moon on Earth. The surface of Pluto is extremely cold, around −230°C (or only about 40-50 degrees above absolute zero). It is highly improbable that Pluto has an atmosphere, because its low surface gravity is unable to hold onto any gaseous hydrogen or helium, and the extremely low temperatures mean that compounds such as water, carbon dioxide, ammonia and even methane are all in the frozen state upon its surface.

Various estimates have been made concerning its size, and these vary from between a diameter of 2,000 to one of 6,000 miles, with a mass of about 1/10th that of the Earth. This mass is nowhere great enough to produce the perturbations upon Neptune which led to the discovery of Pluto. It has been suggested that the surface is covered with ice which causes the planet to shine like a dark mirror, so that all which is seen of Pluto is the reflection of the Sun on the ice, with the rest of the planet invisible. It is interesting to note that in mythology, Pluto, who was lord of the underworld possessed a helmet which rendered him invisible.

In 1978, it was found that Pluto possesses a small moon provisionally named Charon. This satellite revolves in a period of just over 6 days. The brightness of most planets changes, generally because their distances from Earth constantly alter. Pluto, in contrast, has an intrinsic fluctuation, first noted in 1955 by R. H. Hardie, of approximately twenty per cent over a period of 6.39 days. This light variation, which has been increasing in the quarter century since first detected is attributed to a gradually changing aspect of the planet as it revolves around the Sun. Even though the satellite period (6.39 days) is identical to the light period, Charon is much too faint to account for the light variation. Therefore, we have satellite revolution and planet rotation of exactly the same period. Pluto and its moon appear to have complete synchronism, and it will be most interesting to see what further discoveries are revealed about this most enigmatic planet.

Asteroids (minor planets)

Between the orbits of Mars and Jupiter, there are over 40,000 minor planets or asteroids. The largest of them, Ceres, is only 430 miles in diameter and was found by Piazzi in 1801. Most of the other asteroids are much smaller, and of these, only Vesta and Pallas exceed 250 miles. Only Vesta is ever visible with the naked eye, being closer to the Sun than Ceres. Of the vast swarm of asteroids (most of which stay within the region of the Solar System between the orbits of Mars and Jupiter), Ceres, Vesta, Pallas and Eros have received some attention regarding any astrological significance. A considerable amount of research is needed before any firm conclusions can be drawn concerning their astrological relationship. The origin of minor planets is not known with certainty. It has been suggested that they are the debris left after the formation of the principal planets, or they may be the remnants of former planets which, for one reason or another, disintegrated. A minor planet looks exactly like a star, and can only be identified from its position and its movement from night to night.

8.
THE MECHANICS OF THE SOLAR SYSTEM

The Sun is the largest and most massive body in the Solar System, and it occupies a central position with the planets revolving around it. In increasing distance from the Sun, these planets are Mercury, Venus, Earth, Mars, Jupiter, Saturn, Uranus, Neptune and Pluto. The orbits of Mercury and Venus lie inside the Earth's, so these two planets are called *inferior* and never appear far from the Sun. The other planets, from Mars outward, have orbits which lie outside the Earth's, so they can be seen at any time of night. These are known as the *superior* planets.

When any superior planet is in the same part of the sky as the Sun and in line with it, that planet is said to be at superior conjunction. After a few weeks, it will have moved out of the glare of the Sun's rays, and will become visible in the early morning sky, rising shortly before dawn. During the following months, the planet will rise earlier and earlier every night until it reaches the point in the sky exactly opposite the Sun, when it is at opposition. At this point, the planet will be visible all night since it rises at sunset, culminates in the south at midnight and sets at sunrise. After the planet has passed opposition, it has already risen when the Sun sets, and sets earlier each night, until it becomes lost in the glare of the Sun's rays, shortly after which it will reach superior conjunction once more. When a planet is 90° from the Sun, it is said to be at quadrature (square), and at this point, it will cross the southern meridian at six hours at morning quadrature and at eighteen hours at evening quadrature. At opposition, a planet is at its nearest point to the Earth,

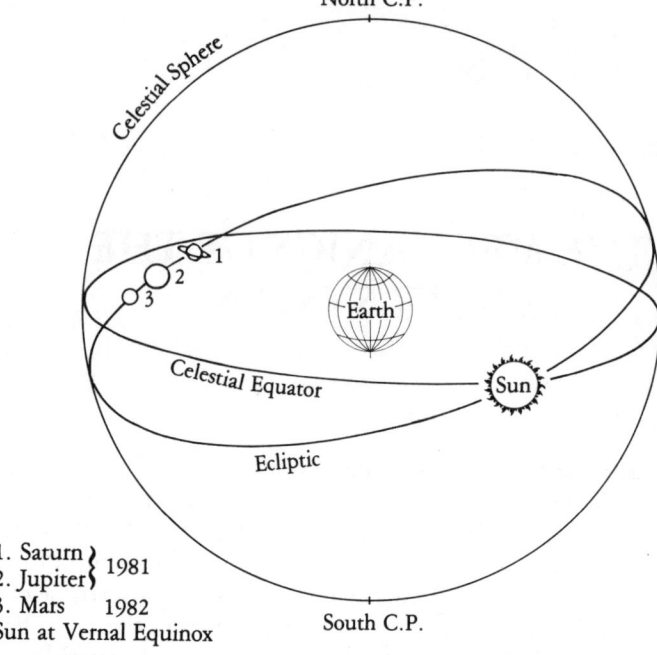

Figure 21. Shows the relative positions on the celestial sphere of the planets in 1981-82.

and consequently, appears at its largest and brightest. However, planets appear as only points of light, and a telescope is needed to show them as discs owing to their small apparent diameter. Five planets are visible without a telescope, having been known since ancient times, and each one is different in colour and brightness: Mercury is pale yellow; Venus is brilliant white; Mars is very bright orange-red; Jupiter is very bright white, and Saturn is dull yellow. The inferior planets orbit the Sun in less than one Earth-year, while the superior planets take much longer than one year to complete their revolutions. All planets revolve around the Sun in the same direction as each other. The Earth must, therefore, 'catch up' with each planet, as the latter moves a short distance along its orbit each year, and this explains why oppositions occur later every year. The more distant a planet is, the slower its orbital motion, and the shorter the delay between one opposition and the next. For instance, Jupiter orbits the Sun once every twelve years, so its annual motion is about

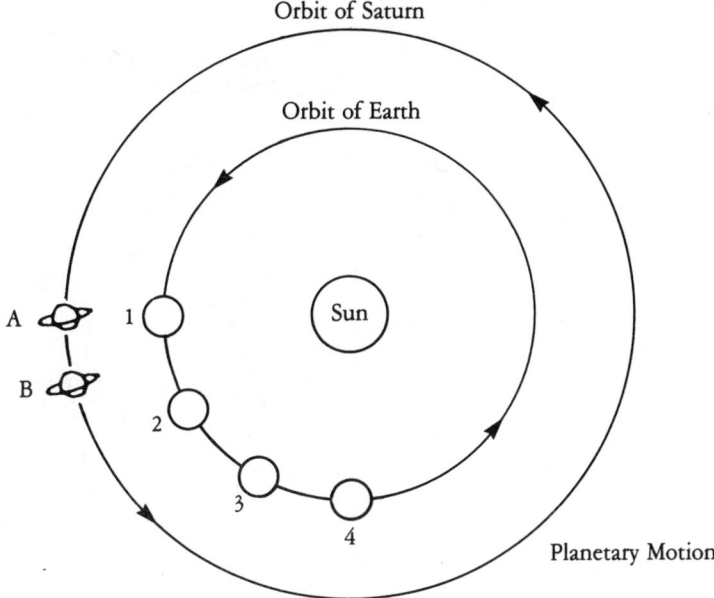

Figure 22. Shows the relative slow movement of Saturn in one year (A to B) compared to the Earth's movement (occupying positions 1, 2, 3, 4) at monthly intervals.

30°, and therefore, it comes to opposition about one month later each year. For the more distant planets, Saturn, Uranus, Neptune and Pluto, the corresponding periods are approximately 13, 4, 2 and 1 day. Mars, on the other hand, has an orbit lying not far beyond the Earth's, and its orbital revolution period of 687 days is less than twice the Earth's year of 365 ¼ days, so that oppositions of this planet are separated by more than two years.

During a certain period before, around and after opposition, a planet will appear to change its normal eastward motion and go into reverse, moving westward against the stars. A planet which does this is said to be moving *retrograde,* and this phenomenon is caused by the Earth overtaking the outer planet. At two points, usually a few weeks either side of opposition, the Earth is moving directly towards or directly away from the planet, which then appears stationary. At the planet's stationary points, its motion changes from direct to retrograde or vice-versa. Astrologically, retrograde motion

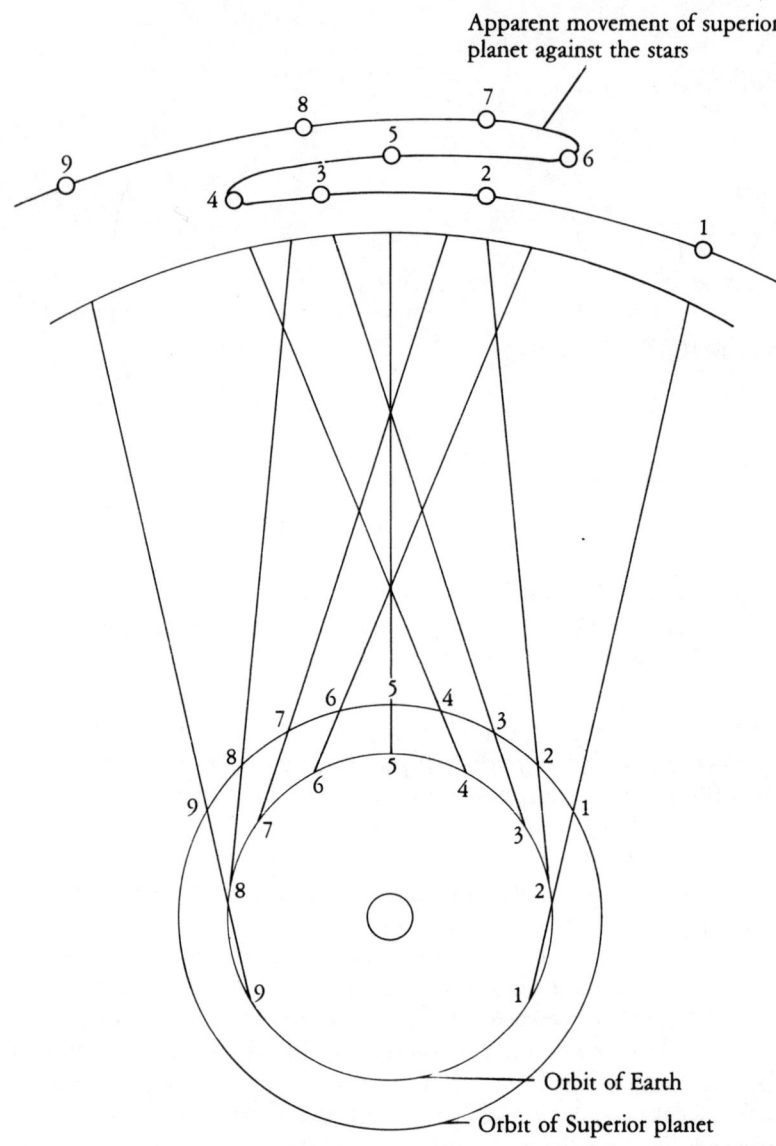

Figure 23: Retrogradation

often appears to cause confusion and misunderstanding. Many astrologers attribute a significance to retrograde planets far greater than the facts warrant.

A study of any ephemeris will show that it is impossible for a superior planet to be in signs on the opposite side of the sky from the Sun without being retrograde. Retrogradation depends upon geocentric view and distance, and the period of retrogradation is greater, the more remote the planet happens to be. Each planet is retrograde for varying periods of time, the mean averages being: Mercury 20 per cent, Venus 7 per cent, Mars 9 per cent, Jupiter 30 per cent, Saturn 36 per cent, Uranus 41 per cent, Neptune 43 per cent and Pluto 44 per cent. If we take the planets from Jupiter out to Pluto, we can see that it is impossible for the Sun to form a trine aspect to any of these planets without the planets having retrograde motion at the same time; not only the trine aspect but also the opposition and quincunx. The phenomenon of retrograde motion is a perfectly natural occurrence, and it has no real meaning astrologically, except when a planet becomes stationary, slows down and 'hovers' on a critical point in a chart. Then it does have significance, and should be considered. The statements which appear in astrological journals and the like concerning retrograde motion and its association with mentality, transportation accidents and other similar conditions, do little for the credit of astrology, particularly when we consider the large percentage of the population who have planets retrograde.

All the planets, with the exception of Pluto, move around the Sun in orbits which are in almost the same plane as the Ecliptic, keeping to the narrow band called the Zodiac which extends about eight degrees either side of the Ecliptic. The angles at which the planets' orbits are inclined to the Ecliptic, their *orbital inclinations*, vary from 0° 46' (Uranus) to 7° (Mercury), while Pluto's is 17° 10'. Most planets have orbital inclinations of between 1° and 4°. The two points where a planetary orbit intersects the Ecliptic are called the *ascending node* and the *descending node,* the former where the orbit is moving from the south of the Ecliptic to north of it, and the latter where the orbit is moving from north to south.

The orbits of the planets are not circular. They are slightly elliptical, the degree of ellipticity being called the *orbit's eccentricity* which varies between 0 (for a circle) to 1, and eccentricities of planetary orbits vary from 0.007 (Venus) to 0.246 (Pluto). When a planet is at its nearest point of approach to the Sun, it is said to be at *perihelion;* when it is at its furthest point from the Sun, it is at *aphelion.*

In astronomical texts, the following elements are used to denote planetary orbits:

a = average distance of planet from the Sun (in astronomical units*).
P = Sidereal period of planet (in days, months or years).
i = inclination of orbit to Ecliptic (in degrees and minutes).
e = orbital eccentricity expressed as a ratio and given a value between 0 and 1.
ϖ = longitude of perihelion (degrees). ⎫
☊ = longitude of ascending node (degrees). ⎬ all measured from the First Point of Aries
l = longitude of the planets at a particular time. ⎭

* One astronomical unit = 93 million miles (average distance between Earth and Sun).

By these symbols or elements, it is possible to predict the exact motions and positions of each planet.

Bode's Law
Johann Bode (1747-1826) was a German astronomer whose name is associated with the rule known as 'Bode's Law'. This law is expressed by the statement that the proportionate distance of the several planets from the Sun may be represented by adding 4 to each term of the series: 0, 3, 6, 12, 24, 48, 96, 192, which gives 4, 7, 10, 16, 28, 52, 100, 196. These latter numbers are roughly equal to the distances, in tens of millions of miles, of each planet from the Sun, from Mercury through to Uranus. This correlation known as Bode's Law does not hold for Neptune or Pluto.

Kepler's Law of Planetary Motion
Between 1609 and 1618, the astronomer Johannes Kepler founded the three laws of planetary motion. These laws, deduced from the observations of Tycho Brahe, enabled Isaac Newton to formulate his law of universal gravitation and which eventually led to Einstein's theories of relativity. These three laws are:

THE MECHANICS OF THE SOLAR SYSTEM 137

Law 1:

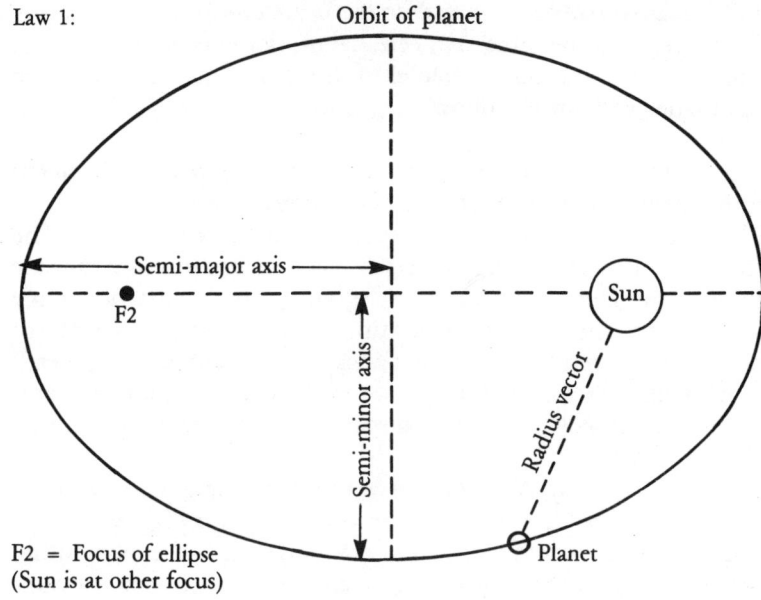

F2 = Focus of ellipse
(Sun is at other focus)

Law 2:

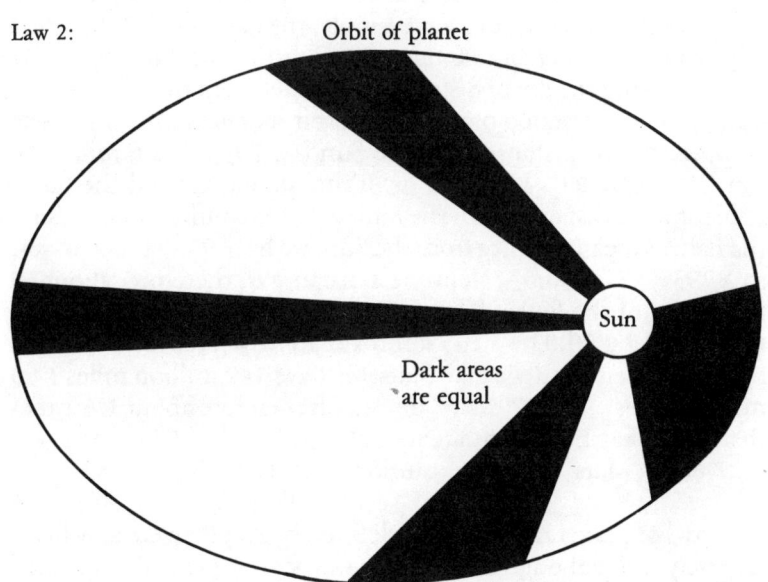

Figure 24. Kepler's Laws of Planetary Motion

1. *The planets move in ellipses with the Sun at one focus of the ellipse.*
Formerly, it was believed that celestial motions occurred in circles. This first law indicates the shapes of the orbits and the path which the planet will always follow.

2. *The radius vector (the imaginary straight line joining each planet to the Sun) sweeps out equal areas in equal times.*
This second law involves a continually varying rate of motion. The speed is not constant, the planets moving faster the closer they are to the Sun. The maximum speed of any planet is attained when it is closest to the Sun, the minimum when it is farthest. These two points on the orbit being perihelion (closest) and aphelion (farthest).

Although the speeds of the planets in their orbits are not constant, the radius vector of each planet passes over equal areas in equal times.

3. *The squares of the planets' revolution periods are directly proportional to the cubes of their distances from the Sun.*
This law is known as the 'harmonic law' and defines the relationship between the planet's orbital motion and its distance from the Sun. The period is the time that it takes the planet to complete one revolution around the Sun. For example, the Earth takes 365 ¼ days approximately, Mercury 88 days and Pluto about 248 years.

By knowing the mean distance of a planet from the Sun, we can obtain the exact period of a planet's orbit. For example, if we take Neptune whose distance from the Sun is 2,793 million miles, we can, using Kepler's law, find its orbital period around the Sun.

Neptune's distance from the Sun = 2,793 million miles: Using the Earth's mean distance from the Sun, we have 93,000,000 miles, so 2,793 ÷ 93 = 30.03. Neptune's distance is, therefore, about 30 times that of the Earth. The square root of 30.03 = 5.48 which, multiplied by 30.03 = 165 approximately = Neptune's orbital revolution period. If we take Mars, we have 142 million miles ÷ 93 million miles = 1.527. Mars' distance is therefore about 1 ½ times that of the Earth. The square root of 1.527 = 1.2357 times 1.527 = 1.88 = Mars' orbital revolution period.

The laws of planetary motion as defined by Kepler were a brilliant discovery and, although the third law was not complete, they enabled Newton to show that planets behave as they do because of the universal law of gravitational attraction.

THE MECHANICS OF THE SOLAR SYSTEM

Gravitation

Gravitation is one of the four fundamental forces of physics. It is the force of mutual attraction between bodies, negligible between ordinary objects, but very powerful between astronomical-sized objects such as planets, stars and galaxies. The principles of gravitation were formulated by Isaac Newton three hundred years ago, in his famous work *The Principia Mathematica,* the central theorem stating that there exists a force of gravitational attraction between two bodies which is proportional to the product of their masses and inversely proportional to the square of the distance between them. This principle is called the 'Law of Universal Gravitation' and may be expressed mathematically in the form:

$$F = \frac{G \cdot M^1 \, M^2}{D^2}$$

Where F = force, M^1 and M^2 are the masses of the two bodies and D is the distance between them. G is the universal gravitational constant.

This equation applies not only to planets and satellites in orbit around their primaries, but also to double stars in orbit around one another, so that the law of universal gravitation operates in all parts of the Universe.

All objects possess mass, which is not to be confused with weight. Mass is the amount of material which an object contains, or alternatively, it is a measure of the inertia of that object, that is, its resistance to stopping, starting or change in velocity. An object's mass remains unchanged regardless of the forces acting upon it, but its weight is equal to the product of its mass and the gravitational acceleration, g. The value of g depends upon the mass of the planet so, for Earth, g = 10 metres per second, per second, that being the rate at which a falling object will accelerate toward the Earth.

The Moon's mass is only 1/81 that of the Earth, and the value of g on the Moon's surface is only one-sixth its value on the Earth's surface. This explains why astronauts on the Moon weigh only one-sixth their weight on the Earth.

Planets and satellites are maintained in orbit about their primaries by the balance between the two forces, gravity pulling inward and centrifugal force pushing outward. Inside an artificial Earth satellite in orbit around the Earth, these two forces exactly counterbalance each other and a condition of weightlessness is the result. If it were not for the force of gravity, the Earth would depart from its elliptical orbit and go off at a tangent.

The theory of gravitational attraction explained the causes of many things which, until Newton's time, had remained unknown or obscure. Chief among these were the reasons for falling bodies, tides, planetary motions and the precession of the equinoxes.

Precession of the Equinoxes

The phenomenon of precession was discovered by the Greek astronomer Hipparchus in the second century B.C. By comparing contemporary observations with those made about a century and a half earlier by Timocharis, he concluded that the longitude of the stars appeared to be increasing at the rate of 36 seconds per year, (the modern value is about 50 seconds), while their latitudes showed no definite changes. There were two possible explanations that would account for this change, (a) the stars had real and identical motions, (b) the fundamental reference point, the Vernal Equinox, was not a fixed reference point on the Ecliptic. The fact that the latitudes of stars showed no appreciable changes led to the conclusion that the Equator and, in consequence, the Vernal Equinox moved in such a manner that the longitudes of the stars increased uniformly. The cause of this displacement of stars remained unknown for many centuries, and it was Newton who first gave a correct explanation of precession.

In studying the cause of precession, we need to understand two distinct and unrelated motions, namely (a) the motion of the Solar system in our Galaxy, (b) the motion of the Celestial Pole, around the Pole of its own orbit, i.e., the Pole of the Ecliptic. Our Galaxy and Solar system are whirling around a common centre in their own galactic orbits at different rates of motion, such motions being technically termed *'proper motions'*. Each of the stars which form the pattern of the constellations, (zodiacal and non-zodiacal) is a sun. As all the stars are moving at gigantic but different speeds around the centre of the Galaxy, all the constellations will completely lose their familiar patterns in the course of time. Our Sun with its planets is moving in its own galactic orbit around the centre of the galaxy, and will take an estimated 220 million years to complete the circuit. The direction of the path in the galaxy taken by the Sun and planets is known as the 'apex', and according to astronomical determinants,

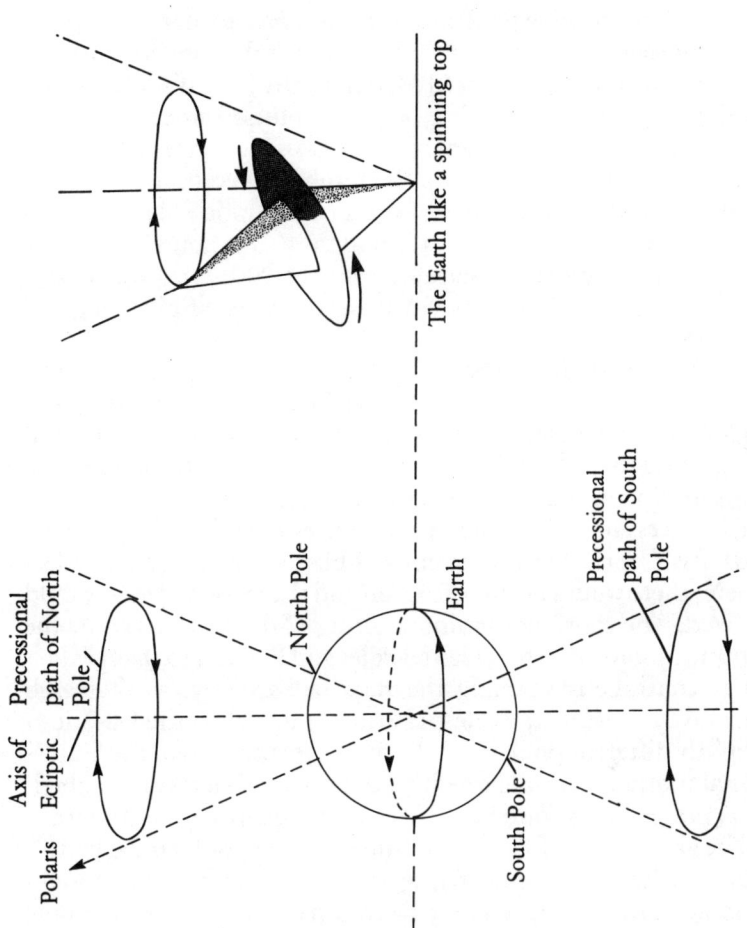

Figure 25. Precession of the Equinoxes

it lies in Sagittarius 29°. Geocentrically, the Sun comes to the Ecliptic conjunction of its apex about 14 January each year. The phenomenon of 'precession', the dating of 'zodiacal ages' and the question of 'zodiacs' have nothing to do with the Sun's proper motion in space.

Simply stated, Precession of the Equinoxes is the annual occurrence of the Vernal Equinox about 21 March, nearly 20½ minutes before the Earth has made a complete orbital revolution around the Sun, so that each year at that instant, the Sun crosses the celestial Equator at a slightly different point. As the result of precession, every star — except those less than 23½° from the Ecliptic Poles — passes through every hour of Right Ascension from 0-24 hours, once every 25,800 years; also the declinations, every 12,900 years swing to and fro 47° (23½° × 2) greatly changing the stars visible at a given place and season.

The Vernal Equinoctial point (0° Aries) is that point on the Ecliptic intersected by the celestial Equator. As the Equator is always at right angles to its own pole, it follows that the movement of the celestial Pole around the Pole of the Ecliptic will cause the vernal-equinoctial point to slip backward along the Ecliptic at the rate of 1° in 71½ years. Precession is therefore a purely terrestrial effect related to the Earth itself. If the Earth were not an oblate spheroid, but a perfect sphere, there would be no precession and the tropical zodiac would be fixed. The continuous minute tilting of the Earth's axis by the Sun and Moon causes the celestial Poles and Equator to change their places continuously among the stars in harmony, so that each successive moment, the celestial Equator intersects the Ecliptic at a slightly different point — in the opposite direction of the Earth's orbital motion — of the one it would occupy if left undisturbed. Thus precession is continuous, not a sudden yearly occurrence.

The gravitational forces of the Sun and Moon pull on the Earth's equatorial bulge, as though trying to bring the Earth into an upright position. However, the spinning Earth behaves like a gyrostat causing the Earth's axis (which would otherwise always point to the same position on the star sphere) and the celestial Poles to rotate round the poles of her orbit (those of the Ecliptic) in circles 23½° distant from them in a period of 25,800 years, displacing the Vernal Equinox in the opposite direction to her orbital motion.

As precession is continuous, the celestial Equator intersects the Ecliptic at a point about one-seventh second of arc west of the position the day before at the same hour, so that right ascension is measured from a slightly different point on the star sphere each day. About the 21 March each year, the Vernal Point is approximately 50 seconds west of its position a year before, or about 3 seconds of right ascension (1° in 71.62 years).

The Ecliptic is the fundamental plane of reference and, as longitude is measured along the Ecliptic from the Vernal Equinox, it changes with precession, but latitude which is measured north or south of the Ecliptic does not change. At the present time, the North Celestial Pole is near the star Ursae Minoris (Pole Star) and

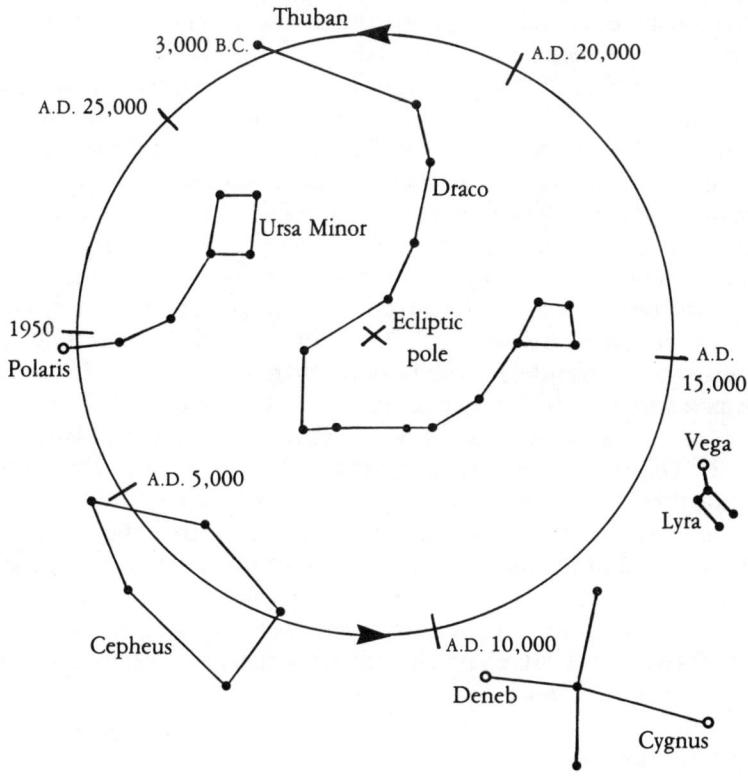

Figure 26. Path of the North Celestial Pole

its nearest approach, (less than half a degree) will be in the year A.D. 2100. About A.D. 7000, Alderamin (Alpha Cephei) will become the Pole Star, and in about A.D. 14,000, Vega (Alpha Lyrae) will be near enough to the pole to mark its position. Similarly, in about 3,000 B.C., the Pole Star was Thuban (Alpha Draconis), the closest of all the bright stars to the true pole throughout the 26,000 year cycle, being within one-sixth of a degree (10 minutes of arc).

In our discussions on megalithic astronomy, we noted how certain structures appeared to have celestial alignments. Due to precession over the centuries, certain stars and constellations no longer rise at the same points of the horizon as they once did, and this deviation assists in the dating of ancient structures. Through this displacement, the part of the sky visible from a particular location gradually changes; certain constellations cease to rise above the horizon and others appear for the first time. 5,000 years ago, it was not necessary to travel so far south to see the Southern Cross as it is now, as it would have been visible from the intermediate latitudes. The dating of megalithic circles and the like can be calculated, if they originally had a particular stellar alignment. With Sun temples, the position is different because the Sun determined the points of reference. The Sun is due south at true noon, and rises due east and sets due west at the Equinoxes as it has always done. Even though the mean obliquity of the Ecliptic varies very slowly between 22°-24½° in a period of about 50,000 years for one complete oscillation, its changing value would need to be combined with other factors to obtain accurate dating.

The position of the stars is listed for a definite epoch, e.g., 1 January 1950. This is done because it is not possible to produce maps and catalogues to keep abreast with precession. In plotting the positions of celestial objects observed before or after the epoch date, astronomers must calculate the amount of precessional change in right ascension and declination for the appropriate interval of time. In the ephemerides used by astrologers, the tabulations of planetary positions are given in celestial longitudes which have been converted from right ascensions.

The Seasons

If it were not for the Obliquity of the Ecliptic, the Earth would spin perpendicularly in the vertical to its orbit, and there would be no change of seasons, and temperatures would be equable. The seasons, therefore, are due to the varying altitude of the Sun, and are a purely

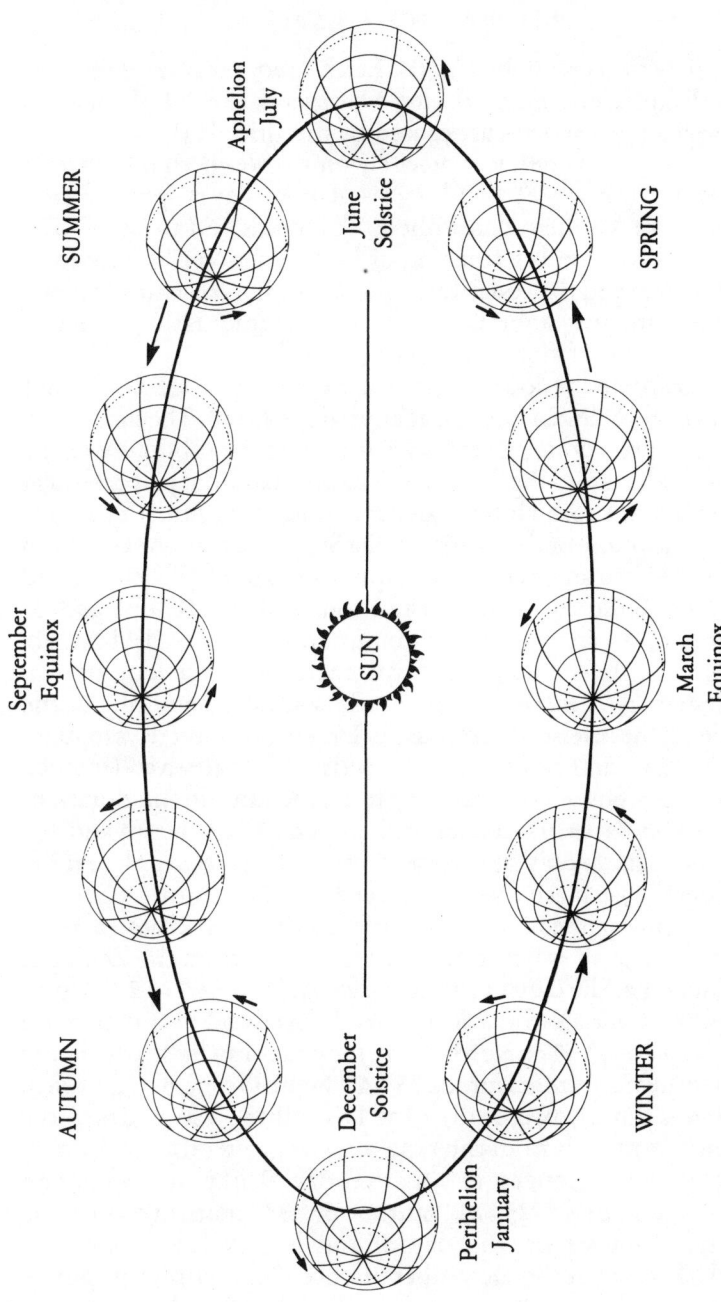

Figure 27. The Seasons: Northern Hemisphere

terrestrial effect occasioned by the Earth's motion around the pole of the Ecliptic, and have nothing whatever to do with the zodiac.

The changing seasons are caused by the altitude (height) of the Sun at *southing* (when it is precisely on the southern meridian or cusp of the 10th house). Southing occurs every day at apparent local noon. In the southern hemisphere, the Sun is said to *north*. The altitude of the Sun is a function of its declination (distance from the Equator) and the co-latitude of the locality; (co-latitude being 90° minus the geographic latitude) and the altitude is the algebraical sum of the declination and the co-latitude.

The *Ecliptic* is the apparent path of the Sun, and the Ecliptic circle intersects the Celestial Equator at an angle of 23 ½ °. The inclination of the Ecliptic and Equator circles is termed the Obliquity of the Ecliptic and is due to the fact that the Earth's axis is not perpendicular to the plane of its orbit but departs from the perpendicular by 23 ½ °. During the course of the solar year, the Sun's declination varies from 0° at the March and September Equinox to 23 ½ ° at the June and December Solstice. At the Solstices on or about 21 June and 22 December, the maximum and minimum periods of daylight are experienced. In the northern hemisphere, there are long days in June, short days in December; in the southern hemisphere, the position is the reverse — long days in December, short days in June. Within the polar circles (66½ °), day and night progressively lengthen until the periods of night and day reach their maximum duration.

As the Sun's declination ranges between 23° 27′ North and 23° 27′ South, it can only be vertically overhead at a given place if the latitude of that place does not exceed 23° 27′ North or South.

At the time of the Equinoxes, the Sun is directly overhead at noon at the Equator. It is never more than 23° 27′ from the Zenith at the Equator at the date of the Solstices. At latitude 23° 27′ North (Tropic of Cancer), the Sun is directly overhead at a maximum declination of 23° 27′ North at the June Solstice. Similarly, in the southern hemisphere at latitude 23° 27′ South (Tropic of Capricorn), the Sun is directly overhead at the December Solstice. The more distant a latitude is from the Equator, the greater the variation in the length of the longest and shortest day. Within the Arctic and Antarctic Circle (90°-23° 27′ latitude 66° 33′ north or south), the Sun does not set on the day of the June Solstice (Northern Hemisphere) or at the December Solstice (Southern Hemisphere) hence we have the phenomenon of the Midnight Sun. From latitudes

66½° to the Poles, the Sun remains above the horizon from 1 to 186 days and below the horizon from 1 to 179 days depending upon the latitude; the nearer the latitude is to the Pole, the greater the duration of day or night.

On Midsummer's Day in London (latitude 51° 32′ North), the altitude of the Sun = 90° — 51° 32′ + 23° 27′ = 61° 55′ which is 28° from the Zenith, while on the same day at Auckland, New Zealand (latitude 36° 52′ South), it will only be 90° minus 36° 52′ minus 23° 27′ = 29° 41′.

The climates of the world are mainly dependent on latitudes. Within the Tropics, the climate is fairly stable, but outside the Tropics, climates due to the Sun's twice-yearly movement across the Equator are seasonal. The five zones of the Earth's surface are: Torrid — lying within the Tropics of Cancer and Capricorn; North Temperate — between Cancer and the Arctic Circle; South Temperate — between Capricorn and the Antarctic Circle; Frigid Zone — between the Polar Circles and the Poles. In the South Temperate Zone, the seasons are reversed. Spring begins at the September Equinox, Summer at the December Solstice.

Broad seasonal changes of temperature are dependent on the amount of solar energy received by the Earth, and on heat carried by winds and ocean currents. At midday, the Sun's rays strike the surface of the Earth at different angles at different latitudes; where the rays are low-angled and therefore spread over a larger area, less heat and light are received. Places in high latitudes thus receive less solar energy than those nearer the Equator, while between latitudes 38° North or South, more energy is received from the Sun than is returned by radiation to space. The unequal heating of different areas of the Earth sets in motion the atmosphere and the oceans; winds assisted by the moisture within them, redistribute the heat received from the Sun and keep temperatures from constantly rising in low latitudes, or falling in the middle or high latitudes. However, variations do occur, and the world's pressure systems do not always respond in the same manner to the fluctuations of solar energy reaching the Earth and its atmosphere.

Tides

The gravitational pull of the Moon and to a lesser degree, that of the Sun, cause the waters of the Earth to ebb and flow (tides). The Moon exerts the greatest influence, particularly when, in its closest

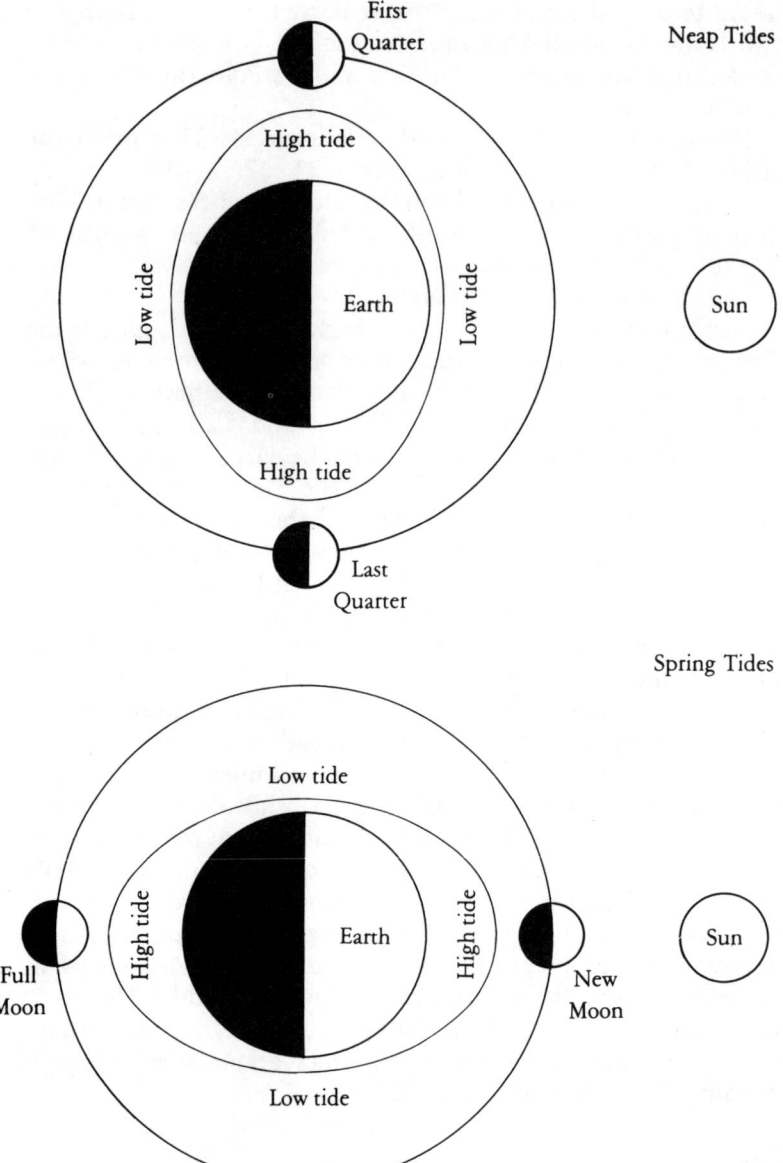

Figure 28. The Tides

orbit to the Earth (perigee), the tides are almost 20 per cent higher than when the Moon is farthest away from the Earth (apogee).

High and Low Water occur on average twice in just under 25 hours, which is the same average interval between two successive meridian passages of the Moon. The surface of the ocean rises and falls at any given place at more or less regular intervals. On average, the period between two successive high tides is 12 hours 25 minutes — exactly one half the time it takes the Moon to complete the circuit about the Earth.

The Moon does not 'lift the waters' away from the Earth, neither are the tidal 'bulges' in the oceans the result of the Moon's 'pulling and squeezing'. The tidal 'bulges' result from the actual flow of water over the Earth's surface towards those regions below and opposite the Moon, causing the waters to pile up to greater depths at those places. As the Earth rotates, these two tidal 'bulges' remain in the same position relative to the Moon, so that they sweep around the Earth and affect the different coastlines in turn. The Sun's gravitational pull too, affects the tides although to a much lesser degree than does the Moon's.

At New Moon or Full Moon, the Sun and Moon — being then in line with the Earth — are pulling together and this results in a high or Spring Tide. At First or Last Quarter, on the other hand, the Sun and Moon are pulling at right angles to each other and the difference in water level between high and low tide is correspondingly much less (Neap Tide). Each point on the Earth's surface therefore has two high and two low tides every day, although local geographical factors such as the shape of the coastline may significantly alter the timing and magnitude of the tides. The two high tides during a day need not be equally high, as for example, in northern or southern temperate latitudes during summer or winter, the axis of the tidal bulges is inclined to the Equator. In the northern hemisphere, the high tide on the side of the Earth under the Moon would be higher than the high tide half a day later. In the southern hemisphere, there would be the opposite effect. In exceptional cases, there may appear to be only one high tide a day.

9.
COMETS

Early Ideas About Comets
From the earliest times right up to the seventeenth century and even later, comets appearing suddenly and without warning in the sky, naturally inspired terror and fear in most people. Having no idea what these peculiar objects were, people took them for warnings of imminent disaster such as drought, famine, earthquakes, war, plague, or the death of kings or princes. In *Julius Caesar,* we have the well-known lines:

> When beggars die, there are no comets seen,
> The heavens themselves blaze forth the death of princes.

These lines were written because there was a general belief among Romans that the death of an emperor was accompanied by a bright comet in the sky at the time of his death. Such ideas were common among the civilizations of the ancient world; some of them (like the tribes of North and South America, Polynesia and the civilization of China), imagining comets to be the spirits of dead people.

While such ideas were prevalent, there were, however, a few persons who were looking at comets in a more scientific way. Of the various schools of thought that appeared, one suggested that comets were merely some kind of phenomenon occurring within the Earth's atmosphere, while another school thought that comets moved outside the atmosphere and were, in fact, visitors from deep space.

The Nature, Composition, Orbits and Origin of Comets

The word 'comet' is derived from the Latin word for 'hair', because a large bright comet's tail strongly resembles long hair being blown in the wind. Comets are large objects, fuzzy in appearance, and composed principally of gas, dust and small particles. The majority of comets consist of four parts: the nucleus, coma, hydrogen cloud and tail.

The nucleus of a comet is very small indeed by astronomical standards, being comparable in size with a large city, and in the majority of cases, probably no more than a few kilometres across. According to the theory advanced by F. L. Whipple and A. Delsemme, the typical nucleus consists of water ice within which are trapped various other substances, and when the comet approaches the Sun, the heat from the latter causes the ice to sublimate, that is, to change directly into water vapour. When sublimation of the ice occurs, gas and dust flow outward from these layers to produce the coma (head) of the comet.

The coma is that part of the comet which gives it its distinctive fuzzy appearance and allows it to be distinguished from a star. A comet will develop a coma by the process described above, normally when it reaches to within about 500 million kilometres of the Sun. Comas vary considerably in size, being generally much larger than the Earth, and even the smallest comas are tens of thousands of kilometres across. The largest comet on record, that of 1811, possessed a coma no less than two million kilometres in diameter, making it larger than even the Sun itself. The average coma is about 100,000 to 500,000 kilometres across. The chemical elements and molecules which make up the gas of the coma are carbon, carbon monoxide, oxygen, amine, cyanogen, water, cyanide and carbon sulphide, and there are also ions (electrically charged particles) of nitrogen, carbon monoxide, water, hydroxyl and carbon dioxide. We know that these elements exist in comets, because they show up distinctly in the comets' spectra. Some of these elements form the gas of the coma, while others form the particles of dust within this gas. This gas is extremely thin, much thinner than the Earth's atmosphere.

As a comet draws near to the Sun, it encounters a constant stream of electrically charged particles continuously moving away from the Sun, called the solar wind. This solar wind impinges upon the coma and forces some of its material to move directly away from the Sun, and the comet therefore develops a tail, which always points away from the Sun. So, when a comet is receding from the Sun's vicinity, it will move tail first and not head first, leaving a trail of dust behind it along most parts of its orbit. When the Earth passes through a comet's path, we see a shower of meteors (shooting stars), which are these dust grains moving quickly through the Earth's atmosphere and being burnt up by friction in the process, each burning grain producing a streak of light lasting for about one or two seconds.

The orbits of comets are quite unlike those of the planets. The latter move in almost circular paths, while that of a comet is a highly elongated ellipse or even (if the comet is non-periodic), one of the open curves known as parabolae and hyperbolae. The speed of a comet, when it is at its nearest point to the Sun, will determine which type of curve it will follow. The distance of closest approach of a comet to the Sun also affects its speed at all points along its orbit, and the higher speeds occur along the parts of the orbit nearer to the Sun.

Cometary orbits are not only often highly elongated; they are also sometimes highly inclined to the plane of the Ecliptic. This means that, unlike the planets which keep to a narrow band in the sky (Zodiac), comets can appear in any part of the sky, although as a general rule, they are most conspicuous when they are near to the Sun. Because the mass of a comet is so low, they are easily swung away from original orbits into new ones under the gravitational influences of the giant planets Jupiter and Saturn and, to a lesser extent, Uranus and Neptune, should they happen to pass near to them.

Although many thousands, or possibly even millions, of comets are thought to exist both within and without the Solar System, the orbits of only about 600 have been determined. Of these, about a hundred are referred to as 'short period', orbiting the Sun once every two hundred years or less. These comets keep within the confines of the Solar System and move in orbits which do not incline steeply to the ecliptic. 'Long period' comets, of which about 500 are known to exist, appear to belong to a different class, since their orbits are highly inclined to the ecliptic and are often retrograde. They originate from well outside the Solar System, possibly from as much as two light-years away (12 million, million miles) or half-way to the nearest star.

About 5,000 million years ago, the Sun and the planets condensed out of a rotating cloud of gas. Most astronomers consider that the comets were formed at about the same time, but remained outside the Solar system in the swarm described above.

Halley's Comet, and Halley's Work on Comets

Edmond Halley (1656-1742) was the second Astronomer Royal from 1720 to 1742. Long before he was appointed to this post, however, he was well-grounded in astronomy, and in 1682, he observed a brilliant comet first recorded by the astronomer G. Dorffel on 15 August of that year.

In 1687, Newton published his monumental work known as the *Principia Mathematica,* a vast three-volume account of a theory of universal gravitation. Halley contributed to this work and also arranged its publication, and in 1695, decided to apply the theory of gravitation and the calculus (a branch of mathematics also developed by Newton) to the question of cometary orbits. He was, in fact, the first astronomer to apply these two new branches of science to astronomy. Newton had observed the comet of 1680, and Flamsteed (the first Astronomer Royal) had observed the one of 1682. Halley took these observations and used them together with observations of comets of earlier times, even those of antiquity. After reducing all these observations — a long, difficult task made more so by the gravitational influences of the massive planets Jupiter and Saturn upon the paths of passing comets — he managed to obtain accurate orbits of more than twenty comets, which were moving in elliptical paths within the confines of the Solar System.

Halley proved by this method, that the brilliant comet of 1682 was the same as that of 1607 and 1531 and, since its period was therefore about 76 years, he predicted its return in 1758. However, sixteen years before its expected return, Halley died in 1742. Concerning the return of this comet, he wrote, 'Wherefore if it should return again according to our predictions, impartial posterity will not refuse to acknowledge that this was first discovered by an Englishman'.

During almost the whole of 1758, however, this comet failed to appear. The astronomers Clairaut, Lalande and Lepaute during this time had been carrying out extensive calculations on the comet's orbit, and Clairaut concluded that the comet would pass close to Jupiter and Saturn and would be delayed (by about one year and eight months) by the gravitational pull of those planets. Towards the end of 1758, many astronomers searched for signs of the comet's reappearance, but it was not until the last few days of that year that it was first seen again by the amateur astronomer Palitzsch. On 12 March, 1759, the comet passed through its perihelion (nearest point of approach to the Sun).

So, Halley had fulfilled the prediction of Seneca 1,700 years before, that someone would one day be able to understand the motions and behaviour of comets in their journeys through space, and the comet of 1682 and 1758 was therefore named after him. Also, Halley's work was a remarkable example of the truth of Newton's laws of universal gravitation. This verification allowed astronomers and mathematicians to apply those laws to the motions of the planets and their satellites and later to those of the stars through space, thereby laying the foundation stones for the growth of modern astronomy.

In November 1835, Halley's comet returned again and passed through perihelion, and was observed by Dumouchel and by Sir John Herschel (the son of Sir William Herschel) among others. The subsequent and the most recent return of Halley's comet was in 1910. It was seen in the sky seven months before it passed perihelion. In May 1910, the comet passed close to the Earth, and on the 19th of the month, the Earth actually passed through the comet's tail, or rather, through part of the tail, since the tail was observed to divide into two parts. On the announcement of the imminent passage of the Earth through the tail, there was considerable alarm and anxiety among the public, the more so, when the further announcement came that a lethal gas known as cyanogen was one of the constituent gases of the tail. In the event, the public's fears proved groundless, since no effects at all were observed, either during or after the passage. This was due to the tail's extremely rarefied gas coming up against the immensely thicker atmosphere of the Earth, and possibly, the deviation of charged particles in the tail around and away from the Earth by the latter's magnetic field. On the same day, the comet passed directly between the Sun and Earth, and did not obscure the Sun's light in the least. During the weeks prior to May 1910, Halley's comet had been a fairly bright object in the early morning sky, and it was visible in telescopes for over a year afterward. After this, it receded into the depths of the Solar System, and in 1948, was at aphelion (greatest distance from the Sun) beyond the orbit of Neptune.

At present (1983), it is near the orbit of Saturn and, as it approaches the Sun, it will move faster and faster until it swings around the

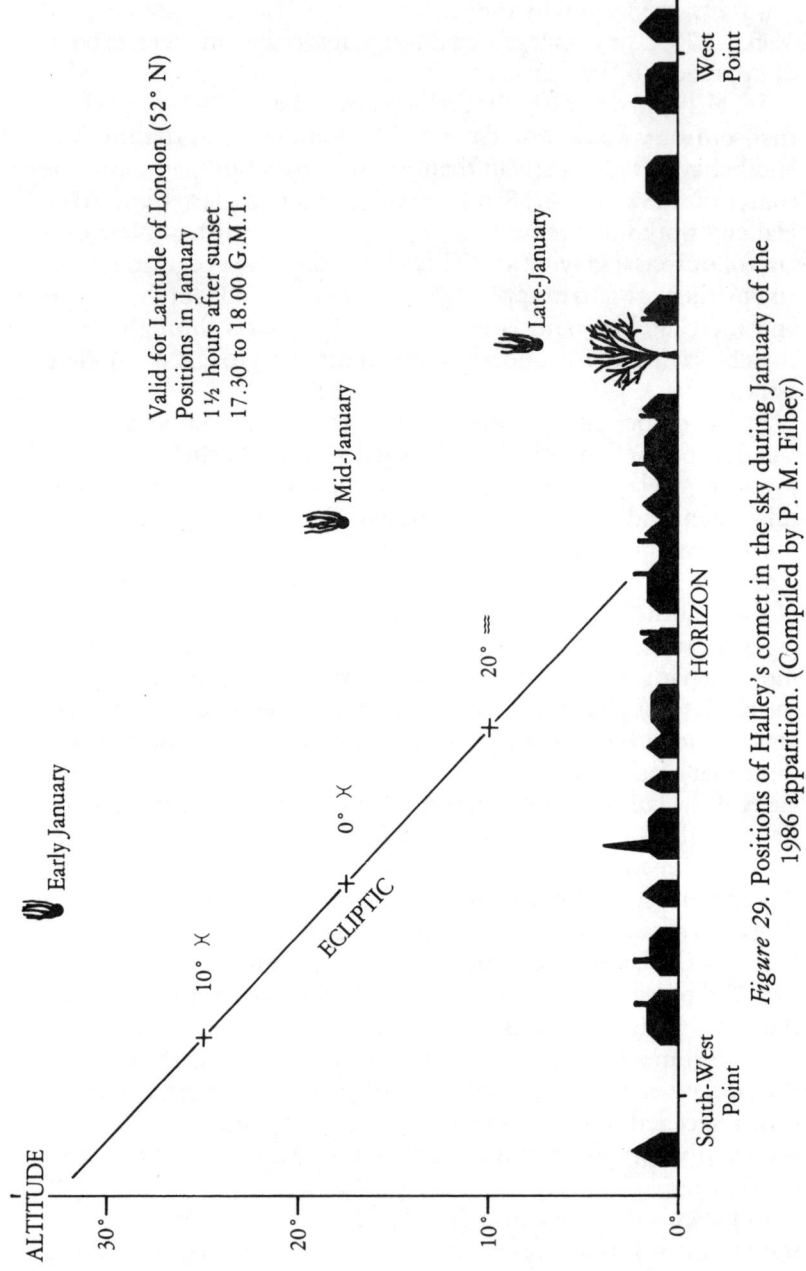

Figure 29. Positions of Halley's comet in the sky during January of the 1986 apparition. (Compiled by P. M. Filbey)

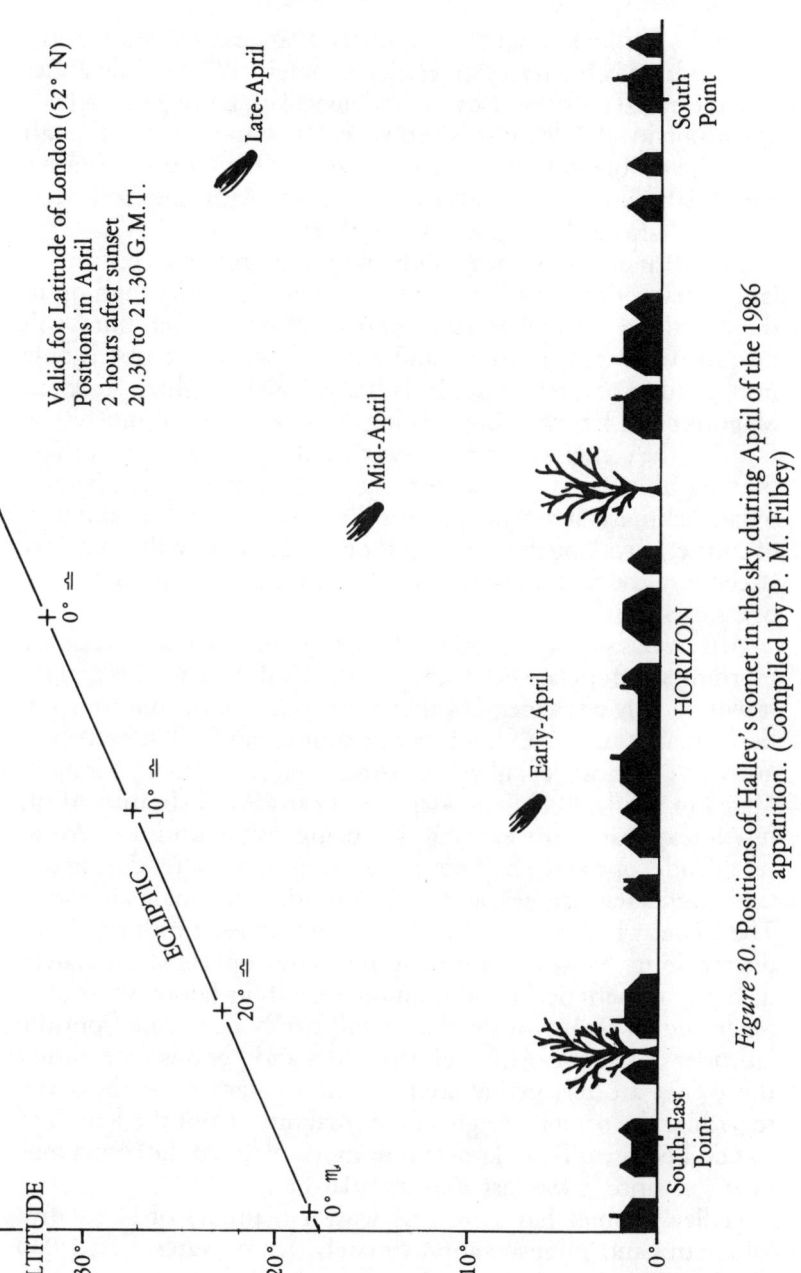

Figure 30. Positions of Halley's comet in the sky during April of the 1986 apparition. (Compiled by P. M. Filbey)

Sun at its perihelion point in February 1986. For several months either side of February 1986, Halley's comet will be visible either with the naked eye or with low-power binoculars. During the comet's apparition in 1985-86, it will be observable from Britain, although it will be visible to much greater advantage higher up in the sky and brighter in more southern latitudes, with the best view obtainable from the tropics and southern hemisphere.

From Britain, the comet will be visible from late December to late January. Early in this period, it will appear quite high up in the sky (about 30° high) an hour and a half after sunset, but it will be quite faint at Magnitude 5 and will be observable properly only in binoculars or a telescope. In January, it will brighten to about Magnitude 4, but this 'brightening' will be cancelled out by the fact that the comet will appear lower and lower in the western sky, the same time after sunset, as the month progresses. From late January to late February, it will be too near the Sun to be visible, and it is, of course, very dangerous to look for it then, because the Sun may sweep into the field of view of the telescope and cause damage to one's eyesight.

After it has swung around the Sun, the comet will appear in the morning sky from late February to early April. During this period, it will be only a few degrees above the southern or south-eastern horizon, one and a half hours before sunrise, and will then appear at its best because its tail will be much longer — from 5° long in March to nearly 20° in late March and early April. In mid-April, it will reappear in the evening sky, being visible until late April. Its altitude, one and a half hours after sunset, will alter during this time from a few degrees, and its magnitude will remain around 5. The comet will now be visible in the southern sky with a tail two degrees long. However, during its morning appearance in March, its high southern declination combined with its faintness (around Magnitude 4 or 5), means that it will barely be visible from the latitudes of Britain. Although the times and periods for sighting the comet are reasonably accurate, no guarantee can be given regarding the comet's brightness or magnitude nor the length of its tail, because it is not known how much material the comet may have lost since it was last seen in 1910-11.

Halley's comet has a nucleus with a diameter of about five kilometres and a density approximately that of water, i.e., 1,000 kilogrammes per cubic metre. This means that the mass of the nucleus must be around 50 thousand million to 100 thousand million metric tonnes. Although this sounds a vast amount, it is in fact no more than the mass of a high mountain, and the gravitational pull which it exerts is negligible compared to that of the Sun or the planets, or even the asteroids. In fact, there is no danger of the Earth's orbit being even slightly altered by a close encounter between the Earth and Halley's or any other comet.

The Earth will make its closest approach to the comet on 27 November 1985 and 11 April 1986. During the last close approach in 1910, the diameter of the coma increased to a maximum of 200,000 kilometres just after perihelion. The nucleus rotates upon an axis once every ten hours.

The earliest recorded sighting of this comet was in 240 B.C., since when it has been seen on twenty-eight of its returns, that is on every return except that of 164 B.C. At the return of A.D. 837, the comet was now known to have passed closer to the Earth (6 million kilometres) than at any time in history either before or after that year. This resulted in the brightest ever appearance of the comet (as bright as Venus) and also the longest ever length of its tail (93 degrees) in that year.

Orbital Data of Halley's Comet

Longitude of Ascending (North) Node	58°
Angular distance of perihelion point from ascending node	112°
Inclination of comet's orbit to Ecliptic	162°
Eccentricity of orbit	0.967
Distance from Sun at perihelion	90 million kilometres
Distance from Sun at aphelion	5,300 million kilometres

Brilliant Comets of the Past

Some comets have been so brilliant that people who were not astronomers did not fail to notice them. The farther back in history the comet appeared, the less reliable (generally) its description was likely to be, so that descriptions of comets seen in, for example, the Middle Ages are usually only approximate and not particularly accurate. Some of these descriptions, however, make interesting reading. For example, the historian, Nicetus, writing about the comet of 1182: 'a comet appeared in the heavens like a twisting serpent, now writhing and coiling back upon itself; now it would terrify the people with its gaping mouth; as if lusting for human blood, it seemed about to slake its thirst . . .'; while from ancient Greece: 'the red star that from his flaming hair shakes down disease, pestilence and war' (Homer, the *Iliad*). Obviously, such descriptions as these were greatly exaggerated, but were perhaps to be expected, when ignorance about comets led to an understandable fear of them.

In 1744, by which time the nature and behaviour of comets was better understood, a rather remarkable comet appeared with a fan-shaped tail. At the times when it was best visible, the apex of this fan i.e., the comet's coma, was below the horizon, and the tail was about 40° long with six bright streamers in it, each of which increased to 5° in width at its furthest point from the coma. It was observed from Lausanne, Switzerland, by the astronomer De Cheseaux, after whom it was named, although it was discovered in the previous year by Klinkenberg. Then, in 1811, another comet appeared and was discovered by the astronomer H. Flaugergues on 26 March of that year. The coma was 2 million kilometres in diameter, larger even than the Sun. The tail was more than 200 million kilometres in length and 25 million kilometres in width in October of that year. This was known as the Great Comet, and was visible until August 1812. According to the astronomer Argelander, this comet has an orbital period of 3,000 years. But probably the greatest comet of recent centuries was that of 1843. This had a tail 350 million kilometres in length, which appeared from Earth to stretch south of the constellation Orion and to be 68° in length. It came extremely close to the Sun — to within 200,000 kilometres of its surface — and was more than twice as brilliant as that of 1811, being clearly visible in daylight.

The Astrological Tradition

> Like the comet burn'd
> That fires the length of Ophiuchus huge
> In the arctic sky and from his horrid hair
> Shakes pestilence and war
>
> Milton

From time immemorial, the appearance of comets has been associated with misfortune and dire events either to persons or to nations as a whole. These 'hairy stars' were viewed with misgivings and foreboding, as they were considered to be the forerunners of all manner of calamities, disasters and death.

Due to the traditional beliefs that exceptional celestial phenomena denoted the 'shape of things to come', much study was paid to comets. Although regarded with interest and apprehension, their capricious movements were noted with great care, and detailed records were maintained, particularly in China, and these records have been very useful in enabling the history of Halley's comet to be carried back 2,000 years.

Whether the appearance of a comet has significance either for persons or nations, remains a debatable point. Certainly, some of the evidence based on observations and well-attested data would appear to confirm the influence of comets when they appear in certain zodiacal signs. However, as in all things astrological, many factors may be operating simultaneously, such as directions and progressions in a personal chart, or in the case of nations, the significance of the appropriate ingress chart coupled with the current trends which may be active in the chart of the country's monarch or leader. Whether the doctrine of 'subsumption' operates at all levels and thereby 'controls' how a particular configuration will act both in time and in nature, only detailed investigation and research can answer.

Nevertheless, putting aside the philosophical speculations concerning chart inter-relationships, there are on record many interesting facts concerning the correlation of events with cometary returns.

The birth of Christ is reputed to have been heralded by exceptional celestial phenomena, and it may be that Halley's comet coupled with the great conjunction of Jupiter and Saturn was visible at that period. The ancients were of the opinion that the zodiacal signs in which a comet was seen were of great importance and denoted the nature of the events and conditions likely to ensue. This particularly, when the Sun in its annual progress arrived at the degrees of the Ecliptic affected by the appearance of the comet. It may be that the Magi considered the great conjunction of Jupiter and Saturn, which occurred in Pisces in 7 B.C., as very significant, and that Halley's comet, even if it was observable at that time, would not have been that important to the Magi's astrological calculations and their decision to travel west, even though they saw 'His star in the East'. 'The star in the East' probably referred to the heliacal rising (just before sunrise) of the great conjunction sometime in early 7 B.C.

The traditional belief that extreme temperatures are associated with the appearance of comets may have some truth, and several instances are cited of exceptional weather conditions occurring at or soon after cometary apparitions. In 1456, Halley's comet appeared and was followed by such a severe winter that even the Baltic Sea and the Danube were frozen for several months. On the next return in 1531, great inundations occurred in Europe, and in England, the country from Somerset to Norfolk had the appearance of a great sea. At Lisbon, thousands of persons perished in a devastating earthquake which continued for eight days.

In 1606, Halley's comet reappeared, and in the following year, there was frost in June, and the following winter was exceptionally severe. In 1682, with the approach of the comet, the temperatures soared to the high nineties, and disease was rampant in Europe. With the departure of the comet, severe frosts occurred, and a fair was held on the Thames.

The last appearance of Halley's comet was in 1909-10, and coincided with the death of Edward VII in May 1910. This event recalls Shakespeare's famous lines 'the heavens blaze forth the death of princes'. Interestingly enough, the Prince Consort (father of Edward VII) died in 1861, soon after the sighting of a comet which appeared in Gemini at the end of June. The appearance of this comet also coincided with a great fire in London which had not been equalled for two hundred years, and also with the outbreak of the American Civil War. Traditionally, the sign Gemini is associated with the City of London and with the United States of America, and although planetary transits in Gemini do correlate with important events connected with London and the United States, the case for 'cometary action' requires a considerable detailed study.

As with previous returns of Halley's comet, the return of 1910 coincided with exceptional weather conditions. The year 1911 was notable for its remarkable summer, and as the comet receded, great heat and severe, prolonged drought were experienced.

The astrological significance of comets may well be of great importance, provided that one can isolate other factors which may be operative at the time of cometary apparitions. From the cases on record — admittedly rather few — it would appear that exceptional weather conditions prevail at or soon after the appearance of comets. With the return of Halley's comet in 1985-86, modern space technology will, no doubt, be able to assist in discovering whether cometary action does affect terrestrial conditions and if so, how and in what manner. This return — the first since 1910 — will generate great interest, and will be an opportunity for astrologers, using the astronomer's findings, to study and to decide whether comets are associated with events and conditions, as has been traditionally stated.

10.
THE UNIVERSE: STARS AND GALAXIES

Stars
The Solar System is a very small place indeed, when its size is compared to the distances which separate the stars. A ray of light takes five and a half hours to travel from Pluto to the Earth but from the nearest star, it takes more than four years. To appreciate the vast distances of space we can use models, and if we assume that the Sun is approximately the size of a football, then the nearest star would be 3,000 miles distant. Even with the largest telescopes, no star appears more than just a point of light. The use of miles or kilometres in the measurement of stars' distances is quite meaningless, so astronomers use the 'light year' which is the distance covered by a light ray in one year, or six million, million miles, the velocity or speed of light being 186,000 miles per second.

About 2,000 stars may be seen without optical aid on the clearest night, and are arranged into 88 groups or *constellations*. Some of these constellations are too far to the south to be observable in northern latitudes, while others neither rise or set (circumpolar stars). The stars which comprise the various constellations are not related to each other, but simply appear to lie in the same line of sight, because of their differing distances from the Earth. A Greek letter is assigned to each of the twenty-four brightest stars in every constellation, the brightest being alpha, then beta, gamma, delta, etc, while fainter stars have numbers; the brightest stars have names, many of which are Arabic. Some constellations (Orion, Leo, Auriga, Cygnus, Ursa Major), because they contain bright stars, are quite

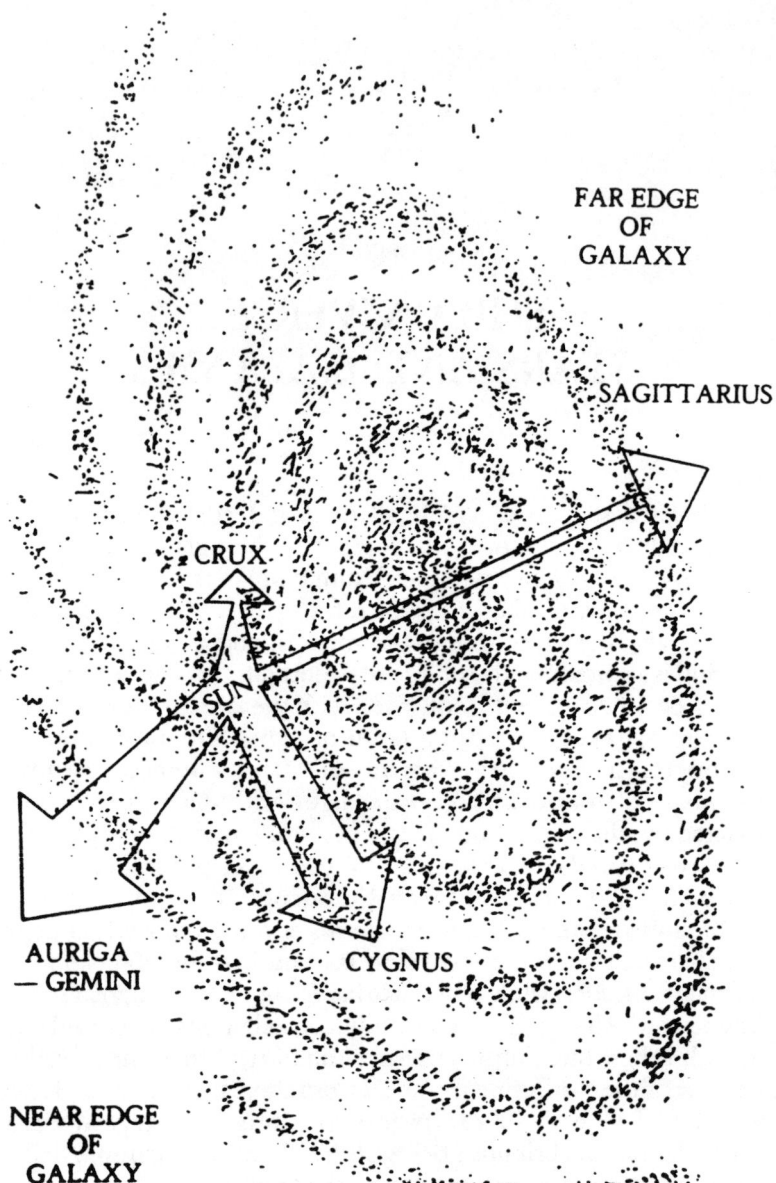

Figure 31. Our Galaxy

conspicuous while many others with only faint stars, are much more obscure.

Looking carefully at the night sky, one can see that the stars vary in colour from bluish-white, through white, yellow, orange and red. The bluish-white stars are the hottest and the red stars are the coolest; their surface temperatures vary from about 50,000 degrees Centigrade for the hottest stars down to about 2,000 degrees for the coolest ones. Our Sun is, of course, yellow in colour and has a surface temperature of 6,000 degrees Centigrade. The brightness of a star is called its *apparent magnitude,* of which there are six classes or groups, with the first magnitude stars (the brightest) being one hundred times brighter than sixth magnitude stars. The latter are the faintest ones visible without a telescope, but telescopes will show still fainter stars (of magnitude 7, 8, 9, and so on), and the world's most powerful instruments can photograph stars as faint as magnitude 24. As the stars become less bright, so their numbers rise dramatically, so that, although only twenty or so stars are of the first magnitude, there are about 500 fourth-magnitude and as many as one million 12th-magnitude stars. Two factors determine a star's apparent magnitude: (a) its distance and (b) its true brightness or luminosity in space, normally called its *absolute magnitude.* A star's absolute magnitude is the brightness it would appear to have were it at a standard distance of 32.6 light years. At this distance our Sun, normally so brilliant, would be reduced to a barely-visible 4th magnitude star, but on the other hand, Deneb in Cygnus (the Swan) would at the same distance be increased to an extremely brilliant star, brighter than Venus which is the brightest planet. Deneb is very far away from us, (1,600 light years), but even so, it shines as a bright 1st magnitude star in our sky because of its extreme luminosity (more than 10,000 times greater than the Sun). At the opposite extreme, some of the nearest stars are so feeble that they remain invisible without the use of a telescope. Since 1838, the distances of the stars have been measured by the method known as *trigonometrical parallax,* where the Earth's orbital motion around the Sun causes a slight apparent displacement (parallax) of a nearby star against the background of more distant stars; the more distant the star, the smaller its displacement.

No star has a parallax of greater than one second of arc, and for stars which are over 150 light years away, the parallax becomes too small to be measured and other methods of distance measurement must be used.

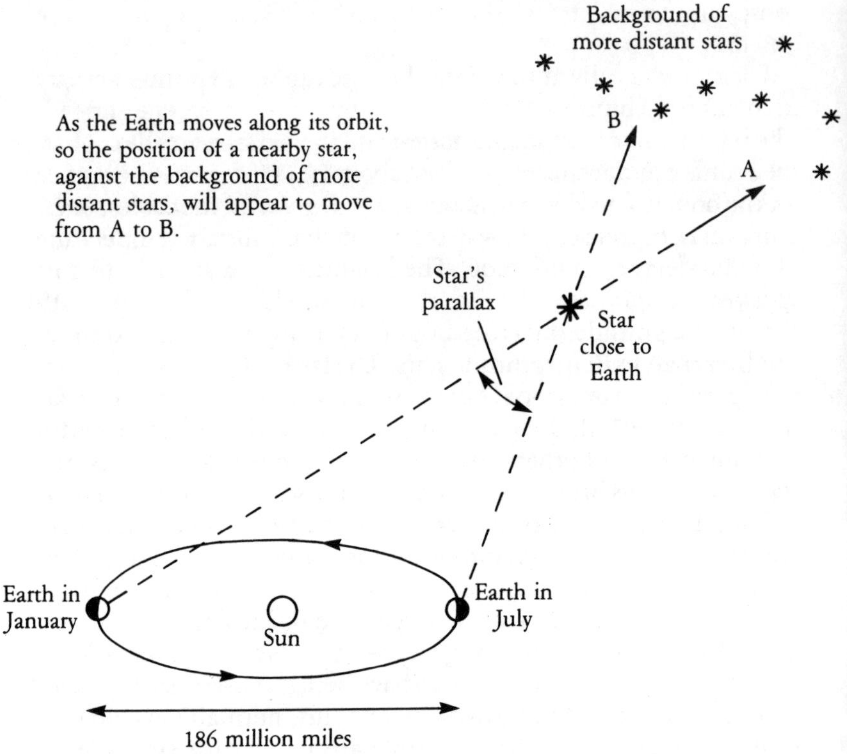

Background of
more distant stars
As the Earth moves along its orbit,
so the position of a nearby star,
against the background of more
distant stars, will appear to move
from A to B.
B
A
Star's
parallax
Star
close to
Earth
Earth in
January
Sun
Earth in
July
186 million miles

Stellar Motions

Star
B
Earth
A
C

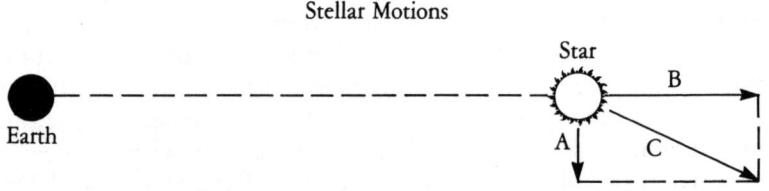

A = Star's proper motion or transverse motion across the celestial sphere.
B = Star's radial motion toward or away from the Earth.
C = Star's true motion through space.

Figure 32. Trigonometrical Parallax

THE UNIVERSE: STARS AND GALAXIES

Stars are not stationary in space. Their constant motion carries them at speeds often of many miles per second; our Sun, for instance, is moving steadily toward the constellation Hercules at twelve miles per second. But because of their tremendous distances, the constellations have not altered significantly for thousands of years. Stars also have different colours, and these indicate their surface temperatures in much the same way as a piece of metal which changes colour when held in a hot flame. Like the Sun, stars are intensely hot spheres of gas, burning hydrogen 'fuel' in their cores where pressures and temperatures are extremely high, and as this hydrogen changes into helium, energy is released. This energy is conveyed to the star's surface, where it pours out into space in the form of light, heat, radio-waves, X-rays and other forms of radiation. Stars of the same colour, however, tend to have similar proportions of the same chemical substances in addition to hydrogen and helium, which are common to all stars. The dark 'Fraunhofer Lines' in a star's spectrum indicate the presence of particular elements and compounds in that star, each star having its own unique spectrum; so that, for instance, two dark lines in the yellow region mean that sodium is present. Stars are grouped according to spectral type by a letter as W, O, B, (bluish), A (white), F (yellow-white), G (yellow), K (orange), M (red) and R, N, S (deeper red).

Early this century, the two astronomers *Ejnar Hertzsprung* and *Henry Russell* compiled a diagram named after them, which is a graph of stars' luminosities against their surface temperatures. This showed that many stars are confined to a narrow band (the Main Sequence), and as the diagram shows, the bluer stars tend to be more luminous, while the redder ones are much less so.

Dwarfs and sub-dwarfs make up the bulk of the stellar population, while giants are quite rare. The table below shows the enormous variations in the principal properties of stars.

Property	*Greatest (Sun = 1)*	*Least (Sun = 1)*
Diameter	1,500	1/1,000
Luminosity	1 million	1 millionth
Mass	70	1/20
Density	1 million	1/10 million
Surface temperature	100,000°C	2,000°C

Variation in mass between stars tends to be relatively small, because

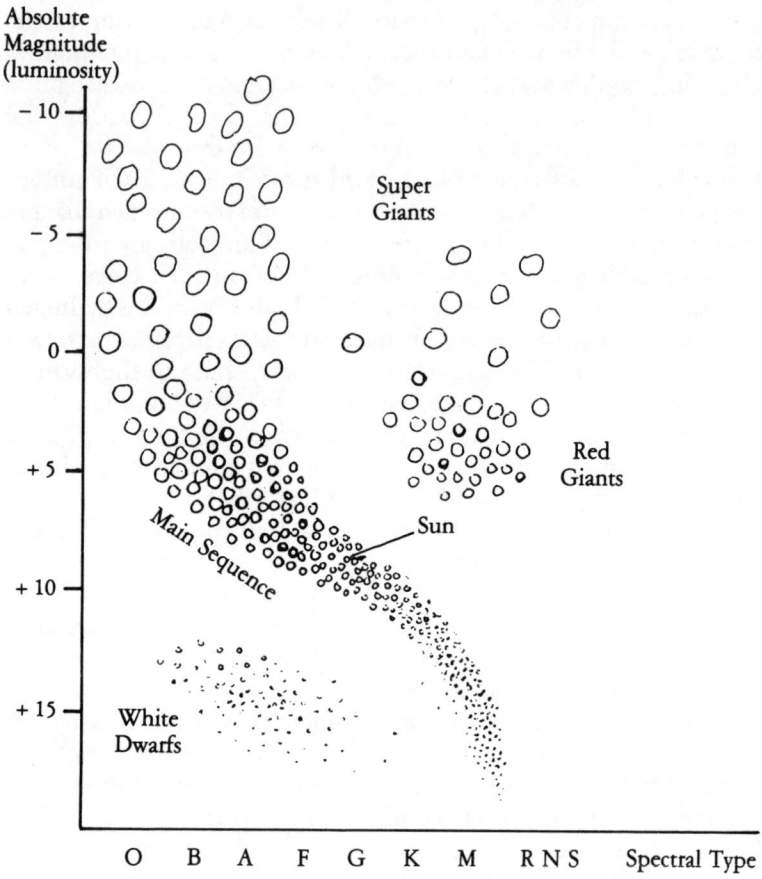

Figure 33. The Hertzsprung-Russell Diagram

the smaller stars are more dense than the larger ones. A cupful of White Dwarf material, for instance, can weigh hundreds of tons, while at the other extreme, some Red Giants and Supergiants are so enormous that they would envelop the Earth were they in the Sun's place.

All stars have condensed out of great clouds of interstellar gas *(nebulae),* and they become progressively hotter as they shrink until nuclear reactions can commence. The larger, more massive stars burn up their hydrogen at a far faster rate than do smaller, solar-type stars, and consequently, a blue or white supergiant may shine for only a few tens of millions of years while the Sun, which is a moderately small star, can be expected to last another 5,000 million years at least. As a star approaches its 'old age', it will be unable to convert any more hydrogen to helium and will swell into a Red Giant after which it will either collapse to become a very small White Dwarf, or (if it is a Giant already) is likely to experience a very violent explosion called *supernova*. Supernovae, which in recent centuries were seen in the years 1054, 1572, and 1604, are so brilliant that they can outshine an average star by no less than 1,000 million times. During their formation, gas is blown off into space which, together with its shock waves, enables new stars to be born out of the interstellar regions. All that remains apart from this is a tiny object called a *neutron star*, which is perhaps ten miles across, rapidly spinning and of an incredibly high density. Some of these neutron stars have magnetic fields, and each send out two very regular beams of radio waves. The star's rotation carries these beams round and round in a manner similar to light from a lighthouse. On Earth, these radio waves arrive in the form of very regular pulses — sometimes many times per second — which have given this type of star its name *pulsar*, of which several hundred have been discovered since 1967. White Dwarfs, pulsars and neutron stars continue to radiate feebly until their deaths.

If a really massive star collapses, it will never be able to stop collapsing and will simply disappear from space altogether. Any object, even light rays, which approach too closely to the disappeared star, called a *black hole*, will likewise vanish from space. Some stars exist in pairs, and many dozens of these double or binary stars can be seen in a small telescope. The stars revolve in orbits around each other, and one member of a binary system may be strikingly different in colour and brightness from its companion, while sometimes, there may be more than two associated stars, sometimes as many as six. Other types of stars, called *'variables'*, shine with an unsteady light. This variation may be caused either by two stars (eclipsing binaries) revolving around one another, with each periodically cutting off the other's light, or there may be changes going on inside the star which cause its energy output to fluctuate; the cycle of light variation can last anything between a few days and many years. Some stars (novae), flare up occasionally, sometimes in only a few days, but unlike supernovae, they do not explode completely.

Our Galaxy

Most stars are isolated from their neighbours by several light years or more, but some exist in *groups* or *clusters,* of which there are two main types. *Open clusters* contain between a few dozen and several thousand stars; our Sun is a member of such a group, and the bright stars Sirius, Procyon and Alpha Centauri are also members of the same group. *Closed clusters* are quite different, since they each contain an average of one million old stars densely packed together into the form of a globe, hence their name, *globular clusters.*

Between the stars, there are large clouds of dust and gas called *nebulae.* Nebulae come in several different forms. Some nebulae, such as the Great Nebula in Orion, contain hot ionized hydrogen, glowing against the dark background of space. This hydrogen, which has a temperature of 10,000°C, fluoresces or glows by absorbing radiation from very hot stars in the vicinity of the nebula, and then re-emitting it mainly in the form of light. Such nebulae are often of an orange colour, although other colours may be present. Other nebulae contain grains of dust which reflect light from nearby stars, and these 'reflection nebulae' are normally of a bluish colour. A third type of nebula (the dark type) consists of a mixture of dust grains and hydrogen gas, and not only are these clouds very cold (below − 200°C), but they are so dense that they block out light from stars behind them. Such nebulae may be seen in Orion (the 'Horsehead'), Centaurus (the 'Coal Sack') and many other parts of the sky. Planetary nebulae are thin shells of luminous gas surrounding stars which have thrown gas off in explosions. Nebulae tend to be rather faint objects, except when they are seen on photographs taken through large telescopes. On a clear moonless night, away from town lights, it is possible to see a faint milky white band crossing the whole sky and passing through the constellations of Canis Major, Monoceros, Gemini, Auriga, Cassiopeia, Cepheus, Lacerta, Cygnus, Vulpecula, Aquila, Scutum, Scorpio and Sagittarius. In more southern latitudes, it can be seen passing through the constellations Ara, Norma, Centaurus, Crux and Argo, which are too far south to rise in Britain. This band, which stretches right round the sky in a great circle, is called the *Milky Way* and is composed of millions of faint stars. The Milky Way forms part of a vast galaxy of stars, 100,000 million in number, which contains a central hub of mainly old stars, from which spiral arms extend outwards in a flat plane, the whole Galaxy being in the form of a disc. The dimensions of our Galaxy, in light years, are: diameter (edge to edge) 100,000; thickness of central hub, 20,000; thickness of each spiral arm, 3,000.

Our Sun is at a distance of 32,000 light years from the centre of the Galaxy, or about two-thirds of the distance from the centre to the edge. All stars in the Galaxy are whirling around and around the centre, but even though the Sun is travelling at over 100 miles per second in this way, it still takes about 250 million years to complete one orbit of the galactic centre. The Galaxy as a whole is slowly rotating with the spiral arms trailing.

The band of the Milky Way is irregular in width and brightness. It is at its widest and brightest, in the constellation of Sagittarius, because the centre of our Galaxy lies in this direction, and at its faintest and most narrow in the opposite part of the sky, near Orion, Gemini and Auriga, because we are here looking out into space through the least number of spiral arms. Surrounding our Galaxy are the globular clusters, several hundred in number, while the open clusters are concentrated in the spiral arms. Apart from stars, the spiral arms also contain most of the nebulae, and also considerable quantities of interstellar gas and dust spread thinly among the stars and obscuring the light from distant parts of the Galaxy.

Other Galaxies

During the 1840s, the astronomer Lord Rosse, using a 72-inch telescope, found that some nebulae had a spiral structure, and in the 1920s, it was confirmed that these objects are far outside our Milky Way System and are, in fact, independent galaxies. The nearest of these galaxies are the two Magellanic Clouds, which are too far south to be seen from British latitudes. Both of these Clouds are visible without optical aid, appearing like detached portions of the Milky Way. The Large and Small Magellanic Clouds are 25,000 and 10,000 light years across, and their distance from the Earth are respectively 170,000 and 200,000 light years.

In the constellation of Andromeda, which is visible on autumn and winter evenings, a faint smudge of light can be seen without a telescope, and in a small telescope, it appears oval-shaped. This object, called the Andromeda Nebula (M31)*, is one of the nearest galaxies to us, but even so, light takes over two million years to travel from this galaxy to the Earth and 150,000 years to cross the galaxy from edge to edge. Not far away, is another galaxy, M33, in the

---

* M31 = Messier 31 (number 31 in Charles Messier's catalogue of nebulae).

constellation of Triangulum. These two galaxies are similar to our own, with a spiral structure, and together with about two dozen other galaxies, form an association called the Local Group, which occupies a region of space about three million light years across.

Far beyond the Local Group and lying in the direction of the constellation Virgo and Coma Berenices, is a giant cluster of galaxies, with several thousand members occupying a region of space about 15 million light years across. The distance of this Virgo-Coma Cluster from Earth is approximately 50 million light years. In between, there are several isolated stellar systems, for instance the 'Whirlpool' Nebula (M51) in Canes Venatici and M81 in Ursa Major.

Galaxies come in several different forms, some being spiral, others elliptical or spherical, and a third type is irregular. Spiral galaxies have a central hub with spiral arms extending outward, and in some cases, the central hub is bar-shaped (barred spirals). The spiral arms may be tightly or more loosely wound around the hub. Spiral galaxies contain much gas and dust in the arms, while elliptical galaxies are relatively gas- and dust-free. Elliptical galaxies are more or less flattened in shape, while irregular galaxies (such as the Magellanic Clouds) have no internal structure.

Most galaxies exist in clusters which contain between a few to several thousand members and, although individual members of a cluster are separated by distances of only a few hundred thousand light years, the distances separating one cluster from its neighbours may be tens or even hundreds of millions of light years. Galaxies appear to us at different angles, some being visible face-on (in plan), others edge-on, and others at various angles in between (obliquely). Galactic distances are measurable to an accuracy of about 10-20 per cent.

Examples of groups of galaxies are:

Perseus Cluster	250 million light years distant
Centaurus Cluster	170 million light years distant
Coma Cluster	300 million light years distant
Cancer Cluster	200 million light years distant
Pisces Cluster	150 million light years distant
Pegasus Cluster	200 million light years distant
Hercules Cluster	400 million light years distant
Ursa Major Cluster	600 million light years distant

These are among the nearer groups. The more distant galaxies are so faint that they appear as no more than faint patches of light, even on photographs taken through powerful telescopes. The number of galactic groups is estimated to be many millions, while the number of galaxies in the Universe is probably thousands of millions.

In 1929, the astronomer Edwin Hubble discovered that the Universe is expanding, since nearly all galaxies appear to be receding from us, this velocity of recession depending directly upon the galaxies' distance in each case (Hubble's Law). In other words, the more distant from us a galaxy is, the faster it is receding from us, although this effect would be noticed from any other galaxy. The Universe is like the surface of a balloon which is being blown up, so that it is the space between the galaxies which is expanding. By looking further out into space, we can therefore see further back in time. It is not, however, possible to observe the Universe's beginning because of the 'absolute horizon', the distance (10,000 million light years) at which galaxies are appearing to us to be receding at the speed of light. Beyond this, no signals can reach the Earth.

Two theories have been advanced concerning the origin of the Universe. One of these — the 'Steady State' theory — maintains that the Universe has had no beginning and will have no end in time, and that material is being continuously created in the spaces left by the receding galaxies. This theory was generally abandoned by 1965, and the other one — the 'Big Bang' — is now generally accepted. The Big Bang Theory, developed in the late 1940s, states that all the material in the Universe — the stars, galaxies, etc. — were at one time compressed into a relatively small space which exploded with tremendous force about 15,000 million years ago and, as the space of the Universe expanded, this material gradually formed into atoms and then into galaxies and stars.

A proportion of galaxies are said to be 'active', and these include the types known as compact galaxies, N-galaxies, Seyfert galaxies and Markarian galaxies.

In 1963, another type of unusual galaxy was discovered, called a quasar (quasi-stellar object), which look like faint blue stars, but in fact are powerful emitters of radio waves. The most distant optical galaxies are about 5,000 million light years from the Earth, but many quasars are much further away than this. Each quasar radiates 100 times as much energy as comes from an entire galaxy. Quasars are likely to be entire galaxies which are falling into black holes.

The Universe may either continue to expand for ever, or, if sufficient material is contained in it, the gravitational force from the material may be sufficient to halt this expansion. In this case, the Universe will contract to a compact mass once more, and may undergo a subsequent Big Bang.

The Constellations of the Zodiac

The twelve constellations of the Zodiac have, from the earliest times, received great attention because it is within the Zodiac belt that the Sun, Moon and planets are always found.

The grouping of stars into constellations had not only a mythological importance, but also a practical significance. To the early 'watchers of the heavens', the same constellations returning year after year at the same time indicated the seasons of the year and could be seen as a gigantic cosmic clock and calendar.

From their observations of these zodiacal constellations, the ancient astronomers could track the yearly progress of the Sun and planets and, in the course of time, divide the Zodiac into twelve signs. Not only was the twelvefold division important, but also the four principal points along the Ecliptic which the Sun reaches during the course of its annual journey. These four points, the Spring and Autumn Equinox and the Summer and Winter Solstice, could be related to the zodiacal belt and the constellations visible at those times.

It therefore seems reasonable to assume that the stars bordering the Ecliptic were the first to be studied and grouped together and that, with a few exceptions, they were considered to be of paramount importance.

Aries (The Ram) Culminates at 10 p.m. in early December.

The brightest star is called Hamal and is of 2nd magnitude and orange in colour. Only a few other stars are visible in this constellation which is small (about 10° by 15°). One of these (Gamma) was the first double star to be discovered as such by Robert Hooke, using a telescope, in 1664. In ancient times, the Sun entered this constellation at the vernal equinox, hence the name 'First Point of Aries'. Mythologically, Aries is associated with the search by the Argonauts for the Golden Fleece.

THE UNIVERSE: STARS AND GALAXIES

Taurus (The Bull) Culminates at 10 p.m. in early January.

During the times of the early civilizations, about 5,000 years ago, the Sun entered this constellation at the vernal equinox. Mythologically, Taurus is associated with Zeus, who assumed the form of a bull in order to carry off the princess Europa. Taurus is a large constellation, extending over an area 35° by 25°, and contains one first-magnitude star, Aldebaran, an orange-red giant about 64 light years distant. There are two star clusters, the Hyades, which form a V-shaped group about 130 light years distant, and the Pleiades, a compact group of several hundred stars at a distance of about 500 light years.

Gemini (The Twins) Culminates at 10 p.m. in early February.

Mythologically, Gemini are twin brothers and were also sons of Jupiter. There are two stars in this constellation, which are both 1st magnitude and separated by only 5°, called Pollux (orange in colour and 35 light years away) and Castor (white, slightly fainter and 45 light years away). Gemini is a large, fairly bright constellation, extending over an area 30° × 20°. There are many double stars here, and Castor is made up of no less than six stars, revolving in complex orbits. The Milky Way flows through this constellation, and in the same region, is the star cluster known as M35, which may be seen in binoculars or a telescope. Sir William Herschel discovered the planet Uranus in 1781 when it was in Gemini.

Cancer (The Crab) Culminates at 10 p.m. in early March.

Mythologically, Cancer is associated with the two Aselli (donkeys), named after two stars in this group, and the association with a crab began with the Chaldeans, who saw that the Sun entered this constellation at the time of the summer solstice, and thereafter reversed its northward movement, appearing to go backward like a crab. Cancer is a small, insignificant constellation covering an area of about 15° × 20°, and containing no stars brighter than fourth magnitude. There is a star cluster here, called Praesepe (The Manger), and designated M44, containing about 400 stars visible in binoculars or a small telescope.

Leo (The Lion) Culminates at 10 p.m. in early April.

About 5,000 years ago, the Sun entered this constellation at the time of the summer solstice. The Chaldeans associated the heat and power of the summer sun with the powerful lion ('king of the beasts'), and Leo is also associated by the Greeks with the lion that Hercules had to slay as one of his twelve tasks. Leo is a large, conspicuous constellation, covering an area of about 35° × 25°. It is one of the few constellations that actually bears a close resemblance to its description, that is, it looks like a lion, particularly when high up in the south. The brightest star is called Regulus, which is a white star of first magnitude and 84 light years distant. There are several double stars and a few distant galaxies (M65, 66, 95 and 96) in this constellation.

VIRGO (The Virgin) Culminates at 10 p.m. in early May.

Mythologically, Virgo represents the goddess of justice and also of the earth. About 5,000 years ago, the Sun was positioned in this part of the sky in late summer when the crops were ripening, and the brightest star is called Spica which means 'ear of corn'. Spica is a first magnitude white giant star at 220 light years' distance from the Earth. Virgo is a large constellation, covering an area about 45° × 25°, but it is not particularly bright, consisting principally of third and fourth magnitude stars. In this region of the sky, a large cluster of distant galaxies — several thousand in number and at about 50 million light years from the Earth — can be found, a few of which are visible in a small telescope.

LIBRA (The Balance) Culminates at 10 p.m. in early June.

Libra was once part of the succeeding constellation Scorpio, representing its claws, but was later defined as a separate constellation, representing a balance, by the Romans in honour of Julius Caesar. Libra is a rather small constellation, covering about 20° × 20°. The brightest star, Zubenelgenubi, is of second magnitude, white in colour and 70 light years distant. The second brightest star, Zubeneschamali, is one of the very few stars which have a green colour.

SCORPIO (The Scorpion) Culminates at 10 p.m. in early July.

Ancient Greeks associated Scorpio with the scorpion which stung Orion, the Hunter, and killed him. These two constellations are never seen in the sky at the same time; when one sets, the other one rises and vice versa. The stars in this group actually bear a resemblance to a scorpion, with a long, curving tail, although being one of the southernmost of the zodiacal constellations, only the northern half of Scorpio is visible from British latitudes. It is a large group, covering an area about 25° × 30°, and the brightest star, Antares ('Rival of Mars') is a first magnitude Red Giant, about 370 light years distant. There are a few double stars and some star clusters and nebulae visible, and the Milky Way runs through most of this constellation.

SAGITTARIUS (The Archer) Culminates at 10 p.m. in early August.

Mythologically, Sagittarius was associated with the centaur Chiron, an animal that was half man, half horse, shooting with a bow and arrow. Sagittarius is a large sized constellation, extending over 30° × 20°. It consists mainly of second and third magnitude stars, although its southern declination means that it is difficult to see from Britain. The brightest star, called Kaus Australis, is a second magnitude White sub-giant at a distance of 136 light years. In this constellation lies the centre of the Milky Way Galaxy, which is at its brightest and widest here. There are many nebulae and star clusters (such as the 'Omega', 'Trifid' and 'Lagoon' nebulae), some of which are visible in a small telescope.

CAPRICORN (The Goat) Culminates at 10 p.m. in early September.

About 3,000 years ago, the Sun was in this constellation at the time of the winter solstice and had reached its southernmost point in the sky for the year. Mythologically, Capricorn was associated by the Ancient Greeks with the god of nature, Pan, who was half man and half goat. The constellation is situated on the western edge of a region of the sky called 'The Sea', which contains constellations representing various sea creatures. Capricorn extends over an area 25° × 15°, and is not particularly noticeable owing to its southern declination and lack of bright stars. The brightest star (Gaedi) is a second magnitude pair of yellow Giants (visible as double without a telescope) at a distance of 116 and 1,100 light years respectively. The other stars in the constellation are of third magnitude or fainter.

AQUARIUS (The Water Carrier) Culminates at 10 p.m. in early October.

Mythologically, Aquarius was associated by the Ancient Egyptians with water, because their rainy season occurred at the same time as when the Sun was in this constellation. Aquarius is a large constellation, extending over an area about 45° × 25°, although it does not stand out, because none of its stars are brighter than third magnitude. The brightest star 'Sadalmelik' is a yellow supergiant at a distance of 1,350 light years from the Earth, appearing as a third magnitude star to us. There are also a few star clusters and nebulae.

PISCES (The Fishes) Culminates at 10 p.m. in early November.

When the Sun was in this part of the sky, fish were abundant, and most civilizations have associated the constellation with two fishes connected by a ribbon. Pisces is a large constellation, extending over 45° × 20°, but consists of only faint, mainly fourth and fifth magnitude stars, so it is quite inconspicuous. The second brightest star, Alrischa, is a fourth magnitude double star consisting of a pair of white giants, 130 light years from the Earth. There is a faint spiral galaxy, called M74, in this constellation.

11.
COSMIC CYCLES AND MUNDANE EVENTS

The Copernican revolution, which laid the foundation for the development of modern astronomy, also contributed to the schism between astrology and astronomy. The questing spirit of the Renaissance and the scientific revolution which followed, called into question the credibility of astrological tenets. As astronomy and science in general advanced with each new discovery, astrology failed to retain its former position, principally because (in the opinion of its critics), it was incapable of logical explanations of how and why it worked.

During the last few decades, there has been a reappraisal of astrology and its relationship with science, leading to the development of an astrology which is seen to embrace all forms of cyclic activity common to man and his environment. Disciplined minds, uncluttered with preconceived notions concerning what astrology is or is not, are subjecting its claims to critical examination and analysis and producing evidence that many traditional astrological laws are valid, but also that many others cannot be substantiated. This is all to the good, not only for astrology, but also for science. We do not want an astrology that is mechanistic, but we do need an astrology that can benefit from the use of scientific methods and from the findings of science.

Our responses, including those of all living organisms and even the Earth itself, correlate with cosmic cycles and configurations. Human behaviour is complex, but this complexity appears to be related to the cosmic patterns existing at birth and with other patterns formed subsequently during life. The Earth reacts violently during certain periods of particular celestial alignments. A study of earthquakes, mine disasters and the like demonstrates that there is some cosmic 'triggering' effect which activates occurrences at a definite time and locality. We do not know about all the various forces operating in the Universe and to which we are responsive. Our knowledge of the stars, galaxies, Solar System and space is minute and fragmentary. The Space Age is less than thirty years old, and since its inauguration, the accumulation of scientific data derived from space missions, probes and the like, show how little we still know about the Cosmos and about ourselves. What we have learned from our efforts to push back the frontiers of space, is that there is a remarkable inter-relationship existing between man and the various cosmic forces. Life and our responses to it are governed not only by the motions and alignments of the Sun, Earth and celestial bodies, but also by the numerous physical forces and energies emanating from outer space.

The Solar Connection
The Sun is an unquiet body. Its turbulence is reflected in its periodic outbursts of solar energy in the form of solar flares and 'surge prominences' during which time there is an increase in X-ray intensity, the output of ultra-violet light and light. Periodically, spots appear on the surface of the Sun, and these sun-spots, as seen from the Earth, are dark patches (umbra) on the solar disc and are connected with solar flare activity. The sun-spot cycle is irregular, and although it now has an average cycle of 11.1 years, individual cycles have varied between 7 to 17 years. In the seventeenth century (1645-1715) for some curious reason, the spots were nearly absent. Chinese records, dating back prior to the Christian Era, show that sunspots were observed, but it is only in comparatively modern times that any systematic investigation of them has been made.

During the 1950s and 1960s, the work of an American radio engineer, J. H. Nelson, attracted considerable attention when he announced that radio reception was affected by planetary aspects. Nelson's theory that planetary aspects are a major factor in causing radio disturbance has recently been challenged (see *Correlation*, December 1981). Nevertheless, sunspot cycles do appear to be related to the synodic periods of the planets, (see *Astrological Journal*, Spring 1971). It has been stated that the variations in sunspot cycles can be correlated with terrestrial phenomena such as weather, epidemics, growing seasons, mortality rates, stock exchange prices and even voting trends in nineteenth century Britain. Whether solar activity operates as a single factor is uncertain. Doubtless, there is a relationship between solar cycles, when they are linked with other factors, and man and his environment. Whatever the reasons for, or causes of solar activity, sunspots and the like are an interesting field for astronomical/astrological research. It is not only solar activity which provides evidence for some form of cosmic connection, but also the Earth/Moon relationship.

The Lunar Connection
From time immemorial, the Moon has been associated with growth and fertility. Experiments carried out by scientists in recent years, have shown conclusively that behaviour patterns are controlled by various cosmic clocks, one of the most important being the Moon and her phases. Moonlight, taken as a single factor, cannot account for the variety of phenomena that has been observed, for much of the phenomena shows a periodicity related to the phases of the Moon.

All living organisms appear to be attuned to an 'inner clock' and to respond to the various celestial alignments. Marine creatures show a remarkable affinity with the Moon and her phases, as shown, for example, by a species of Pacific worm which has an annual swarming date corresponding with one particular new moon every year. When Professor Brown of North Western University transported oysters to his laboratory a thousand miles from the sea, he discovered that they retained the natural rhythms of their 'home waters'. However, after about two weeks, they adjusted to the time at which the tide would have occurred at their new locality (Evanston) if it had been a town on the coast. The passage of the Moon over the meridian of Evanston had, in effect, influenced a new rhythm.

It has always been a well-founded belief that plant life is governed by the lunar phases. Recent studies suggest that plant metabolism can be linked to the 29.5 day lunar phase cycle, and that crop yields have a relationship with the Moon's 27.3 day Sidereal cycle (see *Correlation*, June 1981). The proverbial 'green fingers' possessed by some people may be related to some form of magnetism — perhaps there is some mutual interaction between certain persons and plants which, during significant periods and under appropriate conditions, produces the maximum response. Many aphorisms to be found in almanacs concerning lunar planting are traditional, but they may have some basis of fact. However, any research concerning the lunar influence on sowing and planting has to be done under controlled conditions and be capable of replication. It is an area of research where even the modest amateur can experiment, provided he observes simple conditions and keeps accurate records.

Sex and Fertility

Many of the 'old wives' tales' concerning mentality, conception and birth, may after all have some foundation in fact. Investigations and research carried out during this century have indicated that significant biological rhythms related to sex, fertility and birth can be associated with the Moon and her phases. An investigation of 3,300 births in Japan in the 1930s showed that there was a frequency for the births to occur at full or new moon; the least frequency occurred one or two days before the first and last quarters of the Moon. The study of 10,000 cases of menstruation over a period of four years also indicated a maximum at full and new moon. Donald Bradley (Garth Allen) described in the February 1971 issue of *American Astrology*, an investigation by him into the natal Moon position of 1200 fathers who had families of one sex only. The results are interesting. He found that for fathers with sons, the Moon pattern peaks in the first half of the fixed sign (tropical), that is Taurus, Leo, Scorpio and Aquarius, while the pattern for those fathers with daughters, was concentrated in the mutable signs (Gemini, Virgo, Sagittarius and Pisces). Details concerning this 'boy-fathers, girl-fathers according to the Moon's position' was reproduced in the *Astrological Journal*, Summer 1971. Whether such a comparatively small sample has value, only further research using well-attested data and larger numbers will confirm. However, it does appear that this kind of investigation, properly conducted, has great possibilities for determining the relationship between the Moon and sex.

During the last decade or so, Dr E. Jonas, a Czech psychiatrist, observed that many of his female patients showed cycles of increased vitality and sexuality independently of their menstrual cycles. From his researches, he drew three conclusions:

1. That the ability of a mature woman to conceive tends to occur under exactly that phase of the Moon (Sun-Moon relationship) which existed at her birthtime.

2. The sex of the child depends on whether, at this time, the Moon is in a positive or negative sign of the zodiac.
3. The viability of the embryo is influenced by the position of the celestial bodies at the time of conception.

Jonas' work attracted attention in Europe, but his theories do not appear to have commanded the increased amount of attention and interest that one would have expected. Independent research by other investigators may vindicate Jonas' theories.

The association between human reproduction, parturition and lunar phenomena has its origins deep in the past. For centuries, it has been known that the Moon causes the 'fluids to rise and seek release'; there is, without doubt, a firm link between the Moon acting in concert with other factors, and human somatic and physiological functions. If, as Jonas' theories suggest, there is a limited fertility period each month, then not only do we have a natural birth control system, but also the means of studying sterility.

Natural Disasters

The astrology of disasters, despite its morbidity, is a rich field for the investigative astrologer. Not only are the data reliable as to time and place and can be cross-checked from various sources, but disasters of a similar nature can be studied to see whether they exhibit common factors or patterns. The practice, adopted by some astrologers, of adding up the number of times a certain planet is in a particular sign or house, is of course, useless. Sometimes, the 'event chart' is not as significant as one would like, but when it is related to other charts such as Ingress, Solar and Lunar returns, or eclipses, the time and date of the event 'lock in' with remarkable precision. However, in all studies such as these, the astronomical factors need to be considered. Ecliptical positions taken in isolation without reference to latitude or declination will only give 'half a story or no story at all'. Likewise, the closeness (perigee) or farthest distance (apogee) of the Moon is important. For those readers interested in this kind of study, several cases are listed under 'Data references'.

During the first quarter of this century, half a million people were killed by five major earthquakes — San Francisco (1906), Messina (1908), Arrezanno (1915), Kansu (1920) and Tokyo (1923). In the next twenty-five years, an average of 14,000 died in this way annually. The peak years were 1927, 1932 and 1939.

A study of earthquakes by the geophysicist Dr R. Tomaschek, the results of which were announced in 1959, indicated that planetary positions did seem to be linked to earthquake activity. Although the sample used in this investigation (134 cases) was small, his findings showed that the position of Uranus close to the meridian was the same far more frequently than it would have been by chance. As Tomaschek stated 'An unbiased approach to these problems, of which the correlations of Uranus are only a part and a first step, may help humanity.' Earthquakes are, of course, an ideal subject for study because the data are so precise. There is little doubt that this 'trembling Earth' is affected by celestial alignments. Again, as in all forms of research of this nature, the compiling of vast amounts of data and then merely analysing signs, planets and houses, is meaningless. Each case has to be studied individually in conjunction with all other types of astronomical phenomena which may be present at the time. The study of weather and climatic cycles with their attendant effects, sometimes disastrous, offer great scope for the enterprising researcher. We could, for example, consider whether the hottest days during this century had any similar astronomical or astrological significance, or whether the days of extreme cold had Saturn prominently configurated in some way. We could ask ourselves 'does the hour-angle of the Moon at a definite locality correlate at certain times with the amount of rainfall which occurs?'. Astrologers need to study subjects such as weather, not only from the hard statistical approach, but to see if, and in what manner, the astrological findings can be related to human psychological responses. It may be that weather, crime and suicide statistics have some common factor, either singly or collectively, which is not apparent until they are related to one another and to the various celestial positions. A critical approach is required in all things astrological; we need to cultivate the questing spirit and not to accept everything uttered in the name of astrology, no matter from which quarter or from whom it may have originated. If in the course of our investigations, we discover that some of the cherished opinions, so dearly held by astrologers, cannot be substantiated, we have no alternative but to reject them and adopt a more realistic attitude, thereby relating astrology to real life. It could be said that astrology concerns life and all its processes in relation to the cosmic patterns. The ability to perceive the substance from the shadow is essential, otherwise astrology will still be 'knocking on the doors of the Universities' three centuries hence.

Planetary Cycles

The cycles of the major planets, Jupiter, Saturn, Uranus, Neptune and Pluto are significant and are cycles to which all respond in a greater or lesser degree. During the course of an average lifetime, Jupiter and Saturn will periodically return to their natal positions; Jupiter about every 12 years; Saturn about every 29 years. Uranus completes its cycle in about 84 years, while Neptune (165 years) and Pluto (248 years) move slowly in completing their cycles.

As with all cyclic phenomena, the indications of these cycles have to be related to other factors which may be prominent at the time in question. Traditionally, these cycles are considered to have peaks and troughs, that is, when the planet is in conjunction or opposition to its natal position.

It would appear that there may be some evidence for this when the cycle is studied in relation to the natal chart. The age of 28 years or thereabouts is often significant and coincides with the acceptance of responsibility, a more structured existence within a well-established framework. It is at this age that Saturn and the Moon complete their first cycle and return to their natal positions. This cycle repeats around the age of 56 years, and this period is important either as a time of consolidation or of segregation; its effect, as with all cycles, being accentuated or modified according to other factors. At the age of 84 or so, the third return occurs and, if one survives beyond this time, the combination of the Uranus cycle often instils a new lease of life. The cycle of Jupiter, which is about twelve years on average, coincides with opportunities for development. The essence of Jupiter is that of opportunity and progress which can result from a variety of causes, not all of which are necessarily related to acquisition and materialism. Often, there is a child-like expectation of hoping something extraordinary will happen; an excited anticipation that one is about to gain 'one's heart's desires'. Micawber-like, we expect something to turn up, and it generally does. The opposition of Saturn or Jupiter to their natal position, often coincide with negative responses and lack of motivation. With Saturn, there is a feeling of separation and alienation; all the reactions are geared toward retreat and withdrawal either physically or psychologically. Jupiter tends towards excesses and inflationary conditions. There is an 'eat, drink and be merry' attitude, often indulged in to compensate for the lack of expansion experienced at this time.

It is not only the conjunctions and oppositions which are important in these cycles, but also how the planets, in their progress through the twelve houses, contact the natal positions including the Ascendant and Midheaven. On average, Jupiter will spend a year in each sign and Saturn will take about two and a half years to move through each sign. In their progress through signs and houses, planets will form aspects with all the natal positions. It is these aspects, in combination with other astrological techniques, such as the current progressions, returns and so forth, which show the pattern operating at any given time. The same principles apply with the slower-moving planets: Uranus, Neptune and Pluto. The significance of Uranus lies in its relationship with self-discovery and the abandonment of conservative structures. Often, this is accomplished by violent changes which irretrievably alter the status quo. Divorce, separation and a craving for the new and unusual are typical manifestations of its action. Neptune, on the other hand, indicates the surreptitious surrendering of self or others for some indefinable ideal, cause or situation. There is a falsity with Neptune that defies description. It remains in a sign and house for many years and, when in major aspect, it can indicate 'out-of-this-world sensations and events' or a sense of idealistic atonement for past sins, real or imaginary. Renunciation and escape characterize its action, but more often than not, that which we seek to avoid overtakes us, and we become more confined than ever.

Pluto, with the longest cycle of all, will spend a considerable number of years in a sign and house, but its contacts, however few, will leave no doubt as to its action. In its most drastic form, it heralds death and transition, not necessarily physical death, (although this is sometimes attended by Plutonian contacts). Its action is direct, often violent and destructive and results from an accumulation of tensions which, over a long period of time, have been held in check, but which eventually erupt with startling action and seek release. Thus, its action is like a cleansing agent, whereby that which was repressed is brought to the light of day for examination and analysis. Pluto is remarkable for its singleness of purpose; it is the natural 'loner' and, although naturally secretive, it is paradoxical in that it rends aside the veil of secrecy to reveal the true nature of persons and conditions.

The aspects and contacts of this planet show the periods during life when we are compelled to face reality and to consciously accept those things which we would rather conceal or forget. It forces us to question our motives and actions. Like some magic mirror, Pluto reflects our image nakedly and unashamedly, revealing our true self. This revelation can result in a descent to the depths with all its attendant torments, or it can be a prelude to soaring (like the mythical phoenix) to the heights of heaven. As the planet of finality — nothing is ever the same after it has been subjected to Plutonian action — it coincides with commencements and closures: birth and death, either actual or symbolic.

Through studying the different planetary cycles, we can, by combining their various periods, arrive at a life-cycle and note the years when the peaks and troughs occur. In considering the various cycles, either singly or collectively, we can in broad terms determine the periods of life when we can expect to experience the maximum or minimum effects of a particular cycle(s).

In the same way as all living organisms respond to cyclic phenomena, so also does society and the world at large. The important thing with mundane astrology is that it cannot be studied in isolation. Charles Carter used the term 'the law of subsumption', and by this he meant that every chart is subsumed under other charts of greater and greater amplitude. (see *Astrology* Vol. 19, No. 3, 1945).

The charts of persons prominent in government can be related to the national chart of the country; marriage charts reflect the fortunes of the marriage and those of the family. Charts of organizations, businesses, one's home (to take just a few examples), can be related to the individuals concerned, and indeed progressed to show current trends. With planetary cycles, the greater affects the lesser (individuals) through collective action.

Major disasters, either natural or man-made, which result in the death of countless numbers, would no doubt correlate with the charts not only for the time of the event, but also with the victim's natal and progressed charts.

The obliteration of Hiroshima by an atom bomb — 8.16 a.m. J.S.T., 6.8.1945 (see 'Data References') — has Uranus on the upper meridian, but this position is only one factor of many. To arrive at a true assessment as to why this place was devastated and at that time, we need to compare the charts of the victims, the foundation chart for Hiroshima, the Japanese national chart, perhaps even the chart for the pilot of the plane and the American national chart. The chances are, that we would find links between all of them indicating the magnitude of the event that occurred. The doctrine of 'synchronicity' (a term which has crept into the astrologer's vocabulary) does not satisfy all the criteria concerning the operation of astrological laws.

The spirit of the times can be correlated with mundane cycles, even though several cycles may be inter-linked and operating at the same time. The discovery of Uranus (1781), Neptune (1846), and Pluto (1930) all mark periods of radical changes. The late eighteenth century was notable for the technological advances and for the revolutionary actions concerning man and his rights. The nineteenth century saw the birth of socialistic ideals and, although many of the horrors associated with Victorian England and elsewhere, persisted into the next century, the social conscience was awakened and efforts made towards establishing a more equable society. The early twentieth century had Neptune and Uranus forming a opposition from Cancer/Capricorn and this configuration, which was common to all born in the early years of this century, was expressed in one way through the conditions of the Second World War. Compulsion and regimentation on a colossal scale are the hall marks of Pluto, and with its discovery, dictatorships with all their attendant barbarisms came to power. The capability for unparalleled destruction was achieved with the invention and use of the atomic bomb, and as befits Pluto and its lower manifestations, nothing has been the same since.

Eclipses

From the earliest times, eclipses of the Sun and Moon have always received considerable attention. Like the appearance of comets, they were regarded with some trepidation and the indicators of the shape of things to come. Nevertheless, the Chaldeans were able to predict not only the time of eclipses, but also to formulate rules for judging their probable effects. As with so many aspects of astronomical phenomena, eclipses and their significance attracted a mythology and a host of aphorisms, many of which need to be critically examined. However, despite the illogical approach often noted concerning eclipses and their effect, there does appear to be some foundation for considering the astrological significance of eclipse phenomena.

The combined action of the Sun and Moon studied in conjunction with the planetary positions at the time of an eclipse, indicate the importance or otherwise of a particular eclipse. Not only does the eclipse chart need to be studied overall, but it has to be related to other charts, either personal or mundane, before a true appreciation of its significance can be obtained. The effects of eclipses appear to manifest when the Sun, Moon or a planet in their motion through the zodiac contact the eclipse degree. It would seem that the eclipse chart remains dormant until it is 'galvanized into life' by a body aspecting the critical degree of the eclipse.

The traditional teaching that the effect of an eclipse will last as many years/months as the obscuration lasted in hours/minutes, requires investigation. A more logical explanation would seem to be that the effects of an eclipse last until the commencement of the next eclipse. This, however, is a matter that requires detailed research.

Solar eclipses, of which there must be two at least each year, are probably more important than lunar eclipses. This again needs confirmation by research, for it may be that the Moon's effects are less obvious and operate in a more subtle manner. The Moon is an important body both astronomically and astrologically, and therefore its effects in relation to eclipses operate, but are governed by various other factors such as its distance from the Earth, its latitude and declination.

The Solar eclipse prior to the dropping of the atomic bomb on Hiroshima occurred on the 9 July, 1945 in 16° Cancer, and on the day of the event (6 August), the Moon was conjunct the eclipse point (16° Cancer) close to Saturn and having reached its maximum declination on the previous day. The Moon will, of course, pass over an eclipse point each month, which means that other factors need to be considered before judging the effects of eclipses.

Regarding personal charts, it is highly probable that an eclipse falling on a sensitive or critical point in the chart may, when excited by a transiting planet, indicate conditions or events according to the nature of the contacts. When the laws concerning transits, eclipses and the various other astronomical phenomena are properly understood, we may find that we have valuable predictive tools. Whether we benefit from this knowledge, will depend on how we use it.

GLOSSARY

Altitude: The elevation of a heavenly body above the horizon. A co-ordinate of the horizon system that measures a body's angular distance from the horizon from 0-90°.

Aphelion: The point in a planet's orbit where a planet is at its greatest distance from the Sun.

Apogee: The point in the orbit where the Moon or a planet is at its greatest distance from the Earth.

Apparent Noon: The moment when the Sun crosses the meridian.

Arctic: The polar area north of latitude 66° 33' north.

Ascendant: The eastern angle; the sign and degree of the Zodiac which is rising on the eastern horizon at the time and place of birth.

Aspect: The positions of two or more planets with respect to one another. The distance measured in Celestial Longitude that the planets are apart. The conjunction, opposition, square and trine are the major aspects.

Asteroid: Minor planet, normally found in orbits between those of Mars and Jupiter.

Astronomical Co-ordinates: Values in a reference system used to define a position of a body on the Celestial Sphere. The three principal systems are: 1. Horizon System; 2. Equatorial System; 3. Ecliptic System.

Atoms: Particles of which most matter is made up.

Aurora: Luminosity visible in the night sky mainly from polar latitudes.

Autumnal Equinox: The September Equinox: The First Point of

Libra: One of the points of intersection between the Celestial Equator and the Ecliptic that the Sun reaches when crossing from north to south on or about 23 September.

Binary Star: Double star, where the two component stars are revolving around each other.

Celestial Equator: A great circle on the Celestial Sphere mid-way between the Celestial Poles.

Celestial Mechanics: Laws governing the positions and motions of celestial bodies through space.

Celestial Meridian: The great circle on the Celestial Sphere which passes through the poles, zenith and nadir, and the north and south points of the horizon. The observer's meridian of longitude projected onto the Celestial Sphere.

Celestial Poles: The points on the sky which are directly overhead at the terrestrial poles. The Earth's rotational axis extended into space.

Celestial Sphere: The apparent sphere, with the Earth at the centre, on which the celestial bodies appear to be projected.

Centrifugal Force: The force experienced by a planet or a satellite, in orbit around a larger body, which tries to push it away from the object around which it is travelling.

Cepheid: Variable star whose period varies directly with its luminosity.

Chromosphere: Region of the Sun's surface lying directly above the photosphere.

Circumpolar Stars: Stars which are always seen above the horizon.

Civil Day: The 24 hour Mean Solar Day.

Coma: The head of a comet, consisting of rarefied gas.

Conjunction: When two bodies are within 8° of each other, as measured in Celestial Longitude.

Constellations: Star groupings. Those close to the Ecliptic have the same names as the signs of the Zodiac, but are in no way connected with the signs.

Culmination: The meridian passage of a celestial body.

Cusp: The point of division between either signs, or houses.

Day: The period of time equal to one rotation of the Earth. It can be measured as a Sidereal Day, a Solar Day or a Mean Solar Day.

Declination: The measurement of the angular distance of a body from the Celestial Equator.

Density: The quantity of matter contained in a unit volume, or the mass of a body divided by its volume.

GLOSSARY

Descendant: The point opposite the Ascendant; the sign and degree setting on the western horizon at the time and place of birth.

Direct Motion: The normal apparent motion of a planet around the Sun, as seen from the Earth. This motion is eastward, in distinction to retrograde motion which is westward.

Diurnal Arc: The measurement in degrees of a planet from its rising to its setting.

Diurnal Circle: The apparent path of a celestial body across the sky during daylight hours.

Diurnal Motion: The apparent motion of celestial bodies across the sky from east to west.

Double Star: Pair of stars close together in the sky, either in the same line of sight, or physically associated.

Dwarf Star: Small, relatively dim star.

Eccentricity: Measurement of the degree of flattening of an ellipse, varying between zero for a circle to one for a straight line.

Eclipse: The total or partial obscuration when one body is concealed by another or its shadow.

Ecliptic: The great circle on the Celestial Sphere which is the Sun's apparent path.

Ecliptic System: Co-ordinate system, the fundamental plane of which is the plane of the Ecliptic.

Electromagnetic Radiation: Energy in wave form, which comes in several different types e.g. gamma-rays, X-rays, ultra-violet light, visible light, infra-red (heat), and radio waves.

Electrons: Sub-atomic negatively charged particles in orbits within atoms.

Ellipse: Oval-shaped closed curve.

Elongation: The angular distance of a celestial body from the Sun, either eastward or westward.

Ephemeris: A publication which lists astrological/astronomical data; essential for the calculation of astrological charts.

Equation of Time: The difference between Apparent Solar Time and Mean Solar Time.

Equator: A great circle on the surface of a celestial body whose plane passes through the centre of the body, and which is perpendicular to its axis of rotation.

Equator System: A co-ordinate system, whose fundamental plane is the plane of the Equator.

Equinoctial Signs: Aries and Libra.

Equinoxes: The two points of intersection between the Ecliptic and the Equator. When the Sun reaches the equinoxes day and night are equal.

Fluorescence: The ability of a gas to absorb radiation of a particular wavelength and then re-emit it as visible light.

Focus (of an orbit): Two points within an elliptical orbit. At one of these points is located the larger body around which the smaller body travels in its orbit.

Galaxy: A stellar system.

Greenwich: Suburb of London. Longitude is measured from the Greenwich meridian (0° meridian).

Gregorian Calendar: The New Style calendar which superseded the Old Style (Julian) calendar.

Helium: Second lightest element and second most abundant one in the Universe.

Hemisphere: Half of a sphere, divided from the other half by a 'great circle'.

Hertzsprung-Russell Diagram: Diagram on which are plotted the luminosities of stars against their spectral types or surface temperatures.

Horizon: The great circle which marks the intersection of the horizontal plane with the celestial sphere.

Horizon System: A co-ordinate system with the horizon plane as the fundamental plane.

Hour Angle: The arc measured westward from the meridian. The angle between the hour circle of a body and the celestial meridian.

Houses: The twelve divisions of the birth chart numbered from the Ascendant in an anti-clockwise direction.

Hydrogen: Lightest of all elements and the most abundant one in the Universe. Principal constituent of the Sun and stars.

Hydrogen Cloud: Surrounds the coma of a comet.

Hyperbola: A mathematical curve, obtained when a cone is cut through to its base. This curve is open at both ends, and those comets with the greatest speeds follow orbits which are hyperbolic, with the Sun at the focus of the hyperbola.

Inclination (of an orbit): Angle between the plane of the orbit and that of the Ecliptic.

Inertia: Resistance of a body to stopping, starting, or change in velocity. Varies directly with the body's mass.

Inferior Planets: Planets whose orbits are located within the orbit of Earth: Mercury and Venus.

GLOSSARY

Infra-Red: Radiation in the form of heat with wavelengths longer than those of red light.

Ion: Atom which has had electrons either added to it or removed from it, to give the atom an overall electric charge.

International Date Line: The 180th meridian of longitude that passes across the Pacific Ocean.

Interstellar Regions: Regions between the stars, which contain clouds of dust and gas.

Kilometre: Unit of distance measurement = 1,000 metres (1 mile = 1.609 kilometres).

Latitude Celestial: The angular distance of a body north or south of the Ecliptic. The Sun has no latitude.

Latitude Terrestrial: The distance of any place north or south of the Equator.

Libration: Irregularities of the Moon's motions about its axes.

Lights or Luminaries: The term used to denote the Sun and Moon.

Light Year: The distance that light travels in one year (186,000 miles per second).

Local Group: Groups of galaxies to which our Milky Way Galaxy belongs.

Longitude Celestial: The distance of a body from the First Point of Aries, measured along the Ecliptic toward the east in either degrees and minutes or in signs, degrees and minutes.

Longitude Terrestrial: The distance of any place east or west of Greenwich.

Luminosity: Power output of the Sun or of a star, measured in watts per square metre.

Lunation: The time from New Moon to New Moon; the sequence of phases of the Moon.

Lune: The portion of the surface of a sphere which is contained within two great semi-circles.

Magnitude (Absolute): The brightness which a star would have, were it at a standard distance of 32.6 light years. The indication of a star's true brightness or luminosity.

Magnitude (Apparent): The brightness with which a star or planet appears to shine in the sky.

Main Sequence: A band in the Hertzsprung-Russell diagram, along which many of the stars are to be found.

Mass: The total amount of material contained in an object, and measured in kilogrammes (kg).

Mean Solar Day: The interval of time between two successive culminations of the Sun.

Mean Sun: The fictitious Sun which is used as a timekeeper moving along the Equator as opposed to the True Sun which moves along the Ecliptic.

Mean Solar Time: A measurement of time based on the motion of the Mean Sun.

M.C./Medium Coeli (Midheaven): The highest point of the Ecliptic culminating.

Meridian: A great circle on the Celestial Sphere which passes through the poles, the zenith and the nadir, and corresponds to the terrestrial longitude.

Meteor: Small extra-terrestrial particle which burns up in the Earth's atmosphere as a streak of light. Meteors normally arrive in the form of showers.

Midnight Sun: Term used to describe the Sun when it is visible above the horizon at midnight and is circumpolar, north of the Arctic circle, or south of the Antarctic circle.

Milky Way: Faint luminous band of light crossing the sky and forming part of our Galaxy.

Minor Planet: See Asteroid.

Multiple Star: Star which contains more than two component stars revolving around each other in complex orbits.

Nadir: The point in the heavens that is directly opposite the zenith.

Nebula: A cloud of gas in deep space. External galaxies are sometimes called spiral nebulae.

Neutrons: Sub-atomic particles carrying no electric charge, occupying the centres of atoms with protons. Both protons and neutrons are each 1,840 times more massive than an electron.

Nodes: The points of intersection where a planet crosses the Ecliptic when moving from north to south latitude or vice versa.

Nova: A star which undergoes sudden brightening over a few days or weeks.

Obliquity of the Ecliptic: The 23 ½ ° angle between the Celestial Equator and the Ecliptic.

Occultation: Occurs when one astronomical body passes in front of another and obscures it. Normally this term is used to describe the Moon passing in front of a star or planet.

Opposition: An aspect formed when two planets or bodies are 180 degrees apart.

Orbit: The path taken by any astronomical object through space, when under the gravitational influence of a larger body. This path may be an ellipse, parabola or hyperbola.

Orbital Inclination: The angle at which a comet's or planet's orbit is inclined to the Ecliptic. This varies from 0° to 180° where a comet is moving directly retrograde to the Sun's apparent motion.

Oxygen: One of the constituent gases of the Earth's atmosphere.

Parabola: A mathematical curve, obtained when a cone is cut through vertically to its base. Both parabolae and hyperbolae are therefore referred to as conic section curves. A parabola is open at both ends, and is the orbit followed by those comets which are travelling moderately fast, with the Sun at one focus of the parabola.

Parallax: Apparent displacement of a distant object when the observer moves through a relatively short distance at right angles to the line of sight.

Parallels: Normally refers to Parallels of Declination; circles parallel to the Celestial Equator.

Penumbra: Region of half-shadow surrounding the full shadow cast by an object.

Perigee: The point in the orbit where the Moon or a planet is at its nearest distance to the Earth.

Perihelion: The point in a planet's orbit where a planet is at its nearest distance to the Sun.

Phases: Periodic changes in the amount of illumination of an astronomical body, for instance, of the Moon and the inferior planets.

Photosphere: Luminous surface of the Sun.

Planet: A body, other than a comet or meteor, that revolves around the Sun as the centre and with it forms the Solar System.

Polar Circle: A parallel circle on the Celestial Sphere or on the Earth, 23½° from the pole. The 'midnight sun' is observed from this latitude at the time of the solstice (Summer) and at the Winter solstice the Sun is only at the horizon at noon.

Pole/Pole Elevation: The height of the pole above the horizon as observed from any place is equal to the terrestrial latitude.

Precession: The gradual advance of the equinoctial point (Vernal Equinox) westward at the rate of fifty seconds per year. Caused by the pole of the Equator revolving round the pole of the Ecliptic.

Prime Meridian: The Greenwich meridian which is the zero point for measurements of longitude on the Earth.

Prime Vertical: The great circle that intersects the horizon at the east and west points passing through the zenith at right angles to the meridian.

Prominences: Outbursts of hot gas from the Sun's surface.

Proper Motion: Motion of a star across the celestial sphere over years or centuries, measured relative to other stars.

Protons: Sub-atomic, positively charged particles occupying the centres (nuclei) of atoms.

Pulsar: Very small rapidly spinning star which sends out regular pulses of radio waves.

Quadrature: 90° distance; a square aspect.

Quasar: Very distant radio galaxy, appearing like a faint blue star.

Radiation: Electromagnetic energy in the form of waves (e.g., light waves).

Red Shift: Phenomenon observed in the spectrum of a receding galaxy. The galaxy's recession shifts the spectral lines toward the red end.

Relativity (Theory of): Branch of physics developed by Albert Einstein. The theory of relativity consists of two main parts: the Special and the General.

Retrograde Motion: The apparent westward motion of a body which is contrary to the usual or direct motion.

R.A./Right Ascension: A co-ordinate of the Equator System measured from the First Point of Aries eastward to a point which rises with a planet or part of the Ecliptic. The distance from 0° Aries along the Equator.

Satellite: An astronomical object in orbit around a larger planet. Satellites may either be natural (e.g., the Moon) or man-made (artificial Earth satellites).

Shooting Star: See Meteor.

Sidereal Time/Day/Year: Time based upon the rotation of the Earth with respect to the stars; time between two successive culminations of the Vernal Equinox. A Sidereal Year is the period of the Sun's revolution with respect to the stars and coincides with the Earth's revolution around the Sun.

Solar Time/Day/Year: The time used for civil purposes based upon the daily motion of the Sun: Solar Day is the time interval between two successive culminations of the apparent Sun; the average value of the Apparent Solar Day is termed the Mean Solar Day; the Solar Year is the Tropical Year (year of the seasons).

Solar Wind: A stream of electrically charged particles moving out from the Sun into space.

Solstices: The time when the Sun has its greatest northern or southern Declination, which occurs about 22/23 June and December. The Sun is then farthest from the equator and appears to 'stand still'.

Spectroscope: Device for obtaining the spectrum of the Sun or a star or other luminous body.

Spectrum: Band of colours obtained when white light is passed through a prism.

Spiral Nebula: External galaxy with spiral arms.

Standard Meridian: The meridian adopted for time zones.

Standard Time: The local civil time of a standard meridian, which is the time kept for all places within a particular zone; the difference between zones is normally 1 hour or 15° of longitude reckoned from Greenwich.

Sunspot: Dark blemish on the Sun's surface which is associated with magnetic fields.

Superior Planets: Those whose orbits lie outside that of the Earth: Mars, Jupiter, Saturn, Uranus, Neptune and Pluto.

Synodic Month: The interval between two successive Full Moons; the length of the synodic month is 29.5306 days.

Terminator: Line separating the illuminated and dark sides of a planet or satellite.

Transit: The passage of a body across the meridian; astrologically, the current passage of a planet over a natal position.

Tropics: Two parallels of latitude which are equal to the inclination of the Ecliptic (23½°). The Tropic of Cancer is north of the Equator and the Tropic of Capricorn is south.

Tropical Year: The year of the seasons; the time required for the Sun to complete one revolution with respect to the Vernal Equinox (First Point of Aries).

Ultra-Violet (Light): Light with a wavelength shorter than that of light from the violet end of the spectrum.

Umbra: Full shadow cast by an object.

Universal Time: Mean Solar Time reckoned from mean midnight on the meridian of Greenwich.

Variable Star: A star which has a fluctuating brightness.

Vernal Equinox (First Point of Aries): The point of intersection between the Ecliptic and the Equator which the Sun crosses on or about 21 March each year. The point from which Right Ascension and Celestial Longitude are measured.

Zenith: The point on the Celestial Sphere directly above the observer, 90° distance from the horizon.

Zodiac: (Circle of Animals); a belt or band 8° on either side of the Ecliptic. For astrological purposes, the Zodiac is divided into 12 signs of 30°.

APPENDIX 1
CORRECTION FOR GEOGRAPHIC LATITUDE

In astrological charting, the commonly used geographic latitude has been criticized as being incorrect and that the correct latitude to use is the Geocentric.

The Geocentric latitude is measured relative to the plane of the horizon and the equator and is the angle between the equator and a radius from the centre of the Earth. It is only at the Poles and the Equator that the two types of latitude are identical. Most students use the geographic latitude, but for those who wish to use the Geocentric latitude, the following table is appended. This table calculated to the nearest minute and based on the formula: (Tan. Geocentric latitude = 0.993277 Tan. Geographic latitude), gives the required reduction.

Geographic Latitude Degrees	Deduct Minutes	= Geocentric Latitude
0-1 : 89-90	1	
2-3 : 87-88	1	
4-6 : 84-86	2	*Example:*
7-8 : 82-83	3	Geographic Lat.
9-11 : 79-81	4	New York, 40° 45′ N.
12-14 : 76-78	5	Geocentric =
15-17 : 73-75	6	40° 45′ less 12′ =
18-20 : 70-72	7	40° 33′ N.
21-23 : 67-69	8	

Geographic Latitude Degrees	Deduct Minutes	= Geocentric Latitude
24-27 : 63-66	9	or by calculation
28-32 : 58-62	10	40° 45′ (Tan. 0.86165
33-39 : 49-57	11	× 0.993277
40-48 : — —	12	= 0.85586 Tan)
		40° 33′ N.

APPENDIX 2
THE TIMES OF RISING, CULMINATION AND SETTING OF A PLANET

The Ecliptic is the apparent path of the Sun, and as planets normally have celestial latitude, being either above or below the Ecliptic, their times of rising and setting will not coincide with their Ecliptic degrees.

The Ecliptic longitude of a planet, although correct as such, does not show the planet's actual position relative to the angles. The actual time that a planet bodily crosses the angle is important, and this time can be found by calculating the Sidereal time of its rising and setting.

A planet will culminate at the time which corresponds to its Right Ascension (R.A.), but its rising and setting is dependent upon its Ascensional Difference (A/D). We, therefore, have to find (A) the planet's R.A., (B) the planet's A/D.

The formula for calculating the R.A. of a planet having celestial latitude is:

$$\text{Cos A} = \frac{\text{Cos B Cos L}}{\text{Cos D}}$$

where A = the required R.A.
 B = the latitude
 L = the tropical longitude
 D = the declination

The easiest way to perform calculations such as these is with a calculator using trigonometric functions, or failing that, by the more laborious method of logarithms. If using logs, the addition of the log cosine of the latitude and longitude, less the log cosine of the declination, will give the log cosine of the planet's Right Ascension. However, to avoid subtraction with the use of logs, the formula can be re-stated to read: Cos A = Cos B, Secant D, Cos L, because secant D is the reciprocal of Cos D, and our formula becomes all additive.

When the tropical longitude falls between 90°-180° (Cancer-Virgo) or between 270°-360° (Capricorn-Pisces), the log *sine* should be substituted for the log cosine, and the sum of the three logs will be the log *sine* of the Right Ascension.

Finding the Ascensional Difference (A/D) is a simple matter, the formula for which is:

Sine A/D = Tan Dec. × Tan Geocentric Latitude

If the declination is north (positive) and the latitude is in the northern hemisphere, the A/D is also positive, but if the declination is south or negative, the A/D is negative. For the southern hemisphere, the A/D will be positive if the declination is south but negative if the declination is north.

The Semi-Arc of a celestial body is the time it is above the horizon (diurnal semi-arc), or the time it is below the horizon (nocturnal semi-arc). In the northern hemisphere, the following formula applies:

Semi-Diurnal Arc
90° + Ascensional Difference if the planet has North Declination.
90° − Ascensional Difference if the planet has South Declination.

Semi-Nocturnal Arc
90° — Ascensional Difference if the planet has North Declination.
90° + Ascensional Difference if the planet has South Declination.

(In the southern hemisphere, the reverse applies, for plus read minus, and for minus read plus).

The time a planet rises is given by the Right Ascension *less* Semi-arc, and the time of setting by Right Ascension *plus* Semi-arc. The correct mundane position is of the greatest importance, particularly when considering transits, directions and the like in relation to the angles.

THE TIMES OF RISING

As Pluto is a planet which can have considerable celestial latitude, we can use it as an example to illustrate the importance of calculating the positions *in mundo* of bodies with significant celestial latitude.

Example:
28 October 1980.
At what time will Pluto rise, culminate and set at London, Latitude 51° 21′ N? (see 'Geocentric Latitude')

(A) *Right Ascension: Using Machine*
From Raphael's Ephemeris, 28.10.80, Pluto's
Latitude   16° 36′ North   = Cos 0.95832
Declination   6° 46′ North   = Sec 1.00701
Longitude   22° 14′ Libra   = Cos 0.92565
                                          = Cos R.A. = 26.7107
26.7107 = 26° 42′ plus 180° (as longitude is in Libra) = Right Ascension 206° 42′ divided by 15 = *13 hours 47 mins.* = Pluto's R.A., and Sidereal time of culmination.

(B) *Ascensional Difference*

Tan. Dec. 6°46′ N.	=	0.11865	
Tan. Lat. 51°21′ N.	=	1.25044	
Sine	=	8.53236	
Add		90.	H M
Pluto's Semi-arc	=	98.53236 = 98°32′ =	6 34

	H M
For rising, Right Ascension	13 47
less Semi-Arc	6 34
R.A.M.C. when Pluto rises =	7 13
For setting, Right Ascension	13 47
plus Semi-Arc	6 34
R.A.M.C. when Pluto sets =	20 21

The foregoing shows that, although Pluto's longitude is 22° 14′ Libra, it culminates at Sidereal time 13 hours 47 mins with 28° Libra M.C., rises at Sidereal time 7.13 with 13° Libra, and sets with Sidereal time 20.21 with 7° Sagittarius (7th cusp). It is only marginally conjunction the ascendant at rising, and is not angular (7th cusp) when 22° Aries is rising, being 45° from setting point (22° Libra - 7° Sagittarius). The time of lower culmination is, of course,

R.A.M.C. plus or minus 12 hours. In the above example, the Sidereal time at lower culmination is 13.47 less 12 = 1 hour 47 Sidereal time.

If more attention were given to planets' positions relative to the angles, it is highly probable that transits and directions would be found to coincide more closely in time with events and conditions.

APPENDIX 3
CALCULATION TABLES

(i) Trigonometrical Formulae

1. *To convert longitude into Right Ascension (R.A.) without latitude.*
   Log. cosine of Obliquity of Ecliptic (O/E) 23° 27′
   + Log. tangent longitude from Aries or Libra, (or log. cotangent longitude from Cancer or Capricorn).
   = Log. tangent R.A. from Aries or Libra, (or Log. cotangent R.A. from Cancer or Capricorn).

   In Aries, Taurus, Gemini the result will be the R.A. required.
   For Cancer, Leo, Virgo   Add 90°
   For Libra, Scorpio, Sagittarius   Add 180°
   For Capricorn, Aquarius, Pisces   Add 270°

2. *To convert Right Ascension into Longitude, without Latitude.*
   Log. cosine of Ecliptic (23° 27′)
   + Log. cotangent R.A. from Aries or Libra, (or log. tangent R.A. from Cancer or Capricorn).
   = Log. cotangent longitude from Aries or Libra, (or log. tangent longitude from Cancer or Capricorn).

3. *To find Declination, without Latitude (Longitude being given).*
   Log. sine Obliquity of Ecliptic (23° 27′)
   + Log. sine longitude from Aries or Libra (or log. cosine from Cancer or Capricorn).
   = Log. sine Declination.

4. *To find Ascensional Difference.*
   Log. tangent Declination.
   + Log. tangent latitude of locality.
   = Log. sine Ascensional Difference.

5. *To find Oblique Ascension: (Places in northern latitudes).*
   With North Declination: Right Ascension *less* Ascensional Difference = Oblique Ascension.
   With South Declination: Right Ascension *plus* Ascensional Difference = Oblique Ascension

   (For places in southern latitudes, reverse the above rules, for *less* read plus, and for *plus* read less.)

6. *To find the oblique ascension of the cusp of a house.*
   Right Ascension of the Midheaven (R.A.M.C.)
   + 30° = Oblique Ascension of cusp 11th
   + 60° = Oblique Ascension of cusp 12th
   + 90° = Oblique Ascension of cusp 1st
   + 120° = Oblique Ascension of cusp 2nd
   + 150° = Oblique Ascension of cusp 3rd

7. *To find Semi-Arc (northern latitudes):*
   Diurnal Semi-arc with North declination: 90° + Asc. Diff.
   Diurnal Semi-arc with South declination: 90° − Asc. Diff.
   Nocturnal Semi-arc with North declination: 90° − Asc. Diff.
   Nocturnal Semi-arc with South declination: 90° + Asc. Diff.

   (Reverse rules for places in southern latitudes, for *plus* read minus, and for *minus* read plus.)

(ii) Right Ascension

Aries-Libra (For Libra add 12 hours S.T. 180° R.A.)							
Sidereal Time			R.A.		Long.	
H	M	S	°	′	°	′
0	00	00	0	00	0	00
0	04	00	1	00	1	05
0	08	00	2	00	2	11
0	12	00	3	00	3	16
0	16	00	4	00	4	21
0	20	00	5	00	5	27
0	24	00	6	00	6	32
0	28	00	7	00	7	37
0	32	00	8	00	8	42
0	36	00	9	00	9	48
0	40	00	10	00	10	53
0	44	00	11	00	11	58
0	48	00	12	00	13	03
0	52	00	13	00	14	07
0	56	00	14	00	15	12
1	00	00	15	00	16	17
1	04	00	16	00	17	21
1	08	00	17	00	18	26
1	12	00	18	00	19	30
1	16	00	19	00	20	34
1	20	00	20	00	21	38
1	24	00	21	00	22	42
1	28	00	22	00	23	46
1	32	00	23	00	24	50
1	36	00	24	00	25	53
1	40	00	25	00	26	56
1	44	00	26	00	28	00
1	48	00	27	00	29	03

| Taurus-Scorpio (For Scorpio add 12 hours S.T. 180° R.A.) |||||||
| Sidereal Time ||| R.A. || Long. ||
H	M	S	°	′	°	′
1	52	00	28	00	0	06
1	56	00	29	00	1	08
2	00	00	30	00	2	11
2	04	00	31	00	3	13
2	08	00	32	00	4	15
2	12	00	33	00	5	18
2	16	00	34	00	6	19
2	20	00	35	00	7	21
2	24	00	36	00	8	22
2	28	00	37	00	9	24
2	32	00	38	00	10	25
2	36	00	39	00	11	26
2	40	00	40	00	12	27
2	44	00	41	00	13	27
2	48	00	42	00	14	28
2	52	00	43	00	15	28
2	56	00	44	00	16	28
3	00	00	45	00	17	28
3	04	00	46	00	18	28
3	08	00	47	00	19	27
3	12	00	48	00	20	26
3	16	00	49	00	21	26
3	20	00	50	00	22	25
3	24	00	51	00	23	23
3	28	00	52	00	24	22
3	32	00	53	00	25	20
3	36	00	54	00	26	19
3	40	00	55	00	27	17
3	44	00	56	00	28	15
3	48	00	57	00	29	13

CALCULATION TABLES

Gemini-Sagittarius (For Sagittarius add 12 hours S.T. 180° R.A.)							
Sidereal Time			R.A.		Long.	
H	M	S	°	′	°	′
3	52	00	58	00	0	10
3	56	00	59	00	1	08
4	00	00	60	00	2	05
4	04	00	61	00	3	03
4	08	00	62	00	4	00
4	12	00	63	00	4	57
4	16	00	64	00	5	54
4	20	00	65	00	6	50
4	24	00	66	00	7	47
4	28	00	67	00	8	43
4	32	00	68	00	9	40
4	36	00	69	00	10	36
4	40	00	70	00	11	32
4	44	00	71	00	12	28
4	48	00	72	00	13	24
4	52	00	73	00	14	20
4	56	00	74	00	15	16
5	00	00	75	00	16	11
5	04	00	76	00	17	07
5	08	00	77	00	18	02
5	12	00	78	00	18	58
5	16	00	79	00	19	53
5	20	00	80	00	20	49
5	24	00	81	00	21	44
5	28	00	82	00	22	39
5	32	00	83	00	23	34
5	36	00	84	00	24	29
5	40	00	85	00	25	25
5	44	00	86	00	26	20
5	48	00	87	00	27	15
5	52	00	88	00	28	10
5	56	00	89	00	29	05

(ii) Right Ascension

Cancer-Capricorn (For Capricorn add 12 hours S.T. 180° R.A.)						
Sidereal Time			R.A.		Long.	
H	M	S	°	′	°	′
6	00	00	90	00	0	00
6	04	00	91	00	0	55
6	08	00	92	00	1	50
6	12	00	93	00	2	45
6	16	00	94	00	3	40
6	20	00	95	00	4	35
6	24	00	96	00	5	31
6	28	00	97	00	6	26
6	32	00	98	00	7	21
6	36	00	99	00	8	16
6	40	00	100	00	9	11
6	44	00	101	00	10	07
6	48	00	102	00	11	02
6	52	00	103	00	11	58
6	56	00	104	00	12	53
7	00	00	105	00	13	49
7	04	00	106	00	14	44
7	08	00	107	00	15	40
7	12	00	108	00	16	36
7	16	00	109	00	17	32
7	20	00	110	00	18	28
7	24	00	111	00	19	24
7	28	00	112	00	20	20
7	32	00	113	00	21	17
7	36	00	114	00	22	13
7	40	00	115	00	23	10
7	44	00	116	00	24	06
7	48	00	117	00	25	03
7	52	00	118	00	26	00
7	56	00	119	00	26	57
8	00	00	120	00	27	54
8	04	00	121	00	28	52
8	08	00	122	00	29	50

CALCULATION TABLES

Leo-Aquarius (For Aquarius add 12 hours S.T. 180° R.A.)						
Sidereal Time			R.A.		Long.	
H	M	S	°	′	°	′
8	12	00	123	00	0	47
8	16	00	124	00	1	45
8	20	00	125	00	2	43
8	24	00	126	00	3	41
8	28	00	127	00	4	40
8	32	00	128	00	5	38
8	36	00	129	00	6	37
8	40	00	130	00	7	35
8	44	00	131	00	8	35
8	48	00	132	00	9	34
8	52	00	133	00	10	33
8	56	00	134	00	11	32
9	00	00	135	00	12	32
9	04	00	136	00	13	32
9	08	00	137	00	14	32
9	12	00	138	00	15	32
9	16	00	139	00	16	33
9	20	00	140	00	17	33
9	24	00	141	00	18	34
9	28	00	142	00	19	35
9	32	00	143	00	20	36
9	36	00	144	00	21	38
9	40	00	145	00	22	39
9	44	00	146	00	23	41
9	48	00	147	00	24	42
9	52	00	148	00	25	45
9	56	00	149	00	26	47
10	00	00	150	00	27	49
10	04	00	151	00	28	52
10	08	00	152	00	29	54

Virgo-Pisces (For Pisces add 12 hours S.T. 180° R.A.)						
Sidereal Time			R.A.		Long.	
H	M	S	°	′	°	′
10	12	00	153	00	0	57
10	16	00	154	00	2	00
10	20	00	155	00	3	04
10	24	00	156	00	4	07
10	28	00	157	00	5	10
10	32	00	158	00	6	14
10	36	00	159	00	7	18
10	40	00	160	00	8	22
10	44	00	161	00	9	26
10	48	00	162	00	10	30
10	52	00	163	00	11	34
10	56	00	164	00	12	39
11	00	00	165	00	13	43
11	04	00	166	00	14	48
11	08	00	167	00	15	53
11	12	00	168	00	16	57
11	16	00	169	00	18	02
11	20	00	170	00	19	07
11	24	00	171	00	20	12
11	28	00	172	00	21	18
11	32	00	173	00	22	23
11	36	00	174	00	23	28
11	40	00	175	00	24	33
11	44	00	176	00	25	39
11	48	00	177	00	26	44
11	52	00	178	00	27	49
11	56	00	179	00	28	55

(iii) Longitude Equivalent in Time

Long. °	Equiv. Hours	Mins	Long. °	Equiv. Hours	Mins
1	0	04	39	2	36
2	0	08	40	2	40
3	0	12	41	2	44
4	0	16	42	2	48
5	0	20	43	2	52
6	0	24	44	2	56
7	0	28	45	3	00
8	0	32	46	3	04
9	0	36	47	3	08
10	0	40	48	3	12
11	0	44	49	3	16
12	0	48	50	3	20
13	0	52	51	3	24
14	0	56	52	3	28
15	1	00	53	3	32
16	1	04	54	3	36
17	1	08	55	3	40
18	1	12	56	3	44
19	1	16	57	3	48
20	1	20	58	3	52
21	1	24	59	3	56
22	1	28	60	4	00
23	1	32	61	4	04
24	1	36	62	4	08
25	1	40	63	4	12
26	1	44	64	4	16
27	1	48	65	4	20
28	1	52	66	4	24
29	1	56	67	4	28
30	2	00	68	4	32
31	2	04	69	4	36
32	2	08	70	4	40
33	2	12	71	4	44
34	2	16	72	4	48
35	2	20	73	4	52
36	2	24	74	4	56
37	2	28	75	5	00
38	2	32	76	5	04

Long. °	Equiv. Hours	Mins	Long. °	Equiv. Hours	Mins
77	5	08	115	7	40
78	5	12	116	7	44
79	5	16	117	7	48
80	5	20	118	7	52
81	5	24	119	7	56
82	5	28	120	8	00
83	5	32	121	8	04
84	5	36	122	8	08
85	5	40	123	8	12
86	5	44	124	8	16
87	5	48	125	8	20
88	5	52	126	8	24
89	5	56	127	8	28
90	6	00	128	8	32
91	6	04	129	8	36
92	6	08	130	8	40
93	6	12	131	8	44
94	6	16	132	8	48
95	6	20	133	8	52
96	6	24	134	8	56
97	6	28	135	9	00
98	6	32	136	9	04
99	6	36	137	9	08
100	6	40	138	9	12
101	6	44	139	9	16
102	6	48	140	9	20
103	6	52	141	9	24
104	6	56	142	9	28
105	7	00	143	9	32
106	7	04	144	9	36
107	7	08	145	9	40
108	7	12	146	9	44
109	7	16	147	9	48
110	7	20	148	9	52
111	7	24	149	9	56
112	7	28	150	10	00
113	7	32			
114	7	36			

CALCULATION TABLES

Long. °	Equiv. Hours	Mins
151	10	04
152	10	08
153	10	12
154	10	16
155	10	20
156	10	24
157	10	28
158	10	32
159	10	36
160	10	40
161	10	44
162	10	48
163	10	52
164	10	56
165	11	00

Long. °	Equiv. Hours	Mins
166	11	04
167	11	08
168	11	12
169	11	16
170	11	20
171	11	24
172	11	28
173	11	32
174	11	36
175	11	40
176	11	44
177	11	48
178	11	52
179	11	56
180	12	00

Long. ′	Equiv. ′	″
1	0	04
2	0	08
3	0	12
4	0	16
5	0	20
6	0	24
7	0	28
8	0	32
9	0	36
10	0	40
11	0	44
12	0	48
13	0	52
14	0	56
15	1	00

Long. ′	Equiv. ′	″
16	1	04
17	1	08
18	1	12
19	1	16
20	1	20
21	1	24
22	1	28
23	1	32
24	1	36
25	1	40
26	1	44
27	1	48
28	1	52
29	1	56
30	2	00

Long. ′	Equiv. ′	″		Long. ′	Equiv. ′	″
31	2	04		46	3	04
32	2	08		47	3	08
33	2	12		48	3	12
34	2	16		49	3	16
35	2	20		50	3	20
36	2	24		51	3	24
37	2	28		52	3	28
38	2	32		53	3	32
39	2	36		54	3	36
40	2	40		55	3	40
41	2	44		56	3	44
42	2	48		57	3	48
43	2	52		58	3	52
44	2	56		59	3	56
45	3	00				

Example:

What is the longitude equivalent in time of 145° 18′?

```
                               H   M   S
From Tables: 145°         =    9   40  00 +
             18′          =    0   01  12
                               9   41│12
Or using calculator:
145° 18′ = 145.3°/15 = 9.6866   =  9   41  12
```

(iv) Conversion of Mean Solar into Mean Sidereal Time (9.86 seconds per hour)

Mean Time Hours	′	″ Amount	Mean Time	′ Amount	″	Mean Time	′ Amount	″
1	0	9.86	1	0.16		31	5.09	
2	0	19.71	2	0.33		32	5.26	
3	0	29.57	3	0.49		33	5.42	
4	0	39.43	4	0.66		34	5.59	
5	0	49.28	5	0.82		35	5.75	
6	0	59.14	6	0.99		36	5.92	
7	1	09.00	7	1.15		37	6.08	
8	1	18.85	8	1.31		38	6.24	
9	1	28.71	9	1.48		39	6.41	
10	1	38.56	10	1.64		40	6.57	
11	1	48.42	11	1.81		41	6.74	
12	1	58.28	12	1.97		42	6.90	
13	2	08.13	13	2.14		43	7.07	
14	2	17.99	14	2.30		44	7.23	
15	2	27.85	15	2.46		45	7.39	
16	2	37.70	16	2.63		46	7.56	
17	2	47.56	17	2.79		47	7.72	
18	2	57.42	18	2.96		48	7.89	
19	3	07.27	19	3.12		49	8.05	
20	3	17.13	20	3.29		50	8.22	
21	3	26.99	21	3.45		51	8.38	
22	3	36.84	22	3.61		52	8.54	
23	3	46.70	23	3.78		53	8.71	
24	3	56.56	24	3.94		54	8.87	
			25	4.11		55	9.04	
			26	4.27		56	9.20	
			27	4.44		57	9.37	
			28	4.60		58	9.53	
			29	4.76		59	9.69	
			30	4.93				

(v) Minutes as a decimal of a Degree or Hour; Seconds as a decimal of a Minute

′ ″	Decimal	′ ″	Decimal
1	0.0166	31	0.5166
2	.0333	32	.5333
3	.0500	33	.5500
4	.0666	34	.5666
5	.0833	35	.5833
6	.1000	36	.6000
7	.1166	37	.6166
8	.1333	38	.6333
9	.1500	39	.6500
10	.1666	40	.6666
11	.1833	41	.6833
12	.2000	42	.7000
13	.2166	43	.7166
14	.2333	44	.7333
15	.2500	45	.7500
16	.2666	46	.7666
17	.2833	47	.7833
18	.3000	48	.8000
19	.3166	49	.8166
20	.3333	50	.8333
21	.3500	51	.8500
22	.3666	52	.8666
23	.3833	53	.8833
24	.4000	54	.9000
25	.4166	55	.9166
26	.4333	56	.9333
27	.4500	57	.9500
28	.4666	58	.9666
29	.4833	59	.9833
30	.5000		

(vi) British Summer Time: All changes 2 a.m. G.M.T.

	Commenced						Ended				
	Jan	Feb	Mar	April	May	Jul	Aug	Sep	Oct	Nov	Dec
1916					21				1		
1917				8				17			
1918			24					30			
1919			30					29			
1920			28						25		
1921				3					3		
1922			26						8		
1923				22				16			
1924				13				21			
1925				19					4		
1926				18					3		
1927				10					2		
1928				22					7		
1929				21					6		
1930				13					5		
1931				19					4		
1932				17					2		
1933				9					8		
1934				22					7		
1935				14					6		
1936				19					4		
1937				18					3		
1938				10					2		
1939				16						19	
1940		25									31
*1941	1				*		*				31
*1942	1			*			*				31
*1943	1			*			*				31
*1944	1			*				*			31
*1945	1			*		*			7		
1946				14					6		
*1947			16	*			*			2	
1948			14						31		
1949				3					30		

*Denotes *Double* Summer Time in operation as listed over page.

	April	May	Jul	Aug	Sep
1941		4		10	
1942	5			9	
1943	4			15	
1944	2				17
1945	2		15		
1946	Not observed				
1947	13			10	

*From 1941-1947 except 1946 *Double Summer Time* (+ 2 hours ahead of G.M.T.) from dates shown. Remainder of year 1 hour ahead from dates shown.

Example:
1941 from 1 January to 31 December 1 hour in advance of G.M.T. except for the period 4 May to 10 August + 2 (*Double Summer Time*).

	Commenced		Ended	
	Mar	April	Oct	
1950		16	22	
1951		15	21	
1952		20	26	
1953		19	4	
1954		11	3	
1955		17	2	
1956		22	7	
1957		14	6	
1958		20	5	
1959		19	4	
1960		10	2	
1961	26		29	
1962	25		28	
1963	31		27	
1964	22		25	
1965	21		24	
1966	20		23	
1967	19		29	

1968 from 18 February to 31 October 1971 British Standard Time in operation, 1 hour in advance of G.M.T.

CALCULATION TABLES

	Mar		Oct	
1972	19		29	
1973	18		28	
1974	17		27	
1975	16		26	
1976	21		24	
1977	20		23	
1978	19		29	
1979	18		28	
1980	16		26	
1981	29		25	
1982	28		24	
1983	27		23	

APPENDIX 4
INTERESTING DATA

Abbreviations

A.Q.	Astrologer's Quarterly	
A.J.	Astrological Journal	
M.A.	Modern Astrology (now defunct)	
D.T. Supp.	Daily Telegraph 125 years Commemorative Supplement	
A.A.	American Astrology	
E.S.T.	Eastern Standard Time	5 hours slow on G.M.T.
E.W.T.	Eastern War Time	4 hours slow on G.M.T.
E.D.S.T.	Eastern Daylight Saving Time	4 hours slow on G.M.T.
C.S.T.	Central Standard Time	6 hours slow on G.M.T.
C.W.T.	Central War Time	5 hours slow on G.M.T.
C.D.S.T.	Central Daylight Saving Time	5 hours slow on G.M.T.
M.S.T.	Mountain Standard Time	7 hours slow on G.M.T.
M.W.T.	Mountain War Time	6 hours slow on G.M.T.
P.S.T.	Pacific Standard Time	8 hours slow on G.M.T.
P.D.S.T.	Pacific Daylight Saving Time	7 hours slow on G.M.T.
J.S.T.	Japanese Standard Time	9 hours *fast* on G.M.T.
G.M.T.	Greenwich Mean Time	

		Data	Source
1.	Aviation and Space Exploration		
	(a) First controlled powered flight: Wright brothers	10.35 a.m. E.S.T. 17.12.1903 Kittyhawk, N.C. 36.05 N., 75.42 W.	C. H. Gibbs-Smith. Science Museum H.M.S.O. (1963)

(b)	1½ hours flight — 40 miles — Wilbur Wright	5.17 p.m. Paris time 21.9.1908 Auvours, nr. Le Mans. 48.00 N., 0.12 E.	D.T. Supp.
(c)	Sputnik I.	10.57 a.m. L.T. 4.10.1957 52.16 N., 104.20 E.	A.Q. Vol. 32 No. 1 1958
(d)	First man in space, Yuri Gagarin	Launch: 9.07 a.m. 6.07 a.m. G.M.T. ---- 12.4.1961 50 N., 63 E -------------	D.T. Supp. A.Q. Vol. 35, No. 3, 1961

2. **First men on the Moon**

(a)	Apollo Moonshot: Blast-Off	9.32 a.m. E.D.S.T. 16.7.1969 28.28 N., 80.32 W	Encyclopedia of Space Technology. Salamander Books Ltd. 1981
(b)	Lunar Module on Moon	4.17.43 p.m. E.D.S.T. 8.17.43 p.m. G.M.T. 20.7.1969	Encyclopedia of Space Technology. Salamander Books Ltd. 1981
(c)	Armstrong set foot on Moon	10.56 p.m. E.D.S.T. 20.7.1969 2.56 a.m. G.M.T. 21.7.1969	D.T. Supp.
(d)	Module launched from Moon	1.52 p.m. E.D.S.T. 5.52 p.m. G.M.T. 21.7.1969	A.J. Vol. 11, No. 4, 1969
(e)	Splash-down, 1,000 miles south-west of Hawaii	12.50 p.m. E.D.S.T. 24.7.1969	D.T. Supp.

3. **Concorde:** First passenger flight — 11.40 a.m. G.M.T. 21.1.1976 London — A.Q. Vol. 50, No. 1, 1976

4. (a) Airship-Hindenburg crashed in flames — 7.25 p.m. E.D.S.T. 6.5.1937 Lakehurst, N.J. 40.01 N., 74.19 W. — J. Canning. Great Disasters Octopus Books (1976)

	(b) Airship - R101 crashed	2.07 a.m. Paris time 5.10.1930 nr Beauvais, France 49.26 N., 2.05 E.	D.T. Supp.
	(c) (R101) Left Cardington, Beds., commencement of flight	6.30 p.m. G.M.T. 4.10.1930 52.08 N., 00.28 W.	D.T. Supp.
5.	London Air Raid Victims: All killed on 9.4.1941	(a) 7.00 p.m. G.M.T. 21.11.1924 London (b) 10.30 p.m. G.M.T. 28.8.1929 London (c) 3.00 a.m. G.M.T. 9.12.1936 London	A.Q. Vol. 25, No. 2, 1951
6.	Flying Bomb Victim, killed noon, 19.12.1944 51.44 N., 0.28 E.	Noon, G.M.T. 16.6.1923 51.48 N., 1.04 E.	A.Q. Vol. 21, No. 1, 1947
7.	**Broadcasting**		
	(a) B.B.C. first broadcast	6.00 p.m. G.M.T. 14.11.1922 London	A.Q. Vol. 51, No. 1, 1977
	(b) Became a Corporation	0.00 hours G.M.T. 1.1.1927 London	A.Q. Vol. 51, No. 1, 1977
	(c) Television: First public T.V. service	3.00 p.m. G.M.T. 2.11.1936 London	A.Q. Vol. 51, No. 1, 1977
	(d) B.B.C. Breakfast time T.V. commenced	6.30 a.m. G.M.T. 17.1.1983 London	As noted by authors
	(e) Channel 4 T.V. commenced	4.45 p.m. G.M.T. 2.11.1982 London	As noted by authors

8. **Atomic Age**

(a) First chain reaction obtained — Chicago University	3.35 p.m. C.W.T. 2.12.1942 41.52 N., 87.39 W.	A.A. May 1971
(b) First atomic bomb test	5.29.45 a.m. M.W.T. 16.7.1945 33.38 N., 106.23 W.	A.A. May 1971
(c) Atomic bomb on Hiroshima	8.16 a.m. J.S.T. 6.8.1945 34.34 N., 132.25 E.	Sunday Times 16.11.80: Time from a photograph of a victim's watch
(d) First atomic pile for supplying electricity to industry	12.18 p.m. G.M.T. 17.10.1956 Calder Hall, Cumbria	A.Q. Vol. 30, No. 4, 1956/7

9. **Earthquakes**

(a) San Francisco	5.13 a.m. P.S.T. 1.13 p.m. G.M.T. 18.4.1906 37.47 N., 122.26 W.	Gutenberg & Richter. Seismicity of the Earth, Princetown University Press (1949)
(b) Kansu Province	12.06 p.m. G.M.T. 16.12.1920 36 N., 105 E	Gutenberg & Richter. Seismicity of the Earth, Princetown University Press (1949)
(c) Tokyo	11.58.36 a.m. J.S.T. 02.58.36 a.m. G.M.T. 1.9.1923 35.41 N., 139.45 E.	Gutenberg & Richter.
(d) Long Beach, California	5.55 p.m. P.S.T. 10.3.1933 1.55 a.m. G.M.T. 11.3.1933 33.46 N., 118.11 W.	M.A. Vol. 30, No. 3, 1933
(e) Agadir, Morocco	11.40.14 p.m. G.M.T. 29.2.1960 30.27 N., 9.37 W.	Earth Sciences. Seismicity of the Earth, Unesco (1969)
(f) Tangshan, China	7.42.57 p.m. G.M.T. 27.7.1976 39.36 N., 118.06 E.	A.J. Vol. 19, No. 1, 1976/77

INTERESTING DATA 231

(g) Udine — North Italy 7.55 p.m. G.M.T. P. Verney.
                         6.5.1976   The Earthquake
                         46.03 N., 13.14 E. Handbook,
                                            Paddington Press
                                            (1979)

(h) Volcanic eruption: 7.52 a.m. local time Great Disasters.
    Mont Pelee St Pierre, 11.57 a.m. G.M.T.
    Martinique   8.5.1902
                         14.51 N., 61.10 W

(i) Mount St. Helen's,   8.32 a.m. P.D.T.   Sunday Times,
    Washington State   3.32 p.m. G.M.T.   25.5.1980
                         18.5.1980
                         46.29 N., 122.12 W

10. **Mine Disasters
    and Explosions**

(a) Senghenydd mine,   8.20 a.m. G.M.T.
    nr. Cardiff, S. Wales (approx)   Great Disasters
                         14.10.1913   M.A. Vol. 31,
                         51.28 N., 3.10 W   No. 6, 1934

(b) Gresford,   2.00 a.m. G.M.T.   M.A. Vol. 31,
    nr. Wrexham,   22.9.1934   No. 6, 1934
    N. Wales   53.03 N., 3.00 W

(c) Aberfan, S. Wales,   8.16 a.m. G.M.T.   A.Q. Vol. 40,
    Village school engulfed 21.10.1966   No. 4, 1966/7
    by rain-soaked coal 51.45 N., 3.22 W.
    sludge tip.

(d) Gas Explosion: 11.12 p.m. E.S.T. Disaster.
    Ice Show,   31.10.1963   Phoebus Publishing
    State Fair Coliseum 39.46 N., 86.10 W. Co. 1975
    Indianapolis

(e) Silvertown,   6.45 p.m. G.M.T.   A.Q. Vol. 51,
    East London,   19.1.1917   No. 1, 1977
    Ammunition factory   London
    explosion.

(f) Flixborough,   3.53 p.m. G.M.T.   J. Canning.
    nr. Scunthorpe,   1.6.1974   Great Disasters
    Chemical plant   53.35 N., 0.40 W. Octopus Books
    explosion   (1976)

11. **Fires**

(a) The Iroquois Theatre, Chicago.	3.15 p.m. C.S.T. (approx) 9.15 p.m. G.M.T. 30.12.1903 41.52 N., 87.39 W.	J. Canning. Great Disasters
(b) Cocoanut Grove Night Club, Boston	10.12 p.m. E.W.T. 28.11.1942 2.12 a.m. G.M.T. 29.11.1942 42.22 N., 71.04 W	J. Canning. Great Disasters
(c) The Club-Cinq-Sept, St. Laurent du Pont, nr. Grenoble.	0.40 a.m. G.M.T. (approx) 1.11.1970 45.11 N., 5.44 E.	J. Canning. Great Disasters

12. **Railway Accidents**

(a) Quintinshill, nr. Gretna Junction. (Troop train)	7.00 a.m. G.M.T. (approx) 22.5.1915 55.00 N., 3.03 W.	L.T.C. Rolt Red for Danger Pan Books (1978)
(b) Wealdstone/Harrow	7.19 a.m. G.M.T. 8.10.1952 51.33 N., 0.20 W.	A.Q. Vol. 27, No. 1, 1953
(c) Lewisham, London.	6.20 p.m. G.M.T. 4.12.1957 51.28 N., 00.01 W.	A.Q. Vol. 32, No. 1, 1958
(d) Moorgate, London Underground.	8.46 a.m. G.M.T. 28.2.1975 51.34 N., 00.06 W.	Red for Danger.

13. **British Monarchy**

(a) Queen Victoria	4.15 a.m. L.T. 24.5.1819 London. 51.30 N., 0.09 W.	Manual of Astrology: Sepharial, 1898.
(b) Albert, Prince Consort	6.03 a.m. L.T. 26.8.1819 Rosenau 50.17 N, 11.02 E.	Textbook of Astrology: A. J. Pearce, 1911
(c) Edward VII	10.48 a.m. G.M.T. 9.11.1841 Buckingham Palace 51.30 N., 0.08 W.	Casting the Horoscope, A. Leo

INTERESTING DATA

(d) George V	1.18 a.m. G.M.T. 3.6.1865 Marlborough House 51.30 N., 0.08 W.	Textbook of Astrology: A. J. Pearce, 1911
(e) Edward, Duke of Windsor (Abdicated)	9.55 p.m. G.M.T. 23.6.1894 White Lodge, Richmond 51.27 N., 0.18 W.	A.Q. Vol. 42, No. 4, 1968/69
(f) George VI	3.05 a.m. G.M.T. 14.12.1895 Sandringham, Norfolk 52.51 N., 0.30 E.	Introduction to Political Astrology, C. Carter, 1951
(g) Elizabeth II	1.40 a.m. G.M.T. 21.4.1926 Bruton Street, London. 51.30 N., 0.08 W	Introduction to Political Astrology, C. Carter, 1951
(h) Charles (Prince of Wales)	9.14 p.m. G.M.T. 14.11.1948 Buckingham Palace 51.30 N. 0.08 W.	Introduction to Political Astrology, C. Carter, 1951
(i) Diana (Princess of Wales)	6.45 p.m. G.M.T. 1.7.1961 Sandringham 52.51 N, 0.30 E.	A.Q. Vol. 55, No. 2, 1981
(j) Prince William	8.03 p.m. G.M.T. 21.6.1982 Paddington, London 51.32 N., 0.12 W.	Current Press & T.V. reports
(k) Elizabeth II Married	11.38 a.m. G.M.T. 20.11.1947 Westminster	A.Q. Vol. 22, No. 1, 1948
(l) Father (George VI died early morning 6.2.1952).	News received while in Kenya — Nyeri — 0.25 S, 36.56 E at 12.57 U.T. 6.2.1952	Solunars Series, C. Fagan, American Astrology, Part LI 1960's

(m) Coronation: 11.32 a.m. G.M.T. A.Q. Vol. 33,
2.6.1953 No. 4, 1959/60
Westminster
51.30 N., 0.07 W.

(n) Prince & Princess of 10.18 a.m. G.M.T. As noted by
Wales (Charles & 29.7.1981 authors
Diana) Married St. Pauls Cathedral
51.31 N., 0.05 W.

APPENDIX 5
STAR CHARTS

10.00 p.m. G.M.T. all months — 51.32 N.

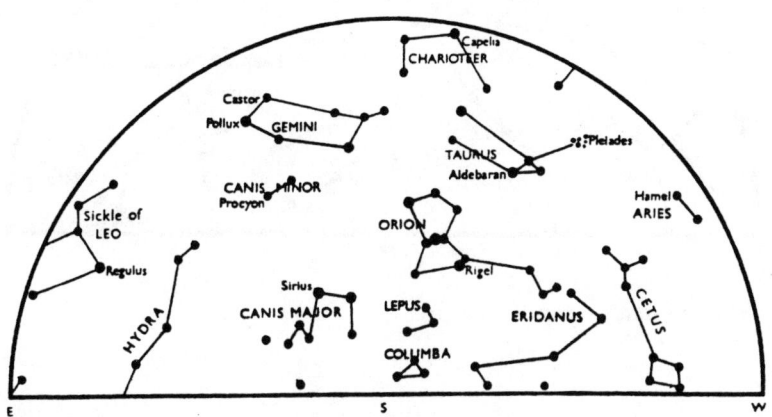

January stars — southern aspect

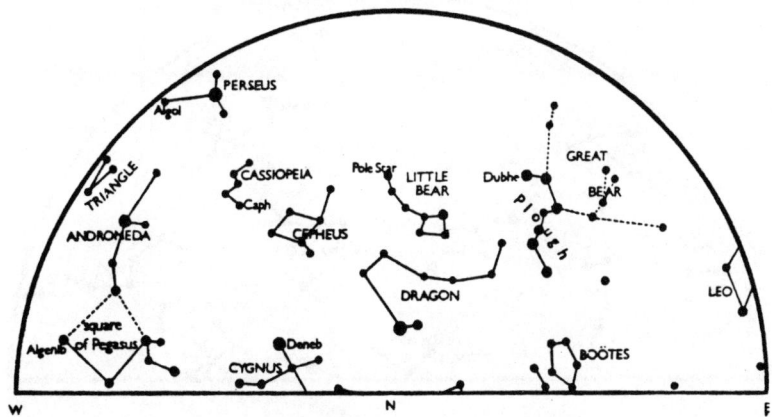

January stars — nothern aspect

January — December star charts
© 1968 Roy Worvill. *Night Skies of the Year*.
Re-produced by permission of Kahn & Averill.

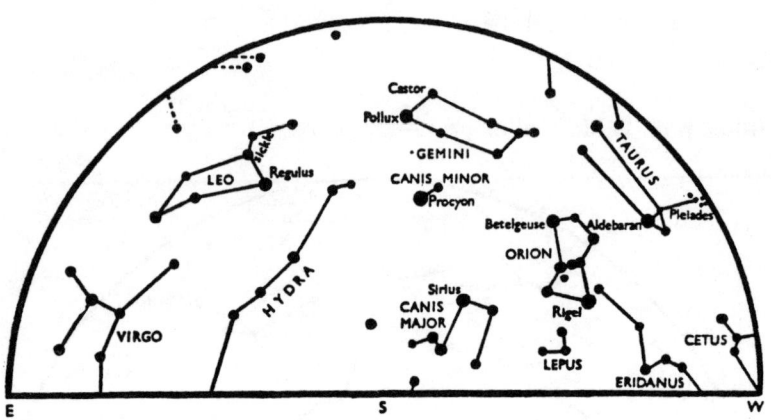

February stars — southern aspect

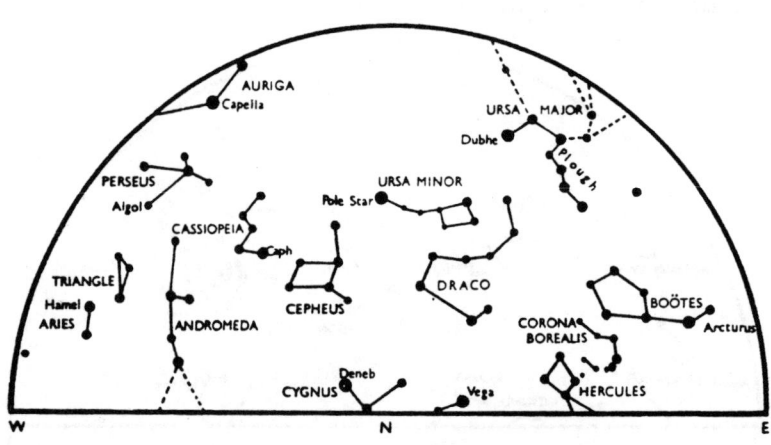

February stars — northern aspect

STAR CHARTS

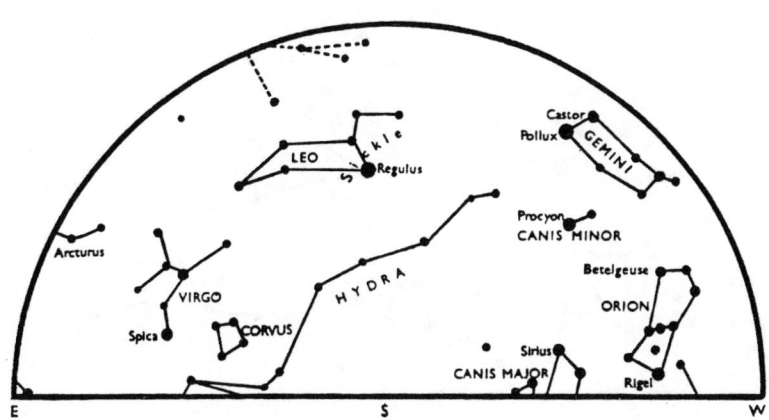

March stars — southern aspect

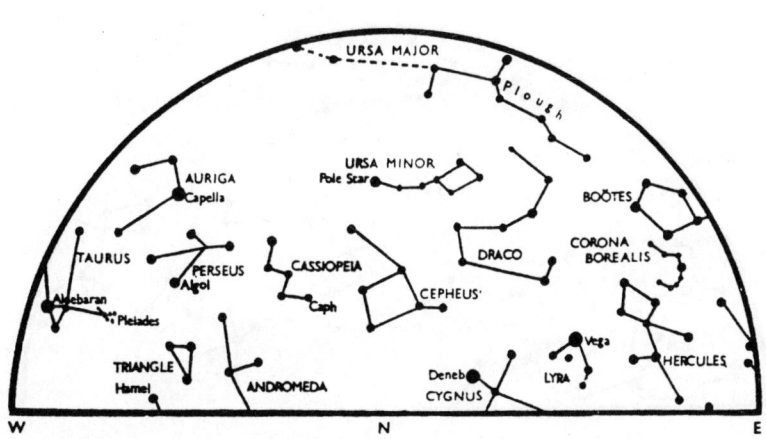

March stars — northern aspect

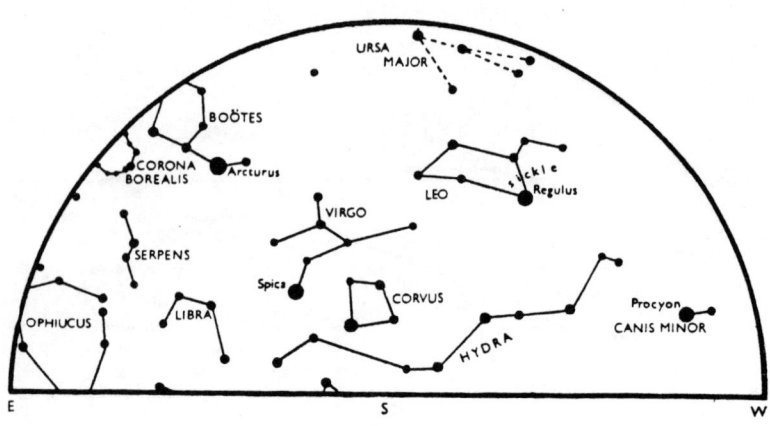

April stars — southern aspect

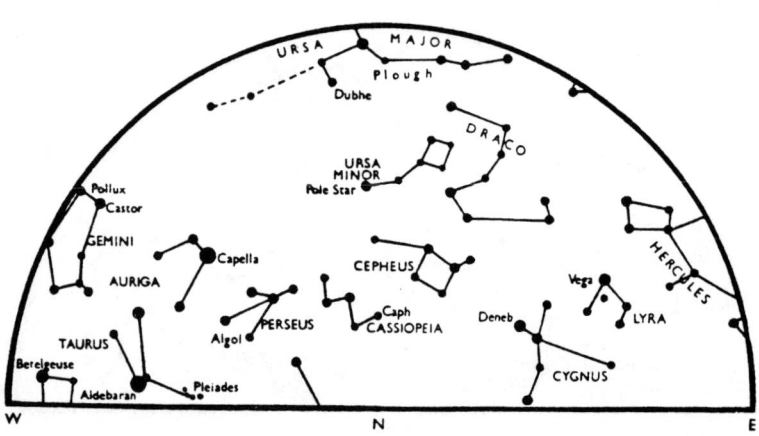

April stars — nothern aspect

STAR CHARTS

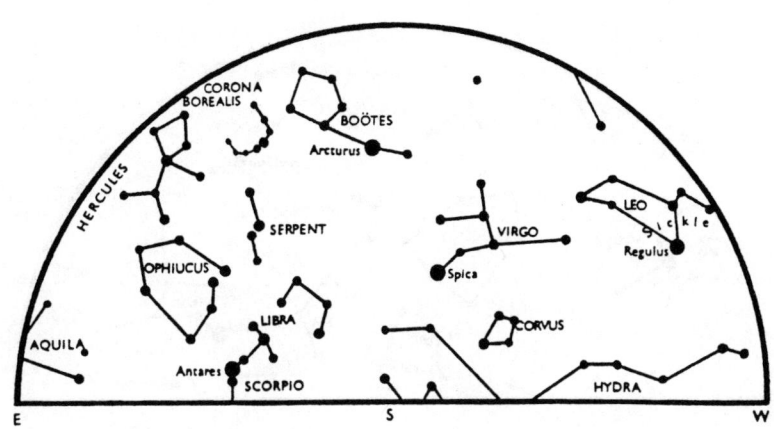

May stars — southern aspect

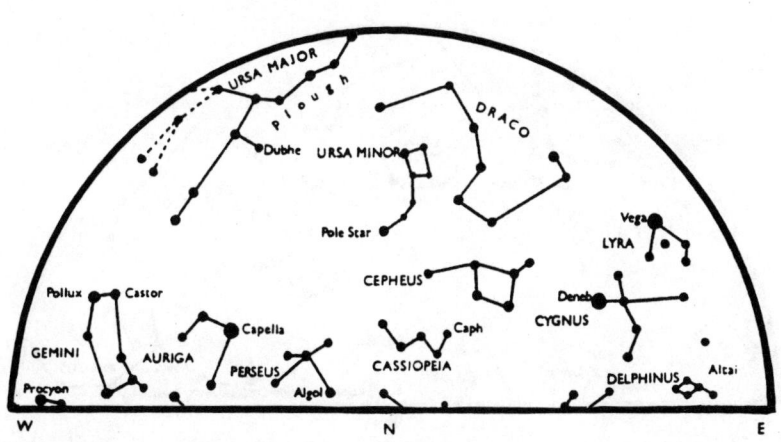

May stars — northern aspect

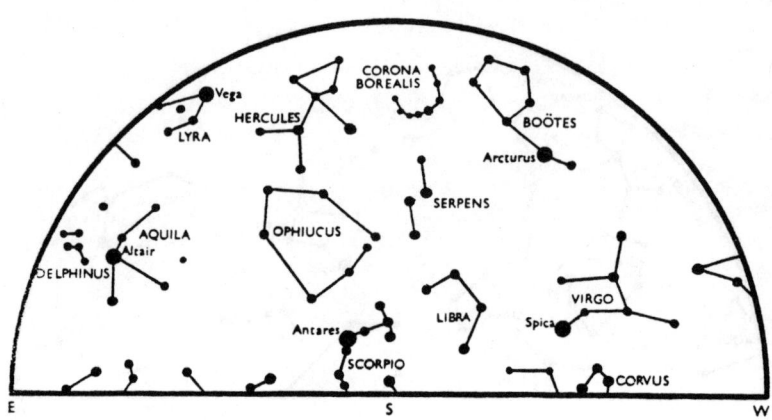

June stars — southern aspect

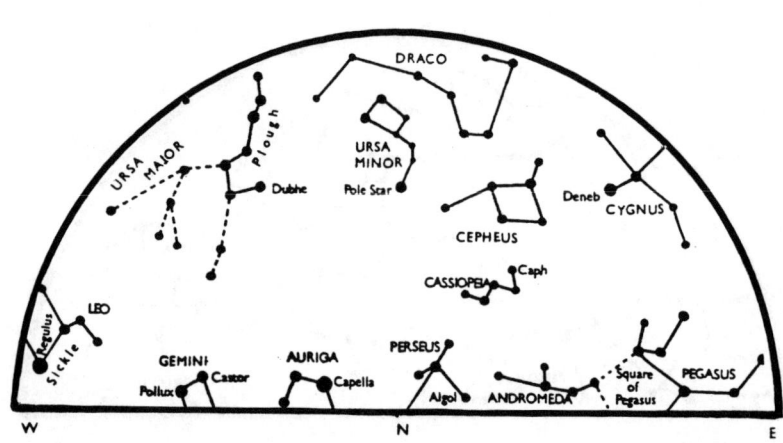

June stars — northern aspect

STAR CHARTS

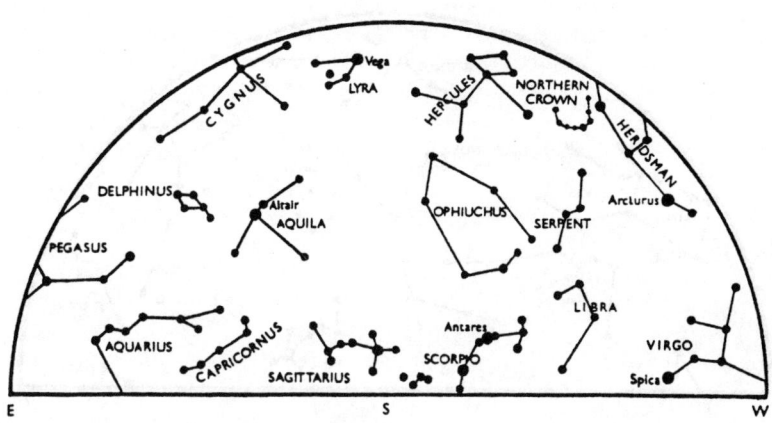

July stars — southern aspect

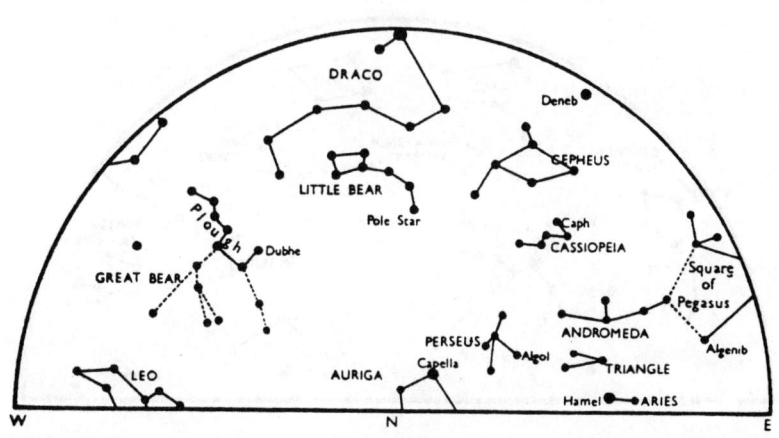

July stars — northern aspect

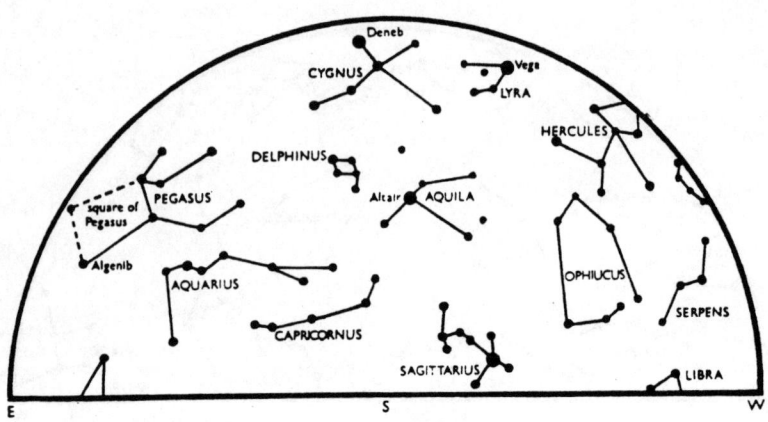

August stars — southern aspect

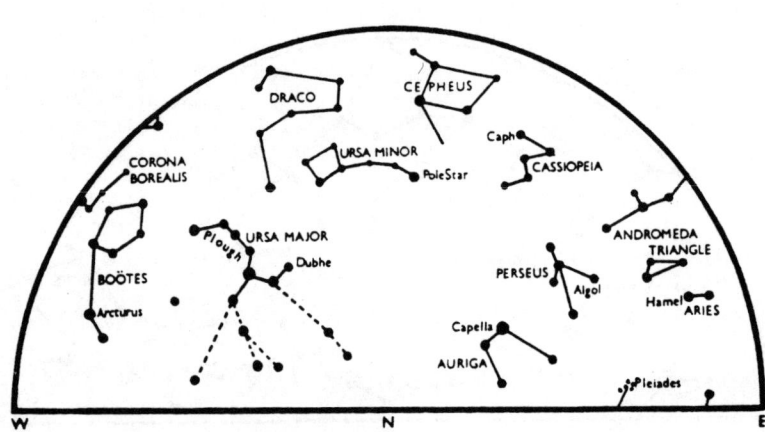

August stars — northern aspect

STAR CHARTS

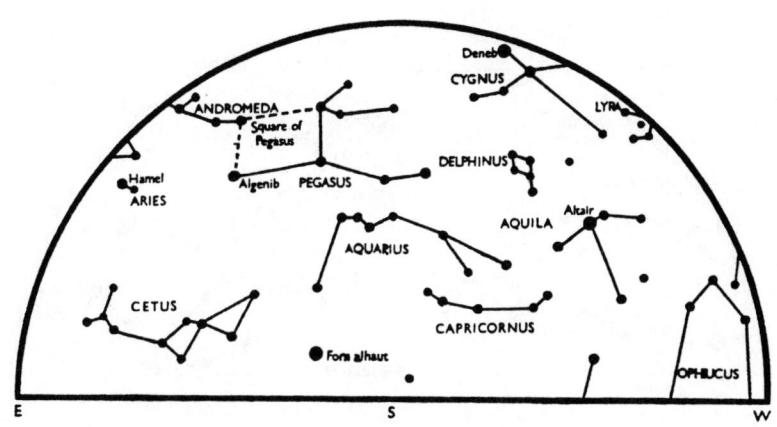

September stars — southern aspect

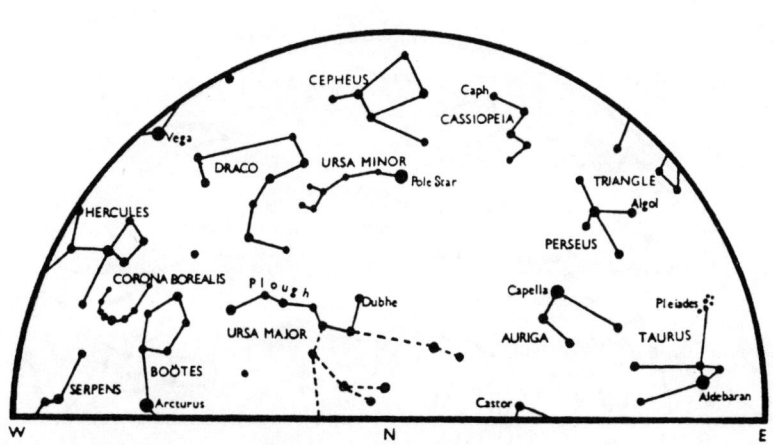

September stars — northern aspect

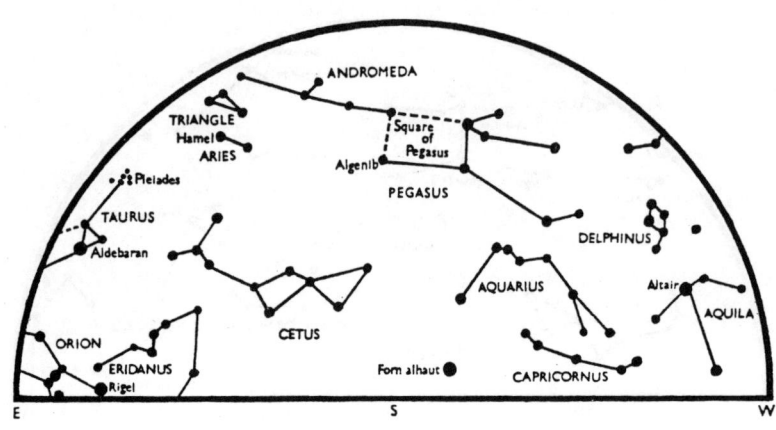

October stars — southern aspect

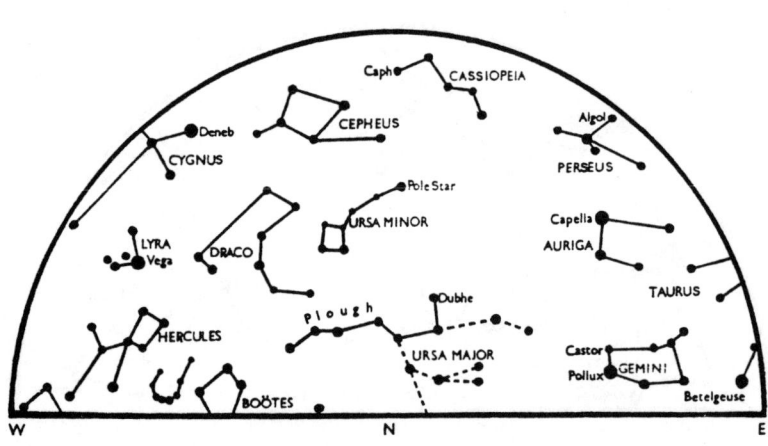

October stars — northern aspect

STAR CHARTS

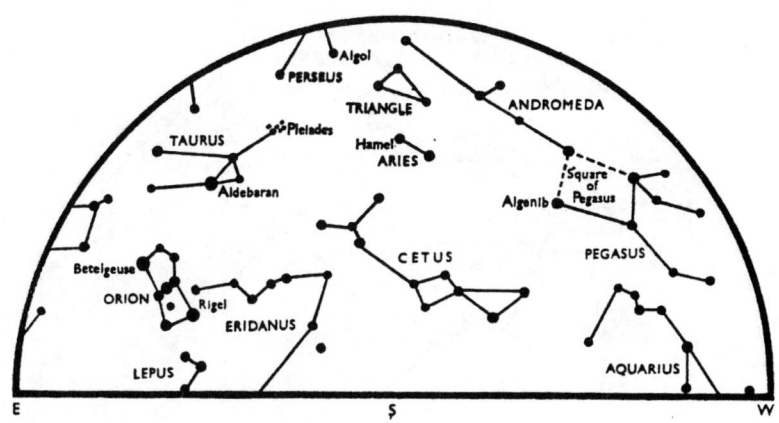

November stars — southern aspect

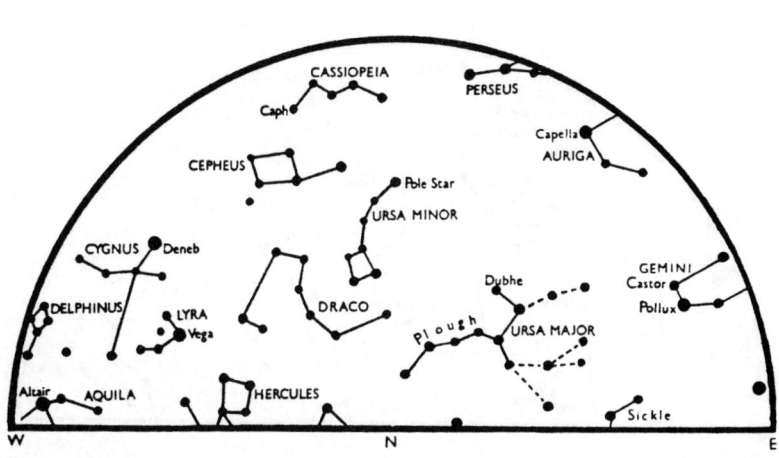

November stars — northern aspect

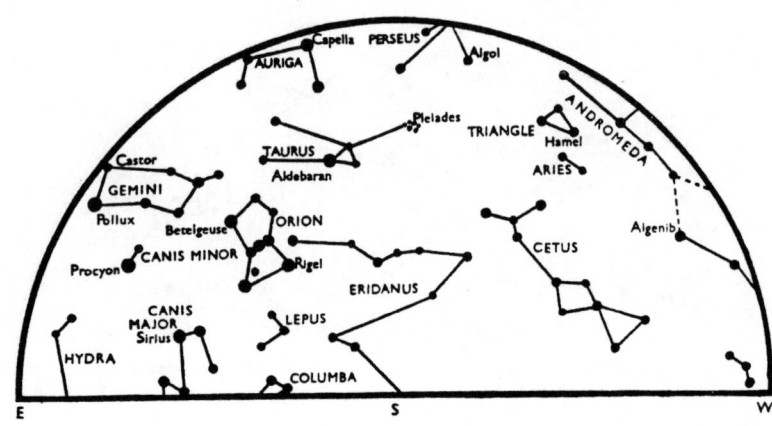

December stars — southern aspect

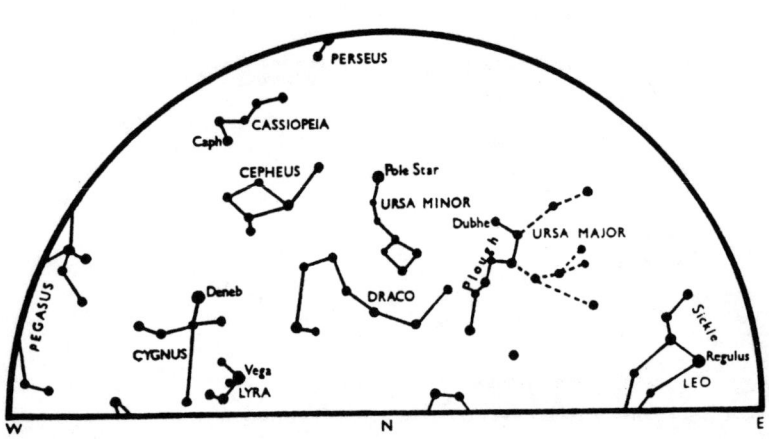

December stars — northern aspect

BIBLIOGRAPHY

Abell, G. O., *Exploration of the Universe* (Holt, Rinehart, Winston, 1975).
Asimov, I., *The Universe* (Pelican Books, 1971).
Bord, J. & C., *Mysterious Britain* (Paladin, 1974).
Bronowski, J. & Mazlish, B., *The Western Intellectual Tradition* (Pelican Books, 1963).
Canning, J., *Great Disasters* (Octopus Books Ltd., 1976).
Coleman, J., *Relativity for the Layman* (Pelican Books, 1959).
Curran, G. & Taylor, I., *World Daylight Saving Time* (Curran Publishing Co., 1935 (out of print).)
Doane, D. Chase, *Time Changes in the World* (American Federation of Astrologers, 1982).
——, *Time Changes in the U.S.A.* (American Federation of Astrologers, 1981).
Filbey, J., *Natal Charting* (The Aquarian Press, 1981).
Gatland, K., *The Illustrated Encyclopedia of Space Technology* (Salamander Books, Ltd., 1981).
Gibbs, C. H. Smith, *The Wright Brothers* (Science Museum, H.M.S.O. 1967).
——, *The World's First Aeroplane Flights* (Science Museum, H.M.S.O. 1969).
Gould, R. T., *John Harrison and his Timekeepers* (National Maritime Museum, Greenwich, 1978).
Gutenberg, B. & Richter, C. F., *Seismicity of the Earth* (Princetown University Press, 1949).

Hawkins, G., *Stonehenge De-Coded* (Fontana Books, 1970).
Hill, D., *The Comet* (New English Library, 1973).
Holden, R. W., *The Elements of House Division* (L. N. Fowler Ltd., 1977).
The Nautical Almanac (H.M.S.O., 1980).
Howse, D., *Greenwich Time & the Finding of Longitude* (Oxford University Press, 1980).
Hoyle, F., *Nicolaus Copernicus* (Heinemann, 1973).
Hughes, D., *The Star of Bethlehem Mystery* (Corgi, 1981).
Klepésta, J. & Rukl, A., *Constellations — Concise Guide* (Hamlyn Artia, 1972).
Kuhn, T., *The Copernican Revolution* (Harvard University Press, 1971).
McNally, D., *Positional Astronomy* (F. Muller Ltd., 1974).
Marten, M., *The Radiant Universe* (Chanose Publishers Ltd., 1980).
Mitton, S., *The Cambridge Encyclopedia of Astronomy* (Trewin Copplestone Publishing Ltd., 1979).
Moore, P., *Concise Atlas of the Universe* (Mitchell Beazley Ltd., 1974).
Murdin, P. & Allen, D., *Catalogue of the Universe* (International Publishers Ltd., 1979).
Dept. of Navigation & Astronomy, *The Planispheric Astrolabe* (National Maritime Museum, Greenwich, 1982).
Norton, A. P., *Norton's Star Atlas* (Gall and Inglis, 1973).
Parker, D. & J., *The Compleat Astrologer* (Mitchell Beazley Ltd., 1971).
Pattie, T. S., *Astrology* (The British Library, 1980).
Pearce, A. J. *Textbook of Astrology* (Mackie & Co., 1911).
Rolt, L. T. C., *Red for Danger* (Pan Books Ltd., 1978).
Ronan, C., *Their Majesties' Astronomers* (Bodley Head, 1967).
——, *Greenwich Observatory* (Times Books, 1975).
Rothé, J. P., *The Seismicity of the Earth (1953-1965)* (Unesco, 1969).
Rubin, F., *'The Lunar Cycle in relation to human conception and the sex of offspring'*: An account of the work of Dr E. Jonas. Published as a supplement to the *Astrological Journal*, Vol. IX, No. 4.
Rudaux, L., & de Vaucoleurs, *Larousse Encyclopedia of Astronomy* (Hamlyn, 1968).
Russell, C. A., *The Background to Copernicus — The Copernican Revolution* (Open University Press, 1972).

Sadler, D. H., *Man is not Lost* (National Maritime Museum & Greenwich Observatory, 1978).
Schneider, M., & Gauquelin, F., *Astro-Psychological Problems,* Francoise Gauquelin, (European time data) Vol. 1., 1-4: Vol. 2, No. 1, 1982/83.
Schroeder, W., *Practical Astronomy* (Werner Laurie, 1961).
Smart, W. M., *Textbook of Spherical Astronomy* (Cambridge University Press, fifth edition, 1971).
Stahlmann, W. & Gingerich, O., *Solar and Planetary Longitudes (−2500 +2500)* (University of Wisconsin Press, 1963).
Swiderska, H. & Tyacke, S., *Copernicus and the New Astronomy* (Trustees of the British Museum, 1973).
Thom, A. & A. S., *Megalithic Remains in Britain and Brittany* (Clarendon Press, Oxford, 1978).
Tuckerman, B., *Planetary, Lunar and Solar Positions, 601 B.C. — A.D. 1, A.D. 2-1649* (American Philosophical Society, 1962).
Wallenquist, A., *The Penguin Dictionary of Astronomy* (Penguin Reference Books, 1968).
Wood, J. E., *Sun, Moon and Standing Stones* (Oxford University Press, 1978).
World Almanac and Book of Facts 1983 (Newspaper Enterprise Association, Inc., New York).
Worvill, R., *Night Skies of the Year* (Stanmore Press Ltd., 1968).
Yeomans, D. K., *The Comet Halley Handbook* (NASA/JPL, 1981).

Journals (Astrological)

American Astrology (Clancy Publications).
Astrologer's Quarterly (Astrological Lodge of London).
Astrological Journal (The Astrological Association).
Correlation, (Journal of Research into Astrology) (The Astrological Association).
Astro-Psychological Problems F. Gauquelin & M. Schneider, Paris, France.
Sky & Telescope (Astronomy), (Sky Publishing Corporation, Cambridge, Mass.).

Reference Materials

Raphael's Ephemerides	(W. Foulsham & Co. Ltd.)
Raphael's Tables of Houses for Northern Latitudes	(W. Foulsham & Co. Ltd.)
Raphael's Tables of Houses for Great Britain	(W. Foulsham & Co. Ltd.)
Raphael's Geocentric Longitudes and Declinations of Mars, Jupiter, Saturn, Uranus and Neptune	(W. Foulsham & Co. Ltd.)
The American Book of Tables	Neil F. Michelson (Astro Computing Services, New York). Available from Thorsons Publishers Limited, Denington Estate, Wellingborough, Northamptonshire.
The American Ephemeris for the 20th century (1900-2000) (includes Pluto)	Neil F. Michelson (Astro Computing Services). Available from Thorsons Publishers Limited.
Longitudes and Latitudes Throughout the World (excluding U.S.A.)	E. Dernay (American Federation of Astrologers).
Longitudes and Latitudes in the U.S.A.	E. Dernay
Time Changes in the U.S.A. *Time Changes in Canada and Mexico* *Time Changes in the World* (excluding U.S.A., Canada and Mexico)	Doris Chase Doane, (Professional Astrologers Incorporated, Hollywood).

INDEX

Aberration, chromatic, 27
Adams, John, 28, 125
Almagest, 19
Altitude, 47
Ancient astronomies, 12-16
Andromeda Nebula, 32, 34, 173
Antoniadi, E. M., 30
Aphelion, 103, 136
Apogee, 103
Aries, First Point of, 41, 44, 45, 52, 55
Aristarchus, 18, 20
Aristotle, 17
Ascendant, 52, 57-59
Aspects, 101
Asteroids, 129
Astronomical unit, 136
Aurora Australis, 108
Aurora Borealis, 108

Babylonians, 16
Beltane, Feast of, 14
Bessel, Friedrich, 28
Bethe, Hans, 31

Big Bang, theory of the Universe, 35
Binary stars, 171
Black Holes, 37, 171
Blue Giants, 31
Bode, Johann, 136
Bode's Law, 136
Bondi, Hermann, 35
Bradley, D., 184
Brahe, Tycho, 21
Bruno, Giordano, 23, 26
Bunsen, Robert, 29

Calendar, 61-65
Cassini, D., 25
Cassini's Division, 124
Celestial Equator; 44,
   Horizon, 46
   Meridian, 46
   Poles, 45
   Sphere, 43
Celtic New Year, 14
Centrifugal force, 139
Cepheid variables, 33, 34
Ceres, 129

Charon, 128
Chromosphere, 107
Climatology, 12, 147
Clusters, stars and galaxies, 172
Coma, 165
Comets, 151-163
Conjunction, 101
Constellations, 165, 176-180
Copernicus, N., 18-19
Cosmic rays, 36
Cosmogony, 35
Cosmology, 35
Crab Nebula, 36

D'Arrest, H., 125
Day, 73-74
Declination, 46, 49, 53
Dee, John., 23, 26
Deimos, 122
Denning, W.F., 30
Density, of planets, 106
    of stars, 169
Descartes, 24
Digges, Thomas 23, 26
Disasters, 185
Diurnal circles, 49
Dollond, John, 27
Doppler effect, 30
Dreyer, John, 32

Earth, 31, 39-43, 139, 142, 144, 147, 149
Eccentricity, orbital, 106
Eclipses, 112, 114, 190
Eclipse year, 77
Ecliptic; 44, 45
    system of co-ordinates, 53, 54
Einstein, Albert, 32

Elongation, 102, 118
Ephemeris, 99-104
Epicycle, 16
Equation of the centre, 114
Equator; 44,
    system of co-ordinates, 50, 51, 52
Equinoctial, 45
Equinox, 45
Eratosthenes, 17
Eudoxus, 16, 18
Evection, 114

Fagan, Cyril, 56
Fraunhofer von J., 28
Fraunhofer lines, 169

Gagarin, Yuri, 37
Galactic clusters, 174
Galaxies, 33, 166, 172-176
Galaxy the, 172
Galilei, Galileo, 23
Galle, Johann, 125
Gamow, George, 35
Gas giants, 122
Globular clusters, 172
Goddard, Robert, 37
Gold, Thomas, 35
Gravitation, 22, 139
Greeks, 16, 17
Greenwich Mean Time, 41, 82, 83
    Meridian, 41
    Observatory, 26

Halley, E., 26
    comet, 154-159
Harrison, John, 19, 26
Harvest and Hunter's Moons, 110

INDEX

Hawkins, G., 13
Helium, 31
Herschel, John, 32
Herschel, William, 27
Hertzsprung, Ejnar, 31
Hertzsprung — Russell
 diagram, 31, 170
Hipparchus, 16
Horizon, 44
 system of co-ordinates,
 44-49
Horology, 80
Hour, Angle, 53
 Circle, 52
House Division, 56-59
Hoyle, F., 35
Hubble, Edwin, 33
Huggins, William, 29
Huygens, C., 80
Hydrogen, 31
Hyperbolae, 153

Inferior planets, 118
Ingress, 185
International Date Line, 41-43

Jansky, Karl, 36
Julian Day/Date, 71-73
Jupiter, 122-123

Kant, Immanuel, 32
Kapteyn, J., 33
Kepler, Johannes, 22
Kepler's Laws, 22, 25,
 136-138
Kirchoff, G., 29

Laplace, Simon de, 37
Lassell, William, 30
Latitude, celestial, 54
 terrestrial, 40

Leavitt, Henrietta, 33
Lemaitre, Georges, 35
Le Verrier, Urbain, 28, 125
Libration, 115
Light year, 28
Longitude, celestial, 53
 longitude equivalent, 41
 terrestrial, 40
Lowell, Percival, 28
Luminosity, 31
Lunation, 75
Lyttleton, R., 35

Magellan, 19
Magellanic Clouds, 173
Magnetic field, 171
Magnitude, 167
Main Sequence, 31, 169
Mars, 120-122
Mass, 139
Megalith, 12
Mercury, 118-120
Meridian, Greenwich, 41
 Local, 40
 Observer's, 40, 47
Messier, Charles, 32, 173, 174
Meteors, 117
Milky Way, 27, 172, 173
Month, kinds of, 74
Moon, motions, 109-111
 orbit, 109-111
 phases, 110
 structure, 116-117
 influence of, 183-185
Mundane position, 205-208

Nadir, 46, 56
Nasmyth, J., 30
Navigation, 26
Nebulae, 32, 170, 172

Neolithic, 14
Neptune, 28, 125-126, 188
Nereid, 126
Neutrons, 126
Newton, Isaac, 8, 24, 138, 140
Nodes, lunar, 112
  planetary, 103, 135
Novae, 171
Nuclear fusion, 31
Obliquity of the Ecliptic, 53, 56
Occulation, lunar, 115
Oort, Jan, 33
Opposition, 102
Orbits, 109-116, 131-135
Orbital elements, 106, 136

Pallas, 129
Parabolae, 153
Parallax, 28, 167
Penumbra, 107, 113, 114
Perigree, 103
Perihelion, 103, 136
Philolaos, 18
Phobas, 18
Photography, 28, 29
Photosphere, 107
Plages, 108
Planetary cycles, astrological, 187
Planets, 105-129, 131, 135
Pluto, 28, 126-129
Polaris, 141-143
Precession of the Equinoxes, 140-144
Prime Vertical, 47, 56, 57
Prominences — solar, 108
Proper motion, 26, 168
Ptolemy, 16, 18

Pulsars, 36, 171

Quadrature, 131
Quasars, 36, 38, 175
Quincunx, 135

Radio waves, 35, 36
Radius vector, 22, 138
Regolith, 116
Relativity, theory of, 35
Renaissance, 19, 181
Retardation of Moon, 109
Retrograde motion, 133-135
Right Ascension; 46, 52, 53
  tables of, 211-216
Rilles, lunar, 117
Rocketry, 37
Rosse, Lord, 32
Russell, Henry, 31, 169

Satellites; earth, 37
  planets' 105-129
Saturn, 123-124, 186-187
Schiaparelli, G., 30
Schwabe, H., 30
Seasons, 144-147
Sex; influence of Moon, 184
Shapley, Harlow, 33
Solstices, 11, 45, 100, 146
Spectroscopy, 28
Stars, 165-174
Steady State theory, 35, 175
Stonehenge, 12, 13
Subsumption, 189
Sun, 105-107, 182-183
Syzygy, 102

Telescopes, 26, 27
Terrestrial planets, 122
Thom, A., 13

INDEX

Tides, 147-149
Tombaugh, Clyde, 28
Time, apparent solar, 83, 84
  civil, 85
  clock, 86
  Daylight Saving, War time, 89
  Ephemeris, 90
  equation of, 85
  Greenwich, 41
    local, 85, 86
    mean, 84, 86, 87
  longitude equivalent, 41, 217-220
  sidereal, 90-93
  Standard, 86, 88
  Summer, 89
  sundial, 80
  True, 84
  Universal, 89
  Zone, 86
Titan, 124
Transits, Mercury, 120
  Venus, 120
Triton, 126
Tropics, Cancer, 45, 146
  Capricorn, 45, 146
Tsiolkovsky, K., 37

Ultra-violet light, 107
Umbra, 113-114
Universe, 35, 165-180

Uranus, 28, 124, 125

Venus, 118-120
Vernal Equinox, *see* First Point of Aries
Volcanoes, 121

Week, 63, 75
Weight, definition of, 139

X-rays, 36

Year; 76-77
  anomalistic, 76
  astronomical, 76
  Besselian, 77
  calendar, 76
  civil, 76
  eclipse, 77
  equinoctial, 76
  financial, 71
  leap, 61-71
  light, 28
  seasonal, 76
  sidereal, 76
  tropical, 76

Zenith, 46, 47, 56
Zodiac; Constellations, 176-180
  Sidereal, 55-56
  Tropical, 55-56